MW01701121

STEWING IN THE MELTING POT

STEWING IN THE MELTING POT

The Memoir of a Real American

To Tony
with best wishes
Roberto

Robert Sanabria

CAPITAL BOOKS, INC.
Sterling, Virginia

Copyright © 2001 by author

All rights reserved. No part of this book may be reproduced or utilized in any form or by any means, electronic or mechanical, including photocopying, recording, or by any information storage and retrieval system, without permission in writing from the publisher. Inquiries should be addressed to:

Capital Books, Inc.
P.O. Box 605
Sterling, Virginia 20172-0605

ISBN 1-892123-46-0 (alk. paper)

Library of Congress Cataloging-in-Publication Data
Sanabria, Robert.
Stewing in the melting pot : the memoir of a real American / Robert Sanabria.
p. cm.
ISBN 1-892123-46-0
1. Sanabria, Robert. 2. Mexican Americans--Biography. 3. Mexican Americans--Cultural assimilation. 4. Sanabria, Robert--Childhood and youth. 5. Orphans--California--Los Angeles--Biography. 6. Los Angeles (Calif.)--Biography. 7. Mexican Americans--California--Los Angeles--Social conditions--20th century. I. Title.

E184.M5 S254 2001
979.4'940046872--dc21

2001028137

Printed in the United States of America on acid-free paper that meets the American National Standards Institute Z39-48 Standard.

First Edition

10 9 8 7 6 5 4 3 2 1

Dedication

To my mother, Josefina,
and to my children, and theirs . . .

Contents

Introduction

The white pillars standing like sentries along the portico of the "Big House," the main building of the institution we called "the Home," is a vision I'll never be able to erase. Just closing my eyes quickly brings the rest of that looming, white stucco edifice into focus. It was a place that nurtured and formed me for ten crucial years of my childhood, a place whose lessons have profoundly affected all of my life, the place where I was to become a "real American." It did this for me and for 179 other Latino children during the thirty-one years it existed. It has long since gone and we who lived there have scattered; some of us are no more. But for a while longer, that orphanage, as well as the church and the people who made it possible, live on with those of us who remain and, like it or not, we remember.

CHAPTER 1

Escape

"Queta!" Mamacita barks for the third time. "Stay close to me and don't lose that package or let go of Roberto's hand." The crowd in the bus station has gotten bigger, pressing in on us, and I feel lost among the legs and baggage of all the people swirling around us. I'm trying hard not to cry. I want desperately to hold Mamacita's hand, but she's got hers full, with the baby in one arm and our suitcase in the other hand. All I can do is hold tightly to Queta as I warn Chuy not to let go of me. The three of us, my older sister and little brother, are like a tail trailing through the crowd after Mamacita, who's so worried and anxious she looks like she'll start to cry at any minute. She's in line waiting to buy tickets, all the while fearfully glancing over her shoulder, looking again and again at the crowd to see if we're being followed. It's Jesús, our Papa, she's afraid of, the man we're all afraid of. We're running away from him. He's beaten Mamacita so often she can't stand it any more, and Queta and I can't stop him or do anything to help her. All we can do is run away crying, hiding until he leaves.

I know it must be almost lunchtime and I'm hungry. People all around us are eating whatever they've brought with them. Exhaust fumes mixed with the smells of their food and sweating bodies are sickening in the mid-day heat and our clothes are already sticking to us. But this is the only time safe enough for us to get away, when Mamacita knows our Papa will be in some cantina drinking with his friends. Our plan to run away from Papa has been our secret for a long time now, because we know how angry he would be if he found out. But now we're ready, it's time to go, and we're all scared Papa might come to stop us and hit Mamacita again. Just thinking about it makes me shudder. Mamacita says there's no one in El Paso who can help us, so we're going far away to where her sister and brothers live.

"In a few minutes we have to get on the bus," Mamacita says to us anxiously, while Conchita nurses. "Queta, take Chuy and Roberto to the fountain over there and get a drink. Then the three of you can share a burrito."

Like all the buses, ours has a big silver dog painted on its sides. Our legs are so short Queta has to help Chuy and me climb up the steep stairs to get into it. From the window next to my seat I can see many buses lined up in a row, and all around in confused disorder a sea of people waiting to get on them. Once everyone is on the bus and the door closes we feel safer, but it's not until we leave the station that Mamacita loses that worried look and seems to relax. I watch her face and feel better when she smiles at the other people cooing over the baby. They smile back, but that only lasts until Conchita starts to cry. And when Mamacita has to change Conchita's and Chuy's diapers, everyone around us complains about the smell. Queta and I laugh together; we think there's something funny about *caca.* The open windows soon clear the odor and in spite of the heat it's comfortable enough as long as we're moving.

The monotonous droning of the bus's engine and the sound of wind rushing past the open windows soon put Conchita and most everyone else to sleep. We travel all through the night, the bus stopping now and then to let people off or take others on. But after the first few times we stop I'm no longer curious and don't wake myself up anymore. I sleep well into the next morning, waking when the bus stops and a man in uniform gets on to ask in English and Spanish if anyone has any plants. He gives everyone an orange and says, "Happy Independence Day. *Bienvenidos a California.*" Smiling, Mamacita turns to Queta and says, "*Feliz cumpleaños, mija.*" It's her birthday. Today she's seven. The orange will be her birthday present.

The sky was yellow as sand and shimmered with the heat of an early August afternoon as I pulled off the interstate into the town of Colton, California. Outside my rented air-conditioned car I knew the air would be stifling. This place, one of many such nondescript suburbs, is near semi-desert San Bernardino. It sits astride Interstate 10, the same interstate that goes nonstop over 800 miles east to El Paso, Texas, where I was born. I had the bad luck of having a flight that put me in the middle of the evening rush hour, doubling the usual one-hour drive from L.A. International Airport. I was tired, my anxiety about this visit greater than usual.

The so-called "Big House," the main building of the Plaza Community Center Children's Home in Sierra Madre, California, circa 1932.

My younger brother's small cottage, where I was headed, sits near the end of a dead-end street with only a letter of the alphabet for a name. Like San Bernardino, Colton was settled by Mormons, but they are no longer much in evidence. In more recent generations Colton has become a workingman's town and a magnet for new immigrants, most of them Latino, Mexican. Over the years I'd been coming here, the number of Anglo families living on Bill's street has declined, and the surrounding area has increasingly become more a barrio, the kind of place I'd avoided living in since it was in my power to make such decisions.

As I continued the drive up Mt. Vernon Avenue, slowing to steer the final right turn onto Bill's street, the sense that I didn't belong in this place was overwhelming. But in almost the same instant I realized that I've never felt that I belonged anywhere.

I'd come here out of duty to visit my mother, something I'd tried to do at least every couple years since my Camel-smoking stepfather—emphysema slowly but inexorably paralyzing his lungs—killed himself in the mid-1970s. But in this summer of 1982 it was different. For the first time in years I'd come here feeling like I needed my family. Newly separated from my wife of twenty-seven years, I felt cut off from my children and very much alone, facts I failed to mention to either my mother or brother during the visit. Though I had a great need to talk to someone about it, it wouldn't be my bachelor brother, who I knew would be less than indifferent. Nor would it be Mother, who had a knack for translating other peoples' problems into her own pain. She wouldn't, couldn't, be very helpful; nor would it be fair to trouble her with my situation.

A woman of secrets, Mother had never had much to say about what actually mattered in her life, and I suspect she really expected no more from me. This was the payoff for having parked her children in an orphanage for ten years, during which we grew apart from her and from each other. Even after we all returned to live with her, we were never really the focus of her life again.

I was right about the air. Even as the shadows lengthened toward dusk, it was eye-burning and unpleasant, like breathing in smoke. As I pushed open the gate on the chain-link fence, the squeal doubled as a doorbell, loud enough to bring Mother in her wheelchair to the screen door. She pushed past it and partway down the concrete pathway to greet me. Her eyes filled with tears at my approach and she wore the expression of mixed pain and joy she'd perfected through years of practice. "*Ay dios mio, hijo,*" she exclaimed, as she reached for me and I bent to hug her.

We shared a supper of something like chicken cacciatore, a dish Mother insisted was my favorite, though it was news to me. Bill had grudgingly prepared it at Mother's insistence, which, I assumed, was why he was so grumpy. As usual, our conversation was superficial, little more than her questioning about my children and my life, and mine about her various physical ailments and her prescriptions. Content to stay out of the exchange, Bill was bored with my litany and so was I. We, none of us, had ever spent much time really talking to each other; mutual interrogations like this hardly qualified. As I departed for the evening and headed to my motel, I wondered how I could stand five more days of this.

◆

Bill had long since gone to work when I showed up the next morning at around ten, but Mother had waited for me to have breakfast with her. Though I'd already eaten, I prepared us scrambled eggs smothered with chile salsa, like we used to fix in our restaurant days, back in another lifetime. We both knew something was off-key, uneasy. Finished eating, I mindlessly traced the grid pattern on the plastic table cover, while she repeatedly rearranged the napkin holder and condiments. But over a second cup of coffee, we began to relax and reminisce, careful to keep it superficial. We both found release and even a little pleasure, transported back to an earlier place and time.

To avoid discussing my current problems, I maneuvered the talk to her childhood and family, about which I'd become more interested as I grew older. Instead of avoiding my questions as she usually did, she seemed pleased that I was interested. Still, I didn't really expect to hear much from her that was very enlightening or revealing.

The kitchen was the least disordered place in the house. Even there I was claustrophobic and very uncomfortable, which is why I stayed in a motel when I visited. I was also emotionally uneasy at being thrown back into the role of a child in a parent's presence; I felt estranged for having chosen, years before, to live a more mainstream, American lifestyle than the rest of my family had wanted or been able to. Before pushing Mother in her wheelchair back into the living room, I rinsed the dishes and left them in the sink for later washing.

The sun was already well above the small, wood-frame and stucco house, unshaded by a tree of any size. The house wasn't air-conditioned, and, despite the constant blow of air from a floor fan, it had heated up fast. Low-ceilinged, it was cramped with too many things in too small a space. Besides two ancient, stained overstuffed chairs and a TV console, what was supposed to be the living room was also furnished with Mother's hospital-style bed and a table filled with her medicines for high blood pressure, arthritis, and Lord knows what else, the bottles in varying sizes and colors creating a miniature skyline at her bedside. The dingy, threadbare carpet contributed to the pervasive air of decline. But what really created a sense of clutter were the cacti, planted in a hodgepodge of pots and rusting coffee cans, that occupied the fireplace mantel, all the window sills, and almost every other flat surface. They at least were alive, growing. Cacti were one of brother Bill's hobbies—he'd had many other, more transient ones. He was also something of a pack rat, which accounted for the ubiquitous cacti, in and outside of the house. Since becoming wheelchair-bound, Mother had given up fighting against the clutter of plants and other "collectibles." She knew she dare not complain too much because Bill was the only one of her four children who was willing and able to take care of her. The alternative to living with him, being warehoused in a nursing home, was a prospect too terrible to contemplate.

◆

At fifty-one, I was retired from the U.S. Army, having survived Vietnam without a scratch. During the thirteen months in the mid-1960s I was overseas, Mother developed cancer. When I returned, she'd become so wrinkled and emaciated I barely recognized her. Besides losing both breasts, she'd had a large tumor removed from her brain, and had two bypass operations to restore circulation to her legs. Now, further crippled by arthritis, she sat there uncomplaining, even a little vain. Just twenty years older than me and a beauty well into middle age, she continued to use some makeup and, despite the arthritic stiffness in her arms, still made the effort to keep her mostly black and naturally wavy hair presentable. Her shapeless body she kept well-concealed in a full-flowing house dress. As we sat talking, I realized just how unremitting life's pain had been for my mother. I felt a grudging admiration.

Her very real enjoyment in reminiscing about her childhood and about when my siblings and I were kids came as a surprise. I was pleased. On only one other occasion—when I was fourteen and had just left the orphanage to live with her—had she ever taken the time to talk to me. Then it wasn't about her childhood, but about her dreams for our future together. That conversation, lasting 'til the sun came up, we both cherished, and for a while afterward referred to it intimately as "that time when we talked." At that moment I thought of it—and all the years wasted since.

◆

In telling me of her past, Mother was also telling me about mine. I'd reached the age when it had become important to look back, to find out who my forebears were and especially more about who I am. For most of my life that was something I'd deliberately tried not to explore for a number of reasons, not the least of which were the lingering bad feelings from my years at the orphanage. It was a touchy subject, one of so many, it seemed. In the past when we'd talked about the Home, as we called it, we always focused on what we all agreed were the happy times—picnics, trips to the beach or mountains, and the like. That's what Mother focused on once again, but this time I was less willing to let her off the hook. Instead, I decided to ask the only two really important questions: Why she had left us at the Home and why had she left us there so long? Still, I approached cautiously.

"You had to put us in the Home, didn't you, Mother?" I said, hoping she wouldn't become defensive and clam up on me.

"Oh, yes, there was nothing else I could do, and thank God I found it." Her answer came in a gush, her speech rapid, and she leaned toward me as if to show how earnest she was.

"Do you remember much about that, how you found out about the Home?" I said, careful to keep a neutral tone.

"Let's see," she said, rubbing her chin thoughtfully. "It was either Cuca or her brother who told me about it."

"Cuca," I repeated. "She's the woman we stayed with for awhile when we first came to Los Angeles, wasn't she? I've heard her name before, but still don't know who she was."

"Yes, she and her brother were the first people I knew when we arrived from Texas."

I waited, saying nothing, letting her find her way. Her face clouded for a moment, as though she was deciding whether or how to continue.

She remembered the day and the trip clearly, she said. She was running away from her husband, she reminded me. We boarded the bus in El Paso in the summer of '35. I was not quite yet four years old and remember little about the journey. But Mother said the bus was very crowded, the heat nightmarish. Since she had to hold and nurse seven-month-old Conchita almost continuously, she hardly slept at all during the two days and a night it took to get to L.A. My older sister, Enriqueta—we still call her Queta—looked after me and Jesús—Bill's original name, though we called him Chuy. He was nearly two. Queta didn't like the task, but was more disgruntled about having to celebrate her birthday on that journey.

"That trip was nearly a thousand miles," Mother said, "the longest one I'd ever made."

Because she had so little money, less than twenty dollars, and was uncertain that we'd have a place to stay, Mother was terrified when we arrived at the L.A. bus station. But what she feared most was "*la migra,*" the immigration authorities. Because of the Depression they were rounding up and forcibly deporting Mexicans—even citizens and those in the country legally—if they couldn't prove they weren't on relief. Her sister, Esperanza, had failed to meet us and when she called her brother, Emílio, he'd told her he couldn't take us in either. I had no trouble visualizing my mother standing outside the bus station with an infant in her arms and three small children clutching at her skirt. It was also no effort at all to feel the sense of near panic she described. As I listened, it was clear Mother had left one set of bad circumstances in Texas for another in California, one that promised to be different but probably no better.

"So what did you do?" I asked, focused on her contorted face. She described a taxi driver, also Mexican, who approached and asked if we needed a ride. Her heart in her throat, she bravely declined. But a short while later he returned from a run to find us still there and realized we very likely had no place to go. He asked again, more gently this time, if he could take us somewhere. Though she lied and said no, he persisted, warning that if we stayed where we were much longer we were certain to be picked up by immigration authorities.

"So, what else could I do?" she said. "I could barely afford the fare to get to a hotel, much less pay the price of a room. And we had to eat."

When the cab driver offered to take us to his sister's home for the night, she accepted. I knew well how she'd always been distrustful of people, but the fear of deportation had left her little choice. "The cabby's kindness must have made you feel better, didn't it?" I said. At this she shook her head, no, explaining that she was still terrified, not knowing what she was getting into. And when she saw his sister's home she wasn't much encouraged, either. It was in the northeast part of the city, an area close to the dog pound, known to all as "Dog Town." Heavily crowded with immigrants of many nationalities, but mostly Mexicans, it was a short ride from the bus station, an area of cheap rooming houses and hotels, a slum.

I vaguely recalled Cuca, the taxi driver's sister, as a fairly large woman. Mother confirmed my recollection, describing her as in her forties, bighearted, disheveled, and fat. Her house was small and not very clean, and Mother shook her head as she recalled entering the tiny room Cuca offered her. It was bare of furniture, except for a bed with no mattress, and otherwise crammed with junk. When she walked into it, dust balls swirled around her feet and scurrying insects crunched under the trash strewn on the floor. The dreary accommodations were disheartening, but when we sat down to eat the meal of *guisado*, a hot meaty stew, and tortillas Cuca prepared for us, she seemed like an angel. Afterwards, we slept on the floor with only a thin blanket to cushion us from the floor's hardness.

First thing the next day, Mother found herself a job as a waitress in a nearby restaurant, and within a few days our outlook seemed to have improved dramatically. But she soon realized our stay with the cabby's sister could only be temporary. Although Cuca had dug up a lumpy, stained mattress from somewhere so Mother and Conchita could use the bed, the rest of us were still sleeping together on the floor, which crawled with ants and cockroaches. And as charitable as her impulses might have been, it was clear Cuca had things other than children on her mind.

Mother recalled returning from work one day not long after our arrival and asking Cuca where we were. Conchita was asleep in the bedroom, she thought, the rest of us playing in the backyard. As she began to change her clothes, Mother called Queta to come in and bring Chuy and me with her. That's when they discovered Chuy was missing. Hysterical, Mother forgot she was dressed only in her slip. Barefoot, she ran through the crowded streets in a frantic search, with Queta close behind. She found a nearly naked Chuy, diapers dirty but otherwise unhurt, headed nowhere in particular. She knew then Cuca was undependable, and it was asking too much of Queta, only seven, to care for us.

If she needed more convincing it came a few days later when, in a neighboring yard, I was pushed by another child and struck the back of my head on the edge of a metal washtub, opening a grisly gash. I have only the scar to remind me of it—I remembered nothing of a taxi ride to the doctor or the pain about which Mother said I complained loudly and long. What really horrified her was what I told her had happened as I was waking from an afternoon nap a day or two later. At the mere mention of it, the image came flashing back: I was lying on my stomach, my face turned to one side having just emerged from sleep, when through partially opened eyes I saw a man's hand holding his enlarged penis. As I watched, fearful and confused, a thick, gray-white fluid erupted from its end. I remained unmoving, pretending to be asleep, until the man had gone. When I told Mother what I'd seen, she looked stricken, though she said nothing about what it meant. Now as we talked about the incident, she said she was shocked and enraged that Cuca had let one of her friends do such a thing, especially while lying beside me. Though Cuca promised nothing like that would happen again, Mother, now fearful of the kind of people Cuca consorted with, was convinced Cuca really couldn't prevent her friends from trying to involve one of us in a similar episode.

There were other incidents, as well, that destroyed Mother's trust in Cuca and made her afraid to stay with her. I suggested Cuca might have been operating a brothel but Mother said she never saw other women in the house, though Cuca was always trying to interest Mother in one or another of her male friends, which Mother refused. The chain of events had a cumulative effect. Mother began to feel the same sensations of fear and hopelessness she'd experienced in the weeks before she fled with us from El Paso. She knew she had to get us away from Cuca's. But to where?

Then the miracle—as Mother is sure it was—happened. One day in early September, Cuca's brother told Mother he'd just heard of a home for "Latin American" children. It was run by the Methodist Church, a place called the Plaza Community Center in the heart of old Los Angeles, and he thought they might help her. When he took her there the next day, she was sure God had heard her prayers; she was told to bring us in to be examined. After an interminable wait of two weeks, she learned to her great relief that early in October we would be admitted to the Center's Home in Sierra Madre, California. There was a minimum age of two for children, but the Center was even willing to make an exception for Conchita so we could all stay together. Mother readily agreed to the support payment she'd be required to make each month.

She recounted this episode quickly and somewhat sketchily, almost as if to dismiss it. Only my persistent questions pulled the details from her and gradually revealed the guilt she felt about having left us. I don't know what emotions my face revealed. Perhaps skepticism, because Mother said again how much she hated to be separated from us, that there was nothing else she could do.

"You know I had to work," she repeated. "I couldn't trust Cuca and hated to leave you kids with her. I worried all the time I was working. Besides, Queta was already a month late starting in school."

"Queta, where are we going?" I asked as we were preparing to leave Cuca's house after lunch. She pretended she didn't know but I could tell she did. She was like a storm warning; I always worried when I saw her unhappy and upset. But my uneasiness was soon replaced by the excitement of riding on a streetcar. By mid-afternoon we had arrived in a small town. Chuy and I, each holding one of Queta's hands, nearly had to run as the three of us trailed behind Mamacita and the woman who had come with us from Los Angeles. The hill from the streetcar station to our destination was steep and seemed endless, but we finally arrived at a spacious yard with buildings bordering it on two sides. The white stucco main house was enormous and frightening. While Mamacita, still holding Conchita in her arms, talked with the three women who acted as if they owned the place, Chuy and I stayed close to Queta.

There seemed to be children everywhere. Many of them, mostly girls, came running out of the houses to gawk at us and chatter among themselves. They milled around asking in English, which only Queta understood a little, but also in Spanish, who we were. Shy and uncertain, we remained silent, huddled together. But it soon became clear they assumed one or more of us would be staying, and their questions about this began to raise doubts in my mind.

After a while Queta began to act strangely. At first I thought it was because Mamacita had handed Conchita over to one of the women, who held her as if she intended to keep her. I knew then that it was time to go, and that Mamacita was going to leave without our baby sister. I couldn't allow myself to think Mamacita would leave us behind, too. I glanced at Queta for reassurance and became alarmed when I saw her standing very still, head and shoulders drooping. I saw she was quietly weeping, but thought it was only because we were leaving Conchita behind. My alarm really rose when Mamacita went to Queta, hugged her and murmured something about wanting her to be very brave and take care of Chuy and me, as always.

Queta nodded, but this added burden only seemed to depress her more, and when I saw her frail body start to heave with sobs, I knew something was terribly wrong. I too began to cry and my wailing set off Chuy, though he understood even less about what was going on.

It was then that Mamacita came and knelt beside us and, for the first time, explained what was happening.

"*Mijitos,* this is going to be your home for a while," she said in almost a whisper. "Queta will be here with you. These nice ladies will take good care of you and you'll have plenty to eat. See how happy all these other children are? Soon you'll get to know them and they'll be your friends."

She wasn't convincing.

"I don't want to stay here," I sobbed through my tears. "I don't like these people. I want to go home with you!"

Chuy, crying all the while, was trying to get Mamacita to pick him up, while I clung tightly to her neck.

"*Ay, mijos,*" she sighed, tears welling in her eyes, "I'm so sorry, but I can't take you home with me. Don't worry, I'll be back to see you very soon and I'll bring you some good things to eat."

"When? When will you come back?" I demanded between sobs, already knowing my protests were futile.

"I'll be back in just a few days," she told us. Then she gathered Chuy and me to her, holding us in her embrace for long seconds before kissing us and disentangling herself. We followed as Mamacita returned to Queta and made one last but vain attempt to comfort her. When she started to leave with the woman who'd brought us, I tried to run after her. As if she had been expecting just such a reaction, one of the other women grabbed my arm and held on.

"¡No me dejes!, mamacita, ¡no me dejes!" I screamed again and again between sobs, begging her not leave me, struggling to get free. It was no use.

As Mamacita and the other woman departed hurriedly in the direction from which we'd come, Mamacita was openly crying. She turned once and gave a half-hearted wave and, her companion urging her along, she was soon out of sight. A few minutes later, the woman who'd been holding me let go and instinctively I ran to Queta and clung to her and Chuy for consolation. The other children stared in silence, perhaps reliving their own experiences of mixed terror and sorrow. The three of us huddled together in the middle of the yard, weeping in misery and despair.

Although she had left us in the care of strangers before, Mamacita had always returned in a few hours. I knew this time was different and, in spite of her assurances, I was really afraid she would never come back. I'd placed all my trust in her and now it seemed she was abandoning me. If I couldn't trust my Mamacita, how could I trust anyone? To these feelings were soon added anger and despair; the only thing left for me was to withdraw to a place deep within myself, the only place where I could find solace.

I learned much later that dramas like our arrival had been enacted many times before; with few exceptions, every child placed in the Home by a parent went through some variation of the same terrified struggle not to be left behind. Whenever possible the women in charge preferred to have this bit of theater exhaust itself there, rather than in Los Angeles, where some protesting children had to be dragged bodily from their mother's—and occasionally their father's—arms onto the streetcar by one of the matrons or a county caseworker. The emotional scene invariably drew a crowd and explanations had to be made to concerned onlookers.

While the matrons may have sympathized with our distress, they knew the best way to snap us out of our misery was to get us doing and thinking about other things. So soon the four of us were lined up to have our picture taken to record the arrival for posterity. Because of our unhappiness, getting us to look halfway pleasant for the camera was next to impossible, and the event had to be put off for a few days. Even then, it still took some doing. This was to be our "before" picture to be followed in a few weeks by an "after" photo to show how much healthier and better we were, a bit of promotional propaganda the Center would use to raise money for the Home.

◆

I asked Mother if she remembers how she felt after leaving us.

"You can't imagine how I cried," she said. "For days afterwards I was haunted by the image of you kids so miserably huddled and screaming after me. The woman from the Center did her best to comfort me, but it didn't help. The worst part was leaving Conchita, she was still only a baby. It broke my heart to do it."

As she related this part of the tale, I felt emotionally shut down and probably had a grim, unsympathetic look on my face. Her eyes had welled up with tears and, despite my feelings, I reached across to put a comforting hand on her shoulder. The touch was to tell her I believed her, and she seemed grateful. Still, I suggested, it must also have been quite a relief to know we were someplace where she didn't have to worry about us. She just wiped her eyes and nodded. Then in an uncharacteristic flash of candor, she admitted that despite her grief she felt like a great burden had been lifted from her, like she'd been set free; that, at twenty-four, for the first time in her life she had no one else to look out for but herself. It was a giddy feeling, she said, one she was fearful of enjoying too much. Even so, because of her small earnings as a waitress, she worried about being able to make the monthly payment to the Center, which she was determined to do faithfully and on time.

❖ ❖ ❖

We didn't see Mamacita again for what seemed like a very long time. Every day when I saw her at mealtimes, I asked Queta, "*Hermanita,* is Mamacita coming today?" And each time she shrugged sadly, or said, dejectedly, "I don't know, little brother." At first she always added in a confident tone, "Don't worry, Mamacita will come back." But after a while, she stopped.

When I'd nearly given up hope, Mamacita finally returned on a Sunday afternoon. We'd only been told of her expected visit after the noon meal and we were all waiting impatiently for her on the stairs at the south entrance to the Home's property, Conchita holding onto Queta.

"There she is, there she is!" Chuy and I yelled excitedly as she came into view. Seeing us jumping up and down and waving a frantically joyous welcome, Mamacita quickened her step as we ran to meet her. And there in the middle of the street, the packages she'd been carrying strewn on the pavement and momentarily forgotten, we all hugged and cried together. Mamacita then took Conchita from Queta and nuzzled her while the rest of us each grabbed the packages she'd brought, trying to guess at what they contained. Our happy little group then walked her up to the front lawn of the main house, where other children and their families were eating and visiting in the sunny warmth of the late October afternoon. And there for two hours that passed all too quickly we forgot our sorrow for a while and basked in the joy of each other's company.

"Are you getting enough to eat?" Mamacita wanted to know first. And then, "Are you being good and doing what the ladies tell you to do?"

Even as we ate the fruit and cookies she'd brought and chattered happily, I could sense Mamacita's relief that we were being taken care of, but also the sadness and maybe even guilt she felt for leaving us here. Then the fleeting, precarious joy we shared in the few hours of this first reunion instantly shattered when she prepared to leave. This time, as Mamacita disappeared into the reaches of the town, it was Queta who kept me from running after her.

During lunch in one of Colton's many chain restaurants where I'd taken her, Mother told me I looked tired and troubled. I confessed to not sleeping well, but felt I couldn't bring myself to tell her about the breakup of my marriage. I realized that I was being as secretive as I'd so often seen her, and smiled inwardly at myself. But then I'd never brought my troubles to her. Maybe that was because, not having her around when I was growing up, I'd never developed the habit. Besides, I was too ashamed to admit that I couldn't hold my life together.

CHAPTER 2

Josefina's Story

Back at the house an afternoon breeze had come up, making it cooler outside, so we sat on the shaded, north-facing porch, skipping from subject to subject for a while before we were able to resume the thread of our talk. The front and side yards were full of head-high cacti, so here, too, we were surrounded by the ubiquitous plants. Many were exotic and in bloom, but there were so many that not even their individual charms were able to dispel my sense of being trapped in a sort of green hell.

While I was trying to decide where next to direct our conversation, neighbors from across the street came over to say hello, though I think it was mostly to satisfy their curiosity about the shiny rented car and the stranger in their midst. From a past visit I remembered Mother telling me about the Pérez family, who'd come from Mexico and spoke little English. It was apparent they'd had a high regard for my late stepfather and treated Mother in a similar fashion. When they acknowledged me I did my best to talk to them in my halting Spanish. They were very polite, indulgent, and patient; my lack of fluency still embarrassed me, though Mother seemed pleased that I'd at least attempted to use Spanish. I was relieved when they'd gone.

When we were alone again, I wondered aloud if the Pérez family was here legally. Mother waved off the question, remarking instead that they were the friendliest and hardest-working people on their street. She also seemed to know a lot of other details about how the family made its way to Colton from Mexico. It reminded her, she said, of the journey her own family made coming to this country so many years before. With no prodding from me, she soon launched into the story. It was as if she was fixed on a track. She stopped looking at me, leaned forward in her wheelchair, and focused on some far-off spot beyond my head, seeing the memories. She began to describe the ranch house originally built by her grandfather on the outskirts of Chihuahua, Mexico. She lived there until she was twelve—long enough to remember it fairly well. Growing up, I'd heard disconnected bits and snatches of Mother's history. And though I knew she was born in 1911, I'd never connected that date with the second year of Mexico's ten-year-long revolution.

I must have had a strange look on my face when she began to tell me about how badly my grandfather treated her, because she believed he'd wanted a son and got her instead. I confessed that seemed a little incredible to me and, when I began to press her for details, she bristled at what appeared to be my questioning of her veracity. She'd misinterpreted me, I told her; it was his blaming her for the "original sin" of being born female that I found incredible. At the same time, it occurred to me that I might have been more sympathetic to my grandfather's attitude if my own firstborn hadn't been a boy.

As if to prove some point, Mother suddenly asked me to bring her the packet of photographs from the hope chest in one of the bedrooms. My stepfather bought her the cedar-lined chest when they married, and it had always been her most cherished piece of furniture. But now, Mother having long since run out of hopes, it held her memories instead. From the thick packet she extracted a number of aged and sepia-colored photographs, two of which were of her father. In one he was standing docilely beside and slightly behind his mother, then quite old, the dark, deeply lined skin of her decidedly Indian features testimony to the hardships of her life. In the other picture, José was seated, looking quite dominating, his wife, Enriqueta, standing beside him. In both pictures the standing person rested a hand on the shoulder of the one seated, probably a photographer's convention of the time, she said, but it struck me the seated person had the place of honor.

When I told her how moved I was to see these pictures, ones I'd seen only once many years before, she removed them from the pile and said, "Here, I want you to have them. Show them to your children." The sudden realization that these photographs may have survived a revolution, and certainly all the exigencies of Mother's life since then, and that they were being delivered to my hand in this moment, made me feel like crying. She was passing a part of our family's story from her generation to mine, the act bringing into stark clarity how remiss I'd been in failing to learn more of it or to pass it on to my children. While I relished the connection with my past, I realized what I'd denied my children by not making sure they at least knew their grandmother better. While for the moment I delighted in repeating silently to myself, "grandmother" and "grandfather," I knew regretfully they were words I'd never had the chance to use, having been

The author's maternal grandparents, José and Enriqueta Mejia (née Zavala), in El Paso, Texas, circa 1923.

in the presence of my grandparents only as an infant before they died. I remembered nothing at all about them. Even so, I knew only I was to blame for my children being denied the opportunity to know something about them.

The warm, sentimental mood changed abruptly when I suggested we talk about my father's side of the family. This was a conversation I'd tried to have with Mother before. It didn't work then and I was having no more success with it now. Irritated, she brushed me off again with, "I've already told you about Jesús." Jesús Sanábria was the man she was married to in El Paso by common law, the one from whom she fled.

When I was nineteen and about to go into the service, I began to doubt that Jesús was my father. I'd had to produce a birth certificate and asked mother for a copy. She clearly didn't want me to see it and I soon learned why: The box marked "Child's Surname" read "Mejia," Mother's maiden name. She tried to explain that at the time I was born, she'd answered, "no," when asked if she was married, because she and Jesús hadn't been married in the church. Later she found out she should have said she was married to him, because under Texas Common Law they'd met the requirements and legally were man and wife. I'd harbored enough shame for having grown up in an orphanage and later, when I had a lawyer verify what she claimed about common law marriage, it was a great relief to know I was legitimate after all.

Now, here we were back at the same touchy area. There was no point in spoiling our talk and, rather than lose the opportunity by pressing the matter, I asked her instead what she remembered about living through the Mexican Revolution, a subject about which I knew next to nothing. This was safer emotional ground for both of us, and I could see immediately she was as relieved as I to be able to continue.

I listened in thrall as memories flooded her mind, pushing her narrative off onto tangents. There was little organization, the recollections given voice as they occurred to her. I had to keep bringing her back to thoughts left dangling. Despite her apparent willingness to talk, her stories were often contradictory, and there remained a reticence about virtually every subject she touched upon, always a wariness that she might reveal more than she wanted me to know. It had always been like that with her and it was no less disturbing now.

"Mother," I began, "I don't know much about the Mexican Revolution. What do you remember about the fighting?" Her recollections were as hazy and disjointed as any child's would be, but some incidents stood out vividly. About the ebb and flow of the fighting she recalled little, mostly because she was so young and the family home somewhat isolated. But she well remembered some of the main combatants, like Francisco "Pancho" Villa, a local hero, the most colorful general and guerrilla-fighter pitted against the "Federalista" General Venustiano Carranza.

Often left alone in her grandmother's care, she and her siblings lived under constant threat of assault by either faction at anytime, day or night. She said she was often awakened, frightened by the pounding of horses' hooves when guerrillas or soldiers would come. And she told me how brave her grandmother was in standing up to them. They usually took what they wanted and demanded to know the allegiance of the household by shouting, as they rode up, ¿Villa o Carranza?; it was a deadly guessing game, which could determine the fate of the household. More than one of their neighbors had the misfortune to guess wrong. The price was heavy: Their houses were reduced to smoldering ruins, their livestock slaughtered, and they themselves hung from the nearest tree or telephone pole.

She'd told me this tale of terror before, when I was a child. But then I'd only half listened and didn't understand what she was talking about.

◆

The week's visit with Mother and Bill was interrupted with two days of traveling into L.A. to show slides of my sculpture to the directors of a number of galleries. Selling art is always more difficult than creating it, and each one I talked with told me they either weren't taking on new artists or they simply were uninterested in my work. It wasn't a new experience, but I still felt rejected and sometimes demeaned and angered by the arrogance some of them displayed. I had to remind myself how sensitive I am to rejection and what an easy step it is into paranoia. I did my best to remain objective, to keep in mind that, in turning me down, these gallery people were simply making business decisions—nothing personal. It still hurt. With artists it's love me, love my art—and vice versa.

The next morning, with one day left before leaving for the Bay Area where I was to attend an international sculpture conference, I wanted to get back to the questions I had about my father. Mother was upset that I'd spent so much time in Los Angeles and neither my apologies nor explanations about how necessary it was could do much to mollify her. She succeeded in making me feel guilty. I didn't love her for it.

The breakfast ritual finished, I pushed Mother in her wheelchair onto the front porch so we could enjoy the morning breeze. Then, to get her off the subject of my faithlessness, I broke her sulking silence by asking her why her family came to Texas.

"Why do you want to talk about that?" she asked, reluctant to get into what must have been another unpleasant period of her life. I ignored her question and plunged ahead, anyway.

"Let's see, if you were twelve when you moved to El Paso, it had to be 1923, isn't that right?"

As if doing the arithmetic in her head, she only nodded a hesitant agreement.

"And, if the war had already been over for two or three years, why did your parents leave Mexico?"

That, at least, got her thinking. But before answering, she shifted in her chair nervously and asked me to bring her a cup of coffee. As I left to get it, I knew she was delaying. But just as determined, I resumed where I'd left off when I got back.

"Well, things were pretty bad for us and everybody else for quite a while after the fighting stopped," she began, when we were settled again. She didn't really know for sure, but many people they knew had already crossed the border, some legally and others not, and that's probably what gave her father the idea. For weeks she recalled overhearing her parents weigh the possibility of going, too, reasoning that life in the United States, if not altogether good, had to be better than it was in Mexico at the end of 1922. Her mother hadn't wanted to leave her parents in Chihuahua and pointed out that it would be difficult to get work because none of them spoke English. But her father pointed out that *Tejas,* once part of Mexico, was full of their *paisanos* and that they could live among them in the barrio, so it wouldn't matter if they didn't speak English. As for work, he'd heard there was plenty of it. America beckoned, and in the end her mother had assented.

When he'd applied for visas at the U.S. Consulate in Chihuahua, her father had to prove that the family wouldn't become public charges. Mother doubted he had any money in the bank, but he did have his property, which he intended to rent or sell, and the title to his truck. That must have been enough because in the middle of the following spring their visas were approved. It was just before new rules requiring a literacy test in English, which certainly would have denied them entry, were to go into effect.

"Did your parents know anyone in El Paso?" I asked.

"No," she said simply, shaking her head.

"So where did you go?"

"Father already knew the first place most Mexicans went when they arrived in El Paso was to the barrio." She said it was in a southern part of the city, close to the Rio Grande, and known as *Chihuahuaita,* Little Chihuahua. Living conditions there were abysmal, but having nowhere else to turn, that's where her family went, too, while her father got his bearings. As much as they disliked it in the barrio, they nonetheless found shelter, food and work. It was also a grapevine of information to be gleaned from conversations in restaurants and saloons from those who had preceded them. Everybody had a story to tell, usually of hardship, of bad luck and lessons hard-learned. From these they also discovered what the unsuspecting newcomer needed to know to avoid being exploited, to survive.

The rest of the city, it turned out, was even less welcoming than *Chihuahuaita.* America may have beckoned, but Americans rejected them. Mother said if her parents could have imagined the extent of the hatred that so rudely confronted them, they would have stayed in Mexico.

Prejudice, injustice, and discrimination directed at Mexicans was rampant; the vehemence took their breath away. They quickly discovered Mexicans were rigidly excluded from social and political life and were only allowed the dirtiest and most difficult work. Although her parents seethed with resentment at these conditions, they decided there was no turning back.

As she relived the experience I could feel her indignation, and I shared it, too, knowing my face must be as flushed as hers. But she dismissed the memory with a frown and a wave of her hand, adding, with a note of cynicism, that ultimately what really mattered was *dinero.* Her father soon discovered that, ostracism notwithstanding, Mexicans with money and education or talent of any kind could actually make their way fairly well in gringo society.

Despite the unwelcoming social climate, the family in time discovered that El Paso wasn't so foreign, after all; they adapted to their new surroundings fairly easily. As her father had predicted, even though the laws and customs were strange, they soon felt as if they were living and working in a part of Mexico. In any event, like many of their countrymen, they regarded the move as temporary and believed, as her mother had promised her parents, that one day they would return to their homeland.

"Once the family was settled in El Paso," I asked, "how was your life different?"

"You know, now that I think about it," she said after a few moments, "those were the only days I remember as being at all happy." She was allowed to go back to school, she said, which during the fighting in Chihuahua she had been able to attend only sporadically. In El Paso she went to a Catholic school, where the nuns liked her and she did well, quickly improving her already passable English.

No pictures of her at that point in her life have survived, but judging from the woman I knew, she must have been a petite, beautiful girl, with her mother's fair skin, large brown eyes, and naturally wavy hair. I'd always known Mother to be warm and affectionate, a charmer, who smiled easily and was not a little coquettish. It was this charm and natural grace, together with his assumption that her family was better off than most, that had caught the notice of a young émigré from Chihuahua named Rodolfo Batres.

As Mother told it, Rodolfo was in his mid-twenties, a handsome, rakish young man with slick manners and a smooth tongue. When he began to court her, though her father remained skeptical, the rest of the family were soon taken in by his good looks and his entertaining and ingratiating manner. He was alone in El Paso and, because so many of the area's residents were immigrants or refugees, there was no way to check his background.

Even so, a few months later when Rodolfo asked her to marry him, even her father agreed she should; she became a bride, leaving home to set up housekeeping on her own.

"You were how old?" I asked, incredulous.

Looking at me soberly, a trace of a smile on her face, she repeated, "Fourteen."

"You were nothing but a child!" I nearly shouted.

"Well, maybe so, but back then that was a common age for girls to marry. My age wasn't the problem," she said and paused.

I waited. Could it be that Mother was actually going to reveal something hidden?

For the first few months she was happy and all seemed well, she told me, but that didn't last long. Rodolfo's aim in life, she discovered, was a fulsome enjoyment of leisure. He was loath to find and keep steady work, and "Fina," the nickname by which she was now known, could no longer count on support from her family. They were glad to be relieved of a mouth to feed, if not of her presence. She'd already given up school to become a housewife, and it wasn't long before she had to go to work as well. That wasn't easy in a city full of immigrants and refugees all vying for the few available jobs as waitresses, maids, and cleaning women.

"During the next two years I did all of those jobs I could find, even after I became pregnant and was well along," she said. And as the date for delivery of the baby became imminent, Fina's concerned mother roamed the barrio searching for Rodolfo. She found him, as she knew she would, living with another woman. Knowing he was in the country illegally, she threatened to have him deported if he didn't straighten out. When his promise to reform proved empty, Enriqueta turned him in, as she said she would. He never saw the twin daughters who were born on Independence Day, 1928, almost exactly a month after Fina's seventeenth birthday.

"Sounds like that whole situation with him was bad," I said. "He was a waster."

"Yes, but what really made me feel like I was bad luck for the family was grandmother Luisa's dying the same day the girls were born."

"That really must have hit the family hard," I said.

"That was just the beginning," she said. "I felt like I was being punished for grandmother's death because the following day one of the babies, the one I named Juanita for my grandfather, also died."

"But it was totally coincidental," I said.

"Probably so, but then everything seemed to be going wrong," she said. "I couldn't work and my husband had deserted me. At least I was allowed to move back in with my family, thanks to my mother."

◆

It was big news when a bank in the city collapsed in late 1930; and that was when everyone knew that the Great Depression had reached El Paso. It was much harder on the local Mexicans. Mother said her father worked all over the city, and he could see Mexicans were being fired in droves. And because Americans were complaining that Mexicans were stealing their jobs and using up relief supplies, the pressure for Mexicans to leave—both those legally in the country and otherwise—grew daily. Everyone they knew had been stopped to have their papers checked. When the government began the wholesale deportation of Mexicans, Mother's parents became increasingly anxious and began to wonder whether this might not be the time for them to return to Chihuahua. Still, they remained.

◆

That evening, back in my motel room, I made notes on the day's talk and began to sketch out a family tree. I wanted to get straight in my head who was related to whom, where they'd come from, and the dates and places of their births and deaths. Though I was eager to get Mother's help on it, I waited to show it to her until lunch the next day. While preparing warmed-over *guisado* and tortillas for us, Mother looked over what I'd sketched out. Her face clouded when I told her I wanted to fill in the tree with as many names and dates as she could remember. Despite an initial coolness, she seemed willing to help and we began while we were eating. This went along pretty well, and though there were a number of inconsistencies, the tree began to take on a satisfying form. That is, until we got to the slots for my father's information. I could see she was nervous again and quickly slid past filling in his name and dates.

At the risk of opening old wounds, I felt compelled to ask her about my birth. I knew from having seen my birth certificate that I was delivered in El Paso's County Hospital at eleven in the morning on August 20. Anticipating where this subject might lead, she diverted the focus to the actual experience of giving birth. Her face took on a relaxed, pleasant look as she described my entrance into the world, which was so swift she barely had time to get to the hospital. The delivery was so easy she almost felt like thanking me afterwards, she said—as if I'd actually had something to do with it.

I wasn't put off so easily. "Was my father present?" I asked. All I got was a shake of her head and that I-don't-want-to-talk-about-it look on her face again.

For a moment she was silent and then said, "Husbands didn't do that sort of thing back then." She grudgingly explained she and Queta weren't living with my father because her mother thought she should be with her family until after I was born. That seemed logical, but I'd learned to sense when Mother wasn't being entirely forthcoming. This was one of those times.

When we got to the date of her mother's death, in October 1931, she again remarked what bad luck she seemed to be for her family. Like Queta's, my birth appeared to signal the death of another family member, she said, this time that of her mother, Enriqueta. I insisted again it was pure coincidence, but she reveled in superstition and maintained there was more to it than that. She was vague about the immediate cause of my grandmother's death, but it had to be something major; she was only 39.

Enriqueta's death left her husband, José, despondent. Enriqueta had been the glue that bound the family together, the intermediary between an authoritarian father and his increasingly restless children. Without her, the family's cohesiveness began to unravel. Increasingly, José became obsessed with the idea of returning to Mexico.

Mother says her parents had always planned to return to Chihuahua, and if her mother hadn't died, it's likely at least she and her sisters would have returned with them. José blamed himself for his wife's untimely death, and when he left El Paso a few weeks later, he decided not to return to Chihuahua to avoid having to face Enriqueta's family. He had little reason to return there, anyway, as his property had long since been sold. Mother never saw him again.

While the family had been together, their combined incomes had made it possible to live fairly comfortably in El Paso. Emílio was a carpenter, while Manuel and Miguel worked as auto mechanics, when they could find such jobs, and ten-year-old Enrique did whatever odd jobs he could find. Still they couldn't make ends meet, and with their father gone, Mother's brothers decided to move to California where things supposedly were better. Never on very good terms with any of them, Mother was happy to see them leave for Los Angeles.

Mother's sisters, Esperanza and Aurora, stayed for a few more months and helped Mother with Queta's and my care. Then Esperanza also moved to Los Angeles, where she married and would be the first member of the family to become an American citizen. Mother saw this as Esperanza's final rejection of her former life and particularly of her tyrannical father, who believed like many of his compatriots that to change citizenship was a betrayal of our Mexican heritage. Briefly, Aurora also considered moving to Los Angeles, but ultimately decided to join her ailing father for a time in Ciudad Juarez. There she eventually married and settled. In July 1933, my mother received a letter from sister informing her that, at age 46, their father had died of kidney failure.

◆

I was drained. Pulling the story out of Mother hadn't been easy, but it filled in so many blanks. And it had the ring of truth, which was more than I could say for many of her tales. But she'd still told me nothing about my father and, though I could see she was tiring, I pressed the matter once again at the expense of really making her angry.

"Mother, can we talk about Jesús?" I asked, my voice as gentle as I could make it.

"*Mijo,*" she said in a near whisper, her face contorting with a frown, "You know I don't like to talk about him."

"Please," I persisted, "I know he wasn't a very nice person, but that's no reason not to tell me about him, is it?"

"No, I guess not," she answered with a heavy sigh. Reflecting a few moments she said, "He was an awful man and he abused me, you and Queta, too." She was visibly upset and fidgeted nervously with her hands.

"Okay, okay," I said. To calm her I rose from my seat and put my arm around her. "I don't mean to hurt you or make you upset, but this is as far as we ever get, and I don't think it's fair. Don't you think I'm entitled to know at least something?"

"Yes," she murmured with resignation. "I suppose you are." Then after a few moments of looking at her hands, she said, "What do you want to know?"

"Well, just tell me something about him, what he looked like, how you met," I suggested for openers, again taking my seat.

An émigré from Durango, Jesús Sanábria had come to El Paso with his family when he was quite young. Mother thought he was handsome, a man whose Indian heritage showed strongly in his dark complexion and straight black hair. He was twenty-eight when she met him, still living with his family, tall and strong from working as a yardman with the Southern Pacific Railroad Company.

They'd met in a small market where she shopped; feeling lonely and isolated at the time, she was taken in by his friendly, outgoing manner.

Meeting him made life seem a little brighter. At first she was encouraged by his ardor and apparent stability, although as time passed his promises of marriage and a home somehow kept being put off. Even when she told him she was pregnant, he wasn't moved to propose marriage or immediately to leave his parents' home.

"But when did you meet him?" I asked not so innocently.

"Oh, let's see, that was right after Esperanza and Aurora left El Paso and . . . "

Somewhere deep inside me an alarm went off. The inconsistency registered in the back of my mind. If she was right in her calculations, she'd just admitted Jesús couldn't be my father, because I was already born. Mother continued talking but I wasn't listening.

"Mother, something you just said isn't making sense," I interrupted, trying not to sound accusing or triumphant, almost ashamed to be trapping her like this.

"*¿Qué es?*" she said, unconsciously reverting to Spanish and looking at me with a startled expression.

"Well, you told me earlier your sisters left El Paso after your mother died. And now you just said that you met Jesús after your sisters left El Paso. That was in late 1931 or early 1932, and I had already been born. Right?"

At this she seemed to deflate, her face clouding. But she recovered with, "Oh, no, that wasn't it. I mean it was after Rodolfo left."

This was another instance of her vagueness about her past and it bothered me so much I could hardly listen to the rest of her story. But she was my mother and I didn't want to be disrespectful by directly questioning her honesty. I let it pass, but noticed she would no longer look me in the eye.

"So when you started seeing Jesús, your father forced you to leave his house?" I asked, once again trying to pick up the thread.

Eyes still cast downward at her fidgeting hands, she only nodded, and though she didn't say as much, her look betrayed the shame she was recalling for having disgraced her family by being involved in this way with a man she wasn't then married to. At this point we both needed a break. And she suggested I wheel her outside, where the late afternoon sun had lost most of its potency.

Changing the subject, I asked her how she was able to get along in the house alone all day while Bill was at work. It was a situation I'd long worried about. But Mother expressed little concern, and I noticed the whistle I'd sent her to alert a neighbor if she needed help was nowhere in sight. I began again.

"So let's see, on the first day of August, 1933, you had another boy," I said, a statement rather than a question. "Was Jesús pleased to have the child named after him?"

Mother looked at me as if debating whether to get caught up again in the discussion. But she said, "Yes, and we nicknamed him Chuy." But even as she said it, her head was shaking as if to deny the memory. While she recovered and took care of Chuy, she said, Jesús was still a reluctant husband at best. It wasn't long before his inattention and the need for money forced her to look for work once again. By then the Depression had settled in as deeply in El Paso as in the rest of the country; jobs of any sort were virtually nonexistent. Desperate for money, and probably to Chuy's detriment, she was reduced to wet-nursing the babies of wealthier families to survive until she found regular work. Then life resumed as it had been before; an aged neighbor woman the nuns had found watched Chuy and me while Mother worked and Queta was at school.

Then to my surprise, Mother began telling me about the first time Jesús hit her. It was at the end of the day he lost his job and the drinking binge that followed. "He hurt me. I only went to his mother for help, not to have him punished," Mother said, now looking at me intently. "But when his father heard what Jesús had done to me, he beat Jesús so badly I thought he'd kill him. Jesús's father was a big man, tall and heavily built. I don't think I've ever seen anyone as angry as he was that day," she said, a grim look on her face at the memory of it. Jesús undoubtedly knew he deserved the beating, but it still left him fuming with resentment. And months later when she told him she was pregnant again, he was anything but pleased. He was spending most of his time drinking at local cantinas, if he had the money, and she was terrified each night because it usually meant more abuse.

That was bad enough, but then Mother was horrified to discover that he was taking me along on his drinking forays to amuse himself and his friends. It took very little beer to intoxicate me. To the amusement of Jesús and his friends, I'd soon be singing and doing a kind of staggering dance around the barroom until I collapsed into a drunken sleep.

The revelation explained something that had bothered me for many years. "You know Mother, that must be why I get so anxious when I'm among strangers who are drinking, one reason I stay out of bars," I said.

"I'm sure that's why," she said. "You know, you would often get sick and throw up."

"I still do that, too, if I'm not careful. So what did you do about it?"

She explained that, because the old woman taking care of us during the day was powerless to stop Jesús, all she could do was to take me with her to the places she worked. For a time that solved the problem. While she went about her work, she had me follow her around holding onto her apron so she'd always know exactly where I was. The system worked well enough, but a few days later I was holding onto her as she prepared a pot of hot lye on the stove to use for cleaning. Without warning the mixture boiled over and some of the caustic brew splashed on my upturned face. My screams of pain were immediately drowned out by hers of panic. She looked aghast at the burns that seemed to cover my entire face. Her employer rushed us to the hospital. Fortunately, there was more blistering than real damage, though my face would be permanently scarred and one glob of the lye had come within an inch of blinding my right eye.

The accident filled her with a sense of hopelessness, she said. Because she feared for our safety, as well as her own and that of another child growing in her, she pleaded with her in-laws to keep Jesús away from her. They did their best, but he still tried repeatedly to see her, beating her when she denied him entry into our small house and refused his advances.

She was alone with us, isolated by one of El Paso's occasional floods, when she went into labor on the first morning of December, 1934. With the midwife unable to get through because much of the city was impassable, Mother knew she'd have to deliver the baby herself and told Queta she'd have to help.

"Poor Queta," she said, "she was so frightened. She did her best, but I couldn't get her to help pull the baby out or cut its cord. She was so terrified by what was happening, the only thing I could get her to do was bring me a knife before she ran out of the room."

"God, what a terrible time for you," I said, sounding a little lame. This was the first time I'd heard that story and it was really shocking. I remembered nothing at all about it but conjured an image of horror worthy of Hieronymus Bosch.

"It really was," she replied, shaking her head, a distant look in her eyes. "So many things were bad in so many ways, for a while I really thought I would go completely crazy."

Later it came to me that the circumstances of her birth could explain certain deficits in Connie's abilities that have hampered my sister all her life.

Out of the blackness of that desperation, Mother said, came the determination not to have any more children, and the realization that the only way to save herself and us from Jesús was to leave El Paso. With Esperanza's help, she made plans to go to Los Angeles. The resolution to leave did a lot to calm her anxieties, she said, and the emerging rudiments of an escape plan strengthened her will, gave her hope. But times were extremely difficult and it was months before she could save enough for the bus trip. In the meantime, she had four mouths to feed, the winter was cold, and she got only scant help from her in-laws—nothing from Jesús.

After our escape from him in El Paso, we saw Jesús only once more two years later, when Mother, Queta, and I accidentally met him on a street in Los Angeles. He was there blocking our path before Mother realized who he was or could avoid him. The encounter was brief. She was very anxious as he told her he had been searching everywhere for her. She told him defiantly they were finished and refused to answer his questions about where she lived. But before she finally broke away, he demanded to know where Chuy was, so he could at least take him back to Texas. She refused to provide that information, too. Furious, Jesús would later attempt, unsuccessfully, to kidnap Chuy.

I told Mother that for many years afterward, whenever I tried to visualize my father, what always came into my mind was that looming, fearful figure of the man we had met on the street. With that image also came the question of why he'd only wanted Chuy and not me or my sisters. She just looked at me and said nothing.

I'd heard bits and pieces of this sorry tale all through my life and hearing it coherently for the first time and in such detail really saddened me. I'd missed having a father, even the one Mother continually criticized, as she did any time his name or the subject came up. I knew she talked this way so that I'd hate him as much as she did, so that I'd put him out of my mind. But what she never realized was I so desperately wanted a father that all the badmouthing she did made him fascinating to me. What child, what boy particularly, has not imagined his father to possess greatness of strength, of wisdom, of prowess in whatever field? The fatherless child is no less prone to such daydreams, and I was not immune either. I'd never seen Jesús' imperfections for myself, so I could imagine him to be any way I wanted. Sometimes when I thought about him, I made him into some sort of hero and that briefly made me feel better about myself. At the risk of seeming disloyal to my mother, I could give him admirable qualities and invent good reasons, even romantic ones, why he was unable to come with us. Mother always claimed it was she who'd run away from him, but could I be sure it really wasn't the other way around? So even as Mother recited her litany of complaints against him, and though I knew better, I found myself making excuses for him, creating extenuating circumstances to mitigate his desertion. I'd often hoped that one day he'd come back. I so wanted to know my father I'd even planned, not so many years ago, to go to El Paso in search of him. And if I'd found him? Well, I guess I'd have forgiven him.

◆

Before leaving the next morning, I stopped by Bill's house to say goodbye. I considered telling Mother about my separation, but couldn't do it. Bringing it up then would have left a cloud over the visit and generated a lot of questions I didn't want to answer. Two weeks later, when I was late in making my usual Sunday night call to her, she called my home and learned the situation from my estranged wife. Mother was more upset that I hadn't confided in her than about the separation itself. No matter what happened, it somehow was always about her.

CHAPTER 3

Metamorphosis

Our arrival at the Home had been anything but pleasant. But even through the fog of despair, I could see that the sooner I reconciled myself to my new surroundings and tried to get along with these people, the easier life would be. I was here against my will, hardly looking for some sort of transformation, but that's exactly what happened. And, whether or not I was ready for them, some changes were already being made for me. This became clear when Miss Gibson, the thin, stern-looking woman in charge, introduced us to the other children and we discovered our names had been changed.

Standing behind the three of us lined up in the living room of the Big House, the larger of the two buildings that made up the Home, and placing her hand first on Queta's head, she said to the children grouped expectantly around us, "This is Henrietta." Eyes downcast, as if being sentenced, Queta listened mute and dejected. Then, patting me and my brother lightly on our respective heads as she did so, she told the knot of upturned faces, "This is Bobby, and this is Haysoos."

Not understanding, I looked quizzically at Queta and asked softly, "What's she saying?"

"She says your name is Bobby," Queta whispered.

"Why?" I asked. "That's not my name." And shaking my head vigorously, I blurted, *"¡Yo soy Roberto!"*

But Miss Gibson, who understood some Spanish, only eyed me impatiently and said emphatically to my sister, "No!" followed by words I didn't understand.

"She says we must have American names," Queta said. I became Bobby, whether I liked it or not.

Turning back to the other children, Miss Gibson said finally and in a more kindly tone, "And this is Connie." Her face softened and she smiled for the first time as she looked down at Conchita, cradled in her arm.

But that still wasn't the end of it. Miss Gibson found "Jesus" an intolerable name for a child and couldn't imagine herself or anyone else calling out the Savior's name, even in Spanish, every time someone wanted to get Chuy's attention. For days afterwards, she tried her best to accustom herself to using "Jesús," pronouncing it, "haysoos," but ultimately she simply couldn't stand it. So when Mother visited us again, Miss Gibson insisted she pick another name—an "American" name—for her younger son. Mother chose William, and he was thereafter known as Billy. But when we were alone with her, Mother called us by the names she'd given us. In Billy's case, though, she afterwards used Guillermo, the Spanish equivalent of William, preferring it to the given name he shared with his father and the husband from whom she'd escaped and whom she despised.

Henrietta already spoke some English, but for Billy and me these anglicized names along with those of the matrons were the first English words we learned to say. Our new names, which only Henrietta could yet pronounce, took some getting used to. The name Bobby just didn't fit me, and it was some time before I readily responded to it. Almost as much as living with these strangers against my will, I resented the identities that someone else had decided would be ours. The names and being forced to learn English further isolated us from the culture we'd known up to that time, and were but the first steps in our metamorphosis into something new. I became increasingly confused about just who I was.

◆

The three people in charge at the Home, all women, we regarded with awe, especially the manager, Miss Gibson. Everybody called her "Gibsie," a nickname she allowed because of the children's difficulty with pronouncing "Gibson," but it no way implied or encouraged familiarity. She was a thin, pale woman who seemed to tower over me. The rimless glasses she wore made over-large her pale-blue steely eyes, giving her an ominous appearance made more so by her prominent jaw. I soon learned the barely perceptible smile she wore was not a sign she was pleased, especially when she looked at me. Her features were capped by a head of prematurely gray hair, always cut short at the neck, tightly finger-waved. In the grip of a hair net, it was like a helmet. Her voice was sharp and penetrat-

The author with his siblings, left to right: Enriqueta, Roberto (the author), Jesús and Conchita, at the Home shortly after arrival there in October 1935.

ing even when she spoke in a normal tone, and it was downright terrifying when she raised it. These aspects and a ramrod-straight posture gave her a forbidding air. It wasn't difficult to tell when she was displeased, which was often, for then her lips would compress to a thin, grim line and her jaw would flex repeatedly. I decided then and there to keep as much distance between us as possible. Fortunately, she dealt mostly with the girls, so Billy and I usually saw her only at mealtimes, and even then she rarely spoke to us.

The woman everyone called "Fuller" was the one I liked best. Mae Fuller was the cook, and she was everything Gibsie wasn't when it came to personality. She wasn't considered pretty; she had a heavy chin and her light-brown tresses, worn in a practical bun, did nothing to enhance her looks. It was her other attributes that made her charming. Blessed with a full womanly figure, she was taller than Gibsie but didn't seem so overpowering, mainly because she was genuinely warm. When she smiled we knew she meant it. Besides, if any of us happened by the kitchen when Fuller was cooking, she could be talked into sharing a taste of whatever she was preparing, if there was any to spare. That she was not directly involved in disciplining us didn't detract from her popularity, either.

It didn't take me long to find out that, for all her Christian idealism, the boys' matron, Melissa Clarke, expected me to jump whenever she said to. She was a large, plain, somewhat-horsey woman whose heavy-hipped lumbering projected a stiffness and a personality that made me want to run from her. I wasn't surprised to learn that the kids had no nickname for her—at least not one they could utter in her presence. On the contrary, she insisted on always being addressed as "Miss Clarke." There was little that was friendly about her. Eyes pinched and mostly unsmiling, she was usually cross and impatient, and it was clear from the outset she took her job seriously and tolerated no foolishness. She regarded us with a cool disdain and refused any sympathy with my homesickness and lack of English. My failure to understand would first elicit a scowl; then she would lean into my face and turn up the volume, repeating her words more slowly and distinctly. But it was mainly through her pointing and gesturing that I understood what she wanted of me. For a while, it was a real struggle for both of us to get me to do as she directed. As with Gibsie, I stayed out of her way whenever I could.

There were half as many boys as girls. Billy and I, being far younger than the other boys, received little trouble from them. They bothered with us only when they had to. The most interesting was a friendly, eleven-year-old Peruvian named Edwin Ortiz, who had a glass eye, which I found fascinating. If pressed, he'd remove it and let me inspect it while he held it in his hand. "You know he can see with that glass eye even when it's not in his head," the other boys claimed. For the longest time I believed them. Edwin, who still spoke some Spanish, told me he and his older sister, Betty, had been in the Home for four years. From all appearances he seemed perfectly happy being there. But his sister told anyone who cared to listen that she hated it and couldn't wait to leave. I understood her perfectly.

Mario Uriarte, a tall, quiet boy, had been at the Home since he was two. When I first met him he was nine and in the Home with his eleven-year-old sister, Berta, a girl I thought was very pretty and who played the piano beautifully. Mario had never learned Spanish and at first we couldn't talk to each other. Even so, he was friendly and tried to show me the ropes. It was soon apparent he was a favorite of Gibsie's, who saw him as something just short of angelic. But Billy and I discovered before long that Mario's benign exterior masked a mischievous streak bordering on meanness, which soon showed itself to us.

Ruben Gonzalez, the only other boy who still spoke Spanish, was stuck with the assignment of getting Billy and me from one place to the next on time. He was a slightly built little guy who looked underfed even to my eyes, and indeed, despite eating regularly, complained constantly about being hungry. The haunted look often on his brownish face seemed to say he'd not forgotten how much of his young life he'd spent with hunger as a companion. So it wasn't too surprising that, when he wasn't supposed to be somewhere else, he could be found hanging around the kitchen—"where the food is," as he'd be quick to say.

Ruben had been there two years, as had his sisters. Nellie, eleven, was quiet, overly serious and kept pretty much to herself. The other was Margaret, seven, and just the opposite. We all got to know her quickly because she spoke Spanish, talked fast and relentlessly, and seemed to consider it her right to pry into everyone's business. She was volatile and unpredictable; one minute she'd blow up for no apparent reason, bursting into tears, then just as suddenly be all smiles again. At first I found her interesting, but she soon became overbearing and I avoided her. Two other girls, sixteen-year-old Victoria Ballesteros, and Regina Rivera, the oldest at seventeen, had already been at the Home eight years. Both girls were brought there years before by their fathers, who thereafter pretty much ignored them, a fact they didn't seem to mind at all.

Before she left us on that first day, Mother told Queta very emphatically to take care of the rest of us, a big and practically impossible job for her. Uncertain about her ability and despite her reluctance, she took Mother literally and from then on was our guardian, taking on anyone who tried to push Billy or me around. It didn't seem to matter whether it was one of the other fifteen children or even the matrons. Until we learned the routine and enough English to respond correctly when told to do something, she had her hands full. All of this took a while, and life for the first few weeks was hectic and more unpleasant than not.

After the initial excitement of our Sunday reunions wore off, our mother found herself with three very unhappy children on her hands. No amount of begging and crying could persuade her to take us home with her. Connie was different from the rest of us. She had been the darling of the place from the outset and happily responded both to the attention paid her and to the richer diet. In only four months it had put pounds on her tiny body. The rest of us were beginning to fill out somewhat as well.

◆

In the boys' building every kid had his own bed, and the first thing Ruben did was show Billy and me ours. A bed all for myself seemed like a wonderful extravagance, but at first I couldn't sleep well because I was not used to sleeping alone. I missed the warmth of another body or two and was afraid, especially when awakening alone during the night. The boys' building seemed vast and was, in fact, a large wooden, barn-like structure.

The sleeping area was one cavernous room with twelve beds arranged in rows, head-to-toe and side-by-side, many of them empty, awaiting new occupants. At the east end there was a row of closets for our clothes and meager other belongings. Adjoining the sleeping room was a communal washroom, with a bank of wash basins, a shower, and toilet; and next to that, a room for the matron. The building appeared to be very old and in desperate need of fresh paint, especially inside, where the walls were bare and had developed a deep brown patina, which wasn't unpleasant, or a pale, nauseating pea-green tint, which was.

During those first weeks, night was the worst time. With the daytime noise and activity stilled, the darkness of the dormitory smothered me and magnified my sense of loneliness; I often cried myself to sleep. Because the other boys often sneered at Billy's and my childishness, I tried to hide my sorrow. Billy wasn't so reticent. To her great annoyance, Miss Clarke, who was anything but motherly, for a time was obliged to rock him to sleep. This period of fear and anguish was one I would see nearly every new boy go through, and for some it lasted for weeks. In my case it seemed it would never end.

One feverish night my misery was suddenly replaced by terror. Whether it was the jostling of my bed or a slight sound that disturbed me I didn't know, but something snapped me awake. With the hair rising on the back of my neck and my body tingling with alarm, I saw an indistinct, slightly luminous, moving figure. I watched in dread as it floated in spectral silence across the room, threading its way through the rows of beds and disappearing into one of the closets. Petrified with fear, I buried my head under the covers and lay perfectly still. I was now absolutely sure a demon of some sort lurked in those chambers, and I couldn't wait to tell everyone about it. But the next morning I had a terrible time trying to explain what I'd seen and was even more frustrated that no one believed me.

For a long time after that, I slept with my head covered and refused to open my closet unless someone else was in the room with me. Eventually I began to wonder whether my apparition was really one of the older boys trying to terrorize me. I never found out for sure, but my suspicions were buttressed when Billy awoke one night a while later screaming that something was under his bed raising him up and down. I pulled my head out from under the covers in time to hear more than see someone on hands and knees scurry away from Billy's bed and quickly climb into another. Thoroughly exasperated, Miss Clarke ran in to quiet Billy. Of course when she demanded to know who'd scared him, everyone else pretended to be asleep. I kept my mouth shut, though I suspected it was Mario. I still couldn't be sure he was also the demon I'd seen. The closets continued to hold terror for me until, to my great relief, they were demolished three years later, when the building was torn down and the dormitory replaced with a new one.

◆

Right from the start, one of the things I took to at the Home was eating regularly. When we spoke of it later, my mother always insisted that we never went a whole day without eating something, though she admitted there were many days when that "something" wasn't much. So by comparison and although they were actually spare, the meals seemed varied and abundant. And that's why, even as a four-year-old, I found mealtimes, especially supper, to be both dramatic and memorable.

The dining room was at the west end of the Big House and itself seemed immense. A big picture window overlooked the backyard on its south side. As the evenings were already chilly, the fireplace set midway in the opposite wall was often lit during supper, adding a cheery element to the ambiance. Even without the fire crackling on the hearth, the room was pleasant enough, though what took place in it wasn't necessarily always so.

Ruben, dutifully carrying out his charge of seeing that Billy and I got to where we were supposed to be, pointed me to a chair near the end of one of the three large tables arranged in a "U" around the periphery of the room. He led Billy to a place opposite me and sat him on a chair, whose seat had been raised with a wooden box made for the purpose, and then stood at the place next to him so he could help my little brother eat, if necessary. In my eagerness, I started to pull out my chair to sit, but Ruben frowned, wagged a "no" with a finger, and told me to stand until everybody was told to sit.

Remarkably, as the other children entered the room they abruptly shut off their noisy chatter and stood quietly behind their assigned chairs. Then somewhat grandly the matrons came into the room, each taking a commanding place at the head of a table around which were alternately arranged as many as eight boys and girls. Each place had been set with an aluminum dinner plate, knife, fork, and spoon, as well as a paper napkin and a glass of milk, all of which I eyed expectantly. As I awaited the unfolding of the next act in the drama, I could see my baby sister, Connie, at another table happily seated in a high chair next to Gibsie. One of the older girls, sitting on her opposite side, was already spooning some kind of mushy food into her. When I spied Henrietta at the third table, she smiled as if to reassure me. Then at a nod from Gibsie, the matrons announced in unison, "You may be seated," a directive I didn't need to have explained.

As soon as I was seated I reached for the glass of milk at my place. Miss Clarke leaned toward me and whispered a sharp, hoarse "No!", a word I understood all too well. There was, it seemed, more ritual to come. Then Gibsie said something I later learned was "Let us pray," and everybody recited a prayer—one of a number of prayers I would shortly also be expected to say before each meal. This one went:

Before we eat this food, dear God,
 We'll bow our heads to pray,
And for Thy gifts and all Thy love,
 Our grateful thanks we'll say. Amen

Only then did the food appear, served by Fuller and a few of the older girls either directly on our plates or in bowls and platters that we passed around from one child to the next. If we were lucky, an evening meal might consist of stew with small bits of meat, though nothing at all like the tasty *guisado* Cuca had often made for us during our short stay with her. There might also be boiled or baked vegetables, and bread. Whatever the fare, the kids immediately dug in, some with obvious relish, others more tentatively, as if unsure whether or not the food was edible. There was little if any talking and most of that was done by one or another of the matrons, who told children how to use their eating utensils, to chew with their mouths closed, or not to talk while chewing. Neither Billy nor I spoke a word to anyone. I imitated the way Ruben used the utensils, while Billy used his fingers when help was slow in coming. I recognized little of the food served, but though it was strange and not especially tasty, I ate everything, as did every other child. Later I would become more discriminating, a sophistication that made no difference whatsoever. The requirement to eat every morsel was rigidly enforced.

As children finished the food on their plates and drained the last of their milk, they said something to the matron at their table and then left, each carrying his or her plate, utensils, and glass to the kitchen. Not knowing what the magic words were that would allow me to leave too, I sat at my place until Miss Clarke noticed I'd finished and said something to Ruben. He thereupon came to my place, gathered up my plate and utensils on top of his, and told me to pick up my glass and follow him to the kitchen. On the way he told me I must ask any time I wanted to get up from the table. The magic words: "May I please be excused?"

Meals might come like clockwork, but it was the middle of the Depression and we were reminded repeatedly that food was scarce. So it was jealously meted out, the daily amount sufficient only to keep us little more than lean. I was probably being fed well enough but was still always hungry. The daily menu was most notable for its predictability; I was soon able to tell the day of the week by what was being served.

It was all I could do to keep from gagging the first time I tried to eat the lumpy oatmeal served for breakfast, a far cry from the tastier tortillas and frijoles I'd been used to. Only a little better was the Cream of Wheat, served without milk or sugar on alternate days. Breakfast would have been a complete loss except for the glass of juice and triangle of toast that also came with it. I loved the jelly on the toast, except it seemed to have been applied and then scraped off, so that only the barest color and taste remained in the crevasses.

On weekdays the mealtime ritual was pretty much abandoned at noon, because most of the kids took their lunch to school. And even though Billy and I weren't yet in school, we got the same trace amounts of peanut butter and jelly in the sandwich, along with an apple or an orange, that served as lunch for everyone else. Older Home kids really prized getting a job at the school cafeteria, where there was plenty to eat. And sometimes the Red Cross came through with school-lunch money for the town's needy children, including some of us from the Home. Since there was never enough money to cover everyone, the school nurse had the unhappy task of recommending which families and how many Home kids would receive the lunches. For Gibsie the decision was easy; she simply picked the kids who were the scrawniest, the most underweight.

As the week progressed, meals were often made from leftovers. By Saturday, the main dish was likely to be a joyless bowl of watery vegetable soup, bolstered by a lone saltine cracker topped with a small cube of American cheese, which disappeared in one gulp. The bowl of rice pudding that followed was the meal's only saving grace. Once in a while for variation, in place of soup there might be a concoction called "tamale pie," an invention of Fuller's. It was made from cornmeal and laced with tasteless black olives, which turned the pie a dirty brown. This was one of the few things that resembled anything like Mexican food and was decidedly awful.

Despite my yearning for food, I developed an instant and intense dislike of cooked turnips and eggplant. When these were served, I gagged quietly while struggling to get the last bite down. Tomato aspic, which for some reason made my jaw muscles ache, also showed up on the menu with disappointing regularity. Rounding out a quartet of barely edibles was baked winter squash, a four-inch square of which arrived on our plates directly from the oven, unseasoned. This orange-pink vegetable stored beautifully in the cool basement pantry and, unfortunately for me, was available the whole winter long. But not liking a meal was no excuse for not eating it, and there were always some children who, long after everyone else had finished, sat at their places struggling to get down the last bites. If winter squash was on the menu, I was always among them.

Things picked up dramatically on Sundays. Breakfast often started with a treat: day-old cinnamon rolls or donuts. These came, I soon learned, from Decker's, the town's bakery, to which one lucky kid was dispatched on Saturday evening to pick up leftovers. The real stuff came at noon, when the best meal of the week was served, usually a wonderful roast beef dinner. We could smell it cooking all the way down in the south lot, a half-acre of once-terraced gardens and the Home's back entrance, as soon as we entered it on the way home from church. Besides the meat there would also be a heaping side of mashed potatoes and gravy, a cooked vegetable, bread, milk, and possibly fruit. From time to time, the roast beef was replaced with meat loaf, baked ham, or roast chicken. Regardless of what the entree might be, Sunday dinner was the one meal sufficient to leave me feeling pleasantly stuffed.

Because food was so hard to come by, Gibsie spent a lot of her time raising money for it or scrounging food itself. One source was the townspeople, who might send us leftovers from their dinners and parties. This could make for an intriguing variety of meals, but, despite Fuller's best efforts, it was hard to dispel the feeling we were actually eating other people's garbage. But hunger left no room for squeamishness, and we ate it. Better were the leftover fruits and vegetables the townspeople gave us. Some came from the town's community garden, when everybody's tomatoes ripened at the same time. And, during the years it was in operation, we could pick grapes left after the harvest in Carter's Vineyard just west of town. Others, like Mrs. Steinberger, the Sierra Madre School principal, invited us to pick oranges in their small family orchards or to gather from their garden plots the winter squash I so disliked. Gibsie and Fuller always accepted these offerings gratefully, and whatever fruits and vegetables we didn't eat right away they "put up"; we had them as preserves through the year.

◆

The author, left, and his siblings in an official group portrait for use in the Plaza community Center newsletter, The Plazagram, *circa 1939.*

Difficulty with the language magnified my resentment of the other aspects of life in my new home, so it was no surprise that I resisted adjusting to the routine. Willingly or not, the other boys shepherded us from place to place and showed us how to take care of ourselves. Billy and I were too young to go to school, and except for the chore or two assigned me, Miss Clarke decided not to demand too much of either of us during our first months at the Home. Besides eating and sleeping, we spent our days alone quietly playing in the yard. This changed markedly when more children began showing up. Within the year, four girls and four more boys arrived; five of them older, two my age, and one younger.

Henrietta did her best to look out for us, as Mother told her to, but during school days this was impossible. She'd started school within days of our arrival. That meant Billy and I had to fend for ourselves. By the time these new kids were on the scene I was better able to defend myself, and for a while I grudgingly took up the cudgel in Billy's defense. When I started kindergarten the next fall, however, Billy was on his own. He was no great shakes as a fighter and usually came out the worse for his encounters, which occurred with regularity. He had a penchant for collecting spiders, lizards, and snakes, which in itself might not have been all that unusual. Most boys are curious about such things. But Billy's fascination carried him a step or two farther. After the poor creatures had starved to death in the boxes he kept them in, he built little mausoleums for their carcasses and muttered prayers and incantations over their remains. This gave the other boys, who already considered him bizarre, reason enough to pick on him.

All the other children who arrived at the Home in late 1935 and during 1936 stayed for as few as three months to less than two years. The turnover created turmoil, the short-timers never getting sufficiently settled-in to be of much help with the myriad chores required to keep up so large a place. The constant flux also made it difficult to get to know them very well. In my withdrawn state, it took me months, even years, for a newcomer to come into sufficient focus to make a lasting impression. What was the point of trying to make friends with kids who were here today and gone tomorrow? Girls were even more remote, since I saw them primarily at meals and otherwise had little to do with them. Later, when I was older and became interested in girls, I got to know better some of the more accepting of them. But the real effect of the turnover was to magnify my inability to trust people and to intensify my efforts to avoid any real friendships. Afraid of being hurt, I became a "loner." I was desolate and friendless.

CHAPTER 4

Happiness Street

Before it happened to me, there was no way of knowing how devastating the process of divorce can be. The tortured course of ending my marriage meant living through four of the worst years I'd ever experienced; another year in Vietnam would have been preferable. It wasn't so much the divorce itself, which indeed was anticlimactic, as getting through the harrowing, years-long settlement negotiations. These resulted in, among other things, losing my home and, worse, for a while almost total alienation from my children. I was at a loss to explain my actions to them, because until I got some help, I couldn't really explain them to myself.

So getting my head straight had been essential to putting my life back together. And with it came a kind of understanding about the role the Home played in my choice of women. There are those who believe that when it comes time to find a mate, men go in search of their mothers. In my case, I found it hard to accept that the first woman I married could have been modeled not after my mother, with whom I hadn't grown up, but after Gibsie, of all people. Yet, looking deeper, that now doesn't seem so far-fetched. First married at twenty-four, I was sure at the time that I'd done so for love. What I was really seeking, it seems, was something much more pragmatic: someone with attributes like status and respectability, and someone whose standards conformed to those instilled at the Home. If that was my underlying goal, I was almost compelled to choose someone who was Anglo and educated, one who represented the ideal American; marrying such a woman would move me, by association, closer to being a "real American" myself.

Of English-German-French extraction, my first wife had two degrees and came from a wealthy, propertied, typically mid-America family. Her father and grandfather were both physicians, her mother a school teacher;

they were solid citizens all. Subconsciously I was "marrying up," thus proving to myself and to the world that I was indeed good enough to be a "real American." Marrying her would at the same time further suppress my own ethnicity and a self-loathing I'd learned to associate with it. I attached so much significance to these aspects of my marriage that when they began to diminish in importance, other fundamental aspects of the relationship were exposed. These aspects were insufficient to keep the marriage together and, indeed, did much to destroy it. That's at least part of what happened. My disenchantment was helped along by the trauma of thirteen months in Vietnam and a life-changing decision after I left the army to become an artist.

Graduate school is about focusing on a narrower area of study. I went because I thought I wanted to teach art, the G.I. Bill providing the means. What I learned, though, was less about art than about myself. While it may be possible to be creative without involving one's personality, as I at first tried to do, real self-expression is not the result. Fortunately my professors, people who didn't hesitate to question my motives, refused to accept the facile work I produced. Instead they demanded that I make myself manifest in my work, that I make it unique to me. To do this forced me to examine who I was. And once the self-examination began in earnest, many of my beliefs—and delusions—about who I thought I was began to crumble, to be replaced with another more real self.

This metamorphosis, already well under way, coincided with my selection of a second mate. She wasn't a complete departure from the first, in fact she had many of the same desirable attributes; she was solidly middle class, educated, from a good family, her father was also a professional. But this time around, those attributes assumed less importance than they had the first time. By now I'd come to embrace my ethnicity and, thanks largely to the Army, had created my own status and respectability, rather than trying to live in the reflection of someone else's. More importantly, besides being a soulmate, herself from a group that has known the worst kinds of prejudice, she had a keen understanding of what it was to be an outsider and, as an artist, had an equally strong passion for personal expression. To start a new life together, we'd built a home—much of it with our own hands—with a large studio a few steps away in which to do our work.

The tail-end of the miserable winter of 1987 was hanging on like an icy shroud in Washington. But the renewal of spring had already arrived in Colton, where I'd returned to visit and introduce my wife of one year to my mother and family. Two days before we arrived, Mother was taken to the hospital, an occurrence of growing frequency, and it was there that she was forced to receive us. Vain even in a crisis, she was very upset to be caught in such unflattering circumstances, but there was no help for it. Even so, the visit was pleasant enough, and an hour or so later we left the hospital with time on our hands.

Sherry, my wife, had only been to the West Coast once, many years before, and now she put me in the role of tour guide. As both of us are artists, the new L.A. Museum of Modern Art and nearby Temporary Contemporary were musts, as were Hollywood, and the beaches at Santa Monica and Venice. But until she suggested it, showing her Sierra Madre hadn't occurred to me. I had no desire to see the town again, but in the end agreed to take her there.

Among the many high-speed freeways in the greater Los Angeles area is one that goes near Sierra Madre's southern extremity, and we arrived there in short order. As we drove into town we were fascinated by the array of Jaguars and Mercedes—there was even a Rolls Royce—we saw parked or driving by. Sherry rightly branded it a Yuppie town; nothing at all like when I lived there, I assured her. She also noticed something else I was never much aware of then, if at all: With a spring-blue sky sparkling above the San Gabriel Mountains towering in the background, Sierra Madre was really quite beautiful.

We parked in the heart of town and began a walking tour. She was very curious and excited to be in this place where I'd walked as a boy. She was hoping for a running commentary about what my life had been like there, but this was next to impossible for me. Reluctant, I cast about for a place to start. I looked for some of the buildings I'd known and recognized a few, like the office of the *Sierra Madre News*, what used to be Roberts' Market, and the old movie house, now the home of a local theater group. The rest I couldn't be sure about. But there was no mistaking the Congregational Church all of us Home kids were required to attend. I declined her request to explore it for the moment, the first of the memories it evoked being one I didn't want relive just then. Instead I suggested we walk up Highland to where the Home was located. The streets were much shorter than I remembered, and we were quickly at the corner of Auburn, where Sierra Madre's elementary school still stands. It's a beautiful building, done in classic Spanish style, with off-white stucco walls, red-tile roof, and an arcade that runs the length of the ground floor of the building on its south side. It didn't seem at all changed and, my excitement growing, we didn't hesitate to go inside.

The youngish principal we found in the office all but yawned when I told him how long ago it was that I'd attended. He said nothing about children or teachers, but seemed only interested in relating how the town fought to preserve the building as the architectural treasure it is, and about how much the town paid to have it reinforced to withstand earthquakes. Then, satisfied he'd properly impressed us, he agreed to let us roam the halls. I left wondering how much interest he really had in teaching children.

Once on our own, I was more voluble about my experiences in this place, which began more than fifty years before. I even remembered the school song we sang those many years ago:

Sierra Madre,
    School of my childhood,
Beneath your Sycamores
    I will linger for ever more.
Close to the mountains,
    Blue skies up above you,
Sierra Madre School,
    You know that I love you.

On the day after Labor Day, 1936, I started kindergarten. For months I'd watched other kids go off to school each day wishing I could go, too. But now that my turn had arrived, I was frightened by the prospect and refused to go. My reaction was hardly a new one to Gibsie and Miss Clarke, and they were ready if necessary to have me dragged there bodily. But Henrietta, ever watchful, again came to my rescue and took me there by the hand, assuring me all the while that I'd soon learn to like school as much as she did. She deposited me in the kindergarten room, leaving me to my fate before I realized she'd gone.

The room was full of children, but none from the Home. I understood no one, and the other children left me to myself. From the first, all classroom instruction was entirely in English, and since it was sink or swim, I felt I was sinking fast. Hearing English spoken during the preceding months at the Home had "tuned" my ear, but any words I'd learned suddenly abandoned me. Understanding was a major problem, along with its correlative, trying to make myself understood. My attempts only seemed to make the other kids laugh. I soon quit trying. Being virtually speechless wasn't so bad most of the time, as kindergarten was mainly about games, songs, and repetitious drills of one kind or another. I got along simply by mimicking what I saw and some of what I heard. I was more than happy to say nothing. The teacher had other ideas, and made it clear she expected an answer when she spoke to me. While she and everyone else waited for something intelligible to come from my grimly clamped mouth, I was in misery, angry and ashamed of my helplessness. During most of that first year I spoke to almost no one in class. To get to the bathroom I gestured and pointed to be understood before I shamed myself. If there hadn't been other Home kids at school, I'd also have been silent on the playground and at lunch. Thankfully this predicament didn't last forever.

In the first grade a year later, I emerged from my cocoon of ignorance and was able to speak English pretty well. Language was even less of a problem when I reached the second grade, and my grasp of English made me feel more a part of things. That year began unremarkably. Each morning in class we recited the "Pledge of Allegiance" and then sang one of a variety of songs before settling into the day's instruction.

But one day the teacher said, "Today we're going to learn a new song I'm sure you'll like. It's called, 'I Am an American.'" She began to sing:

> Rich or poor, young or old
>   Let this lesson be told,
> Shout! wherever you may be,
>   I am an American,
> I am from the heart of me . . . .

We worked on that for a few minutes and then went on to the next stanza. But even then, each time we came to the refrain, "I Am an American," it struck me as a challenge to my integrity. I might have learned English, but I was still a long way from considering myself an American. By the time we returned to the beginning of the song, I decided to show that I, too, was proud of who and what I was. So when we came again to the refrain, I substituted "Mexican" for "American," each time it was repeated in the song. At first surprised, the teacher tried to ignore the substitution, but as my voice was loud and clear—I virtually shouted—she couldn't ignore it for long and fixed me with an annoyed stare. The next time I did it, she stopped the class in mid-song. I was aware of the other kids looking at me, some amused, others with confused looks on their faces.

"Bobby," she inquired reasonably, "don't you want to be an American?"

It felt good to stand up for myself and, eyes bright with pride and excitement, I hesitated for a only moment before shaking my head, no.

"Of course you do," she said sternly. Then facing the class again, she continued, "All right, let's try it again."

But I was not to be so easily silenced and, when we resumed singing, I defiantly repeated the word. This time she stopped the class and hissed angrily at me, "Bobby, you will not use that word again! Do you understand?" Then, "That's all the singing for today, class. Take your seats."

I couldn't understand what she was so upset about. I was only saying what I thought was true, believing I was being loyal to my mother and others like us.

When we were all seated, the teacher waggled a finger at me and said in a calmer, but still assertive tone, "You should be glad to be an American, Bobby. Believe me, it's *much* better to be an American!" Before then it had never occurred to me that to be Mexican was to be something lesser, but her tone made it clear it might even be something to be ashamed of.

Yet later in the year, the teacher taught us a song in Spanish and showed pictures of Mexico as well as some of its food and customs. She even brought to class a sombrero and a multicolored, Mexican blanket called a serape. All this no doubt was well-intentioned and may even have been calculated to give a little dignity and praise to Mexican culture. But it had just the opposite effect when she suggested I don the sombrero and serape, articles I'd never worn or would ever consider wearing. I felt even more foolish when she asked me to explain the food, some of which I'd never eaten, much less knew how to prepare. It embarrassed and shamed me to know less about such things than the teacher.

One day a short while later, my class traveled to Los Angeles, where we visited Olvera Street, what was left of the original plaza of the Old Los Angeles founded by Spanish Franciscan Friars. From all outward appearances it was a festive, colorful place, a single street down the middle of which were booths where dark-skinned men and women sold things purported to be Mexican. There were dolls in peasant dress, ornate pottery, serapes, posters of costumed men fighting menacing bulls. The air was filled with the smells of cooking and spices, odors I recognized and liked. I could tell without looking that the vendors must be selling dishes like tamales, tacos, and enchiladas. Still, I found the place disturbing. The people in the booths were foreign, wore strange clothes, and appeared for all the world like displays in a museum. I felt embarrassed for reasons I couldn't explain. Was I one of them? Was that what the teacher meant?

In particular, I was fascinated by an old man who was playing a harp. His face, under a great crown of white hair, was deeply lined and had the shiny patina of worn leather; the look in his eyes was distant, as if he were in some other place. I liked and recognized the music and he played it very well. But what caught and held my attention was the extra finger on his left hand. It had no fingernail and dangled there uselessly, flopping back and forth as the harpist's hand moved across the array of strings, adroitly plucking out a long medley. The extra digit was part of his hand, but it seemed as odd and out of place as I felt just then. I couldn't wait to leave.

As my wife and I walked and talked our way through the school building, I recounted some of my more distressing experiences. Sherry had listened without interrupting until I lapsed into silence.

Stopping me with a restraining hand on my arm, she asked, "So, how did you get through those times?"

And standing there in those hallways I felt again, for the first time in half a century, the terrible conflicts and confusion of those early school years. The pressure to conform was considerable and mostly negative, and my first impulse was to rebel. Yet somehow I knew I wouldn't do well either by trying to hang on to what I thought I was, or by being defiant. The conflict left me feeling paralyzed and, if no longer speechless, in a rage. "I became the bully of my class," I said, "literally battled my way through most of my elementary school years. Other Home kids reacted differently to the situation, but fighting at least gave me some sense of control."

A lot of the problems for us from the Home had to do with learning English. Though most of us learned it well enough, it wasn't a happy experience. To spur the learning process on, the teachers forbade us to speak Spanish to each other and reprimanded us whenever we lapsed. Some children, especially those who spoke only Spanish and started school when they were older, had greater difficulty and sometimes became disruptive. A few simply ran away and hid rather than go to school. For them, those early school years had a lingering bad aftertaste and may have adversely colored all their later learning experiences. At least our teachers and principals never put any of us in a special class for the feeble-minded or the recalcitrant. As late as 1960, some Mexican-American children in California schools who could not speak English well were still being put into classes for the mentally retarded.

Sherry seemed enchanted by this jewel of a school building. And I had to admit our exploration of it had not left me entirely sorry to relive some of the experiences I'd had there; some were actually quite happy and affirming. But for the most part, I was unsettled as we left, probably because the next place on the itinerary was to where the Home itself had been.

As we continued our walk up the hill, I pointed out the house at the corner of Foothill and Highland where a girl named Priscilla had lived. She was probably the most popular girl in our eighth-grade class, round-faced, freckled and blue-eyed, my idea of what a fabled "fair maid" must be. I'd mooned over her for months. Romance at any age was always of interest to Sherry and, of course, she wanted to know all about Priscilla. Somewhat uneasily, I explained I thought she was the daughter of a naval officer and, even at her young age, an accomplished pianist who, with the music teacher, played perfectly Gershwin's "Rhapsody in Blue" at our commencement. And I confessed I remembered her mostly for being the girl I was certain I loved—and also one who wouldn't have anything to do with me. I never knew for sure, but I suspected this was because I was Mexican, or somehow tainted for being from the Home, or both. As I said all this, and not without some bitterness, my story took a detour. I described how I saw Priscilla again a few years later in Las Vegas, by then married to another of our Sierra Madre classmates, a boy named Jimmy, and already the mother of one or two kids. Like them, I was then twenty-five, a newly minted army first lieutenant driving with my former wife to the East Coast for embarkation to an assignment in Germany. I was feeling a little smug, knowing I was off to see more of the world. Seeing Priscilla so domesticated, so tied down to family, was cathartic for me, and I left believing the visit had dispelled any remaining hurt. As I told Sherry about it, I was surprised to discover that wasn't the case; given all the other wounds that remained, I should have known this psycho-baggage couldn't be so easily discarded.

When we arrived at Alegria Street—*alegría* is Spanish for joy, happiness—and began to walk its length, I had a surreal sensation of something just beyond the edge of consciousness. Two or three people were working in their front gardens as we walked by and, it seemed to me, they eyed us suspiciously. Maybe they'd seen other people like me spending a little too much time searching for something that was no longer there. I resented their wary looks, though I knew I'd probably have the same reaction, were I in their place.

The Big House had been located at mid-block on this street and, while I should have expected it, I was still shocked that no trace of it remained. Constructed on a grand scale, the Big House and its grounds had occupied three lots, a good quarter of the ample length of Alegria Street. Of course, the stunning view of mile-high Mount Wilson, the view I'd hardly noticed as a child, was still there, though the mountainscape had been blemished, studded here and there with houses. Back then, Alegria Street was pretty much at the town's northern extremity and the Big House, which at one time must have been one of Sierra Madre's proudest residences, dominated this quiet street of older, affluent, well-tended homes.

Some of the houses that existed back then were still there, largely unchanged, and I had no trouble recognizing them. Their presence helped me fix and reconstruct not only where the Big House had been, but also its features. I could almost see the lattice wood fence, punctuated at intervals by tall, square, brick pillars, that ran along the street, fencing off the lawn and buffering the house from the roadway. Gazing at where it once stood, I was aware of struggling to keep disturbing feelings from coming to the surface. It was a strange reaction, involuntary and unbidden, but with some effort I was able to squelch it. I realized that suppressing such feelings was exactly what I'd done to survive there.

To my newly arrived, four-year-old eyes, the two-storied, white stucco Big House was huge, mysterious, and fearsome. I learned soon enough this was where the girls lived, where we ate our meals, entertained visitors, and did all the really important things. I mostly found out about its various rooms by using or helping to clean them. It was many weeks before I discovered the full extent of the Big House's myriad spaces, before I ventured into its more secluded recesses and crannies.

There was a long, brick-paved portico on the north side and at approximately its mid-point was the dark-green, double-doored main entrance. This led into an impressive foyer, complete with a heroic landscape mural covering one entire wall. Even though its colors were faded and browned with age—probably by cooking fumes from the kitchen just around the corner—the mural was still discernible, a picture of a majestic mountainscape with a cascading waterfall. From this entrance it was possible to go directly to the living room, located just to the left, but most people, even guests, walked up through the South Lot and arrived through the back yard.

The living room was an enormous, high-ceilinged space, with a large fireplace at its east end. Though at first my understanding was limited, I still liked the evenings spent reading, or in my case being read to, as well as learning songs and dances. There was also a piano, the first I'd seen, on which the children who were taking lessons practiced.

Though no one actually said I couldn't, it was some time before I felt like I had permission to explore my surroundings. I felt like I was in a kind of wonderland, an awe that helped allay my resentment at having to live there. My introduction to the kitchen was to help wash dishes, but it was still my and every other kid's favorite place. My reason, like theirs, was food; the fear of not having enough was an anxiety that remained long after I came to know the next meal was a virtual certainty. At its entrance from the front yard was a small pantry. But when I went to explore it, the only food I found stored there was for Rico, the Home's pet mongrel dog.

The one place I was told I couldn't go was to the second floor, where the girls, Gibsie, and Fuller slept. The prohibition naturally excited my curiosity and set me to wondering what went on up there. In the absence of any actual intelligence, I conjured lurid images of little girls frolicking naked, as we boys did on bath night in our building. The flat roof over the living room was a sun deck, a favorite spot for taking snapshots and group portraits, and the only way to get there was through those upstairs rooms. It wasn't long before my curiosity about them was at least partially satisfied, when I made my first trip upstairs for that picture-taking purpose. Afterwards I was able to add more accurate detail to my visions of unadorned nymphs at play.

More mysterious and spooky was the large basement, which for some time I avoided entering alone. You could get to it by a stairway leading down from the hall on the main floor, as well as through two outside entrances. At first I only went there in the company of a matron or older kid to help sort and do other chores associated with the laundry. But in another part, deeper in the basement's recesses, canned and dry foods were stored, much of it preserved fruit, jams, and jellies. It was the lure of these sweet temptations that eventually overrode any fear I had of the basement itself. Along with other boys, I spent many hungry-eyed minutes clutching and staring through the chicken-wire that separated us from that bonanza.

Large parts of the basement area were unfinished crawl spaces filled with construction debris and layers of dust, and thick with sticky spider webs. In time these became places for secreting forbidden personal treasures and for hiding when I was being sought by one of the matrons or another child. When I discovered the dimly lit room that contained the coal-fired furnace, it became a favorite place not so much to hide in, but simply to be alone; eventually it was a place to be alone with one of the girls. Like many other Home kids, I was destined to have many a meeting of secret intent in one part or another of the basement area.

If the seemingly vast expanse of backyard had ever been a lawn, there wasn't a blade of grass anywhere on it now as a reminder. Dominated by two towering California pepper trees, the backyard was where we spent most of our play time and hung the laundry on washday; we gang-raked it clean once a week. Shaded by a large date palm, the boys' building was at its east end, which made it easy for Miss Clarke to keep an eye on us through the window of her room. For most of the backyard's length along its south edge, there was even an arbor, partially covered by a wisteria vine, where Billy and I spent most of our time playing.

The broad brick steps at each end of the arbor led down to more terraced gardens, mostly overgrown with bamboo. The area, known as the "South Lot," extended all the way through to Grandview Avenue, the next east-west street to the south. It was these grounds we first saw when we arrived at the Home and into which Mother disappeared when she left us behind. No matter how many times I traversed them, they were always a place of sadness.

The pepper trees in both the front and back yards were so large it took three or four medium-size children with arms outstretched to encircle the trunk of any one of them. The trees produced hundreds of small red balls, a kind of fruit I was sure had to be good. On a day not long after I'd arrived, and always interested in food, I decided to see if these little berries might be something good to eat. Unmindful of other kids watching, who'd already explored this potential manna, I picked up a berry, sniffed it, and popped it into my mouth. The little ball was quite hard and there was no discernible taste until I bit into it. The other kids laughed devilishly when they heard the crunch of my teeth shattering the berry, whose wretched bitterness I hastily spit out in disgust. Another lesson learned the hard way.

But there were also real fruit trees—apricot, persimmon, pomegranate, guava, orange—that really excited me and everyone else. It was only the watchful eyes of the matrons that kept our impatience in check long enough so that we could actually pick something ripe.

CHAPTER 5

Getting Along

Fitting in at a place like the Home boiled down to learning the routine, and despite my stubborn resentment, I soon discovered there was no resisting the schedule that seemed to account for every minute of life. We were just as involved in taking care of ourselves and our home as the matrons were; with the exception of cooking and doing the laundry, we kids did all the day-to-day work. I was told repeatedly that I had to "learn to take some responsibility," and that translated into doing the one or more chores each of us was assigned for the week.

My Pavlovian conditioning began the morning after we arrived, when I was rudely jolted awake by the loud ringing of a bell. There was no doubt of its meaning, for as I sat upright in amazement, covers were suddenly flung off of beds and their occupants propelled into a flurry of action. That bell, it turned out, governed all activity. It sounded in both houses giving a five-minute warning for the next event on the schedule. No one had an excuse for being late for meals or work, or for not getting off to school or church on time.

Unlike most of the boys, who hated getting up, I was usually already awake by 6:30, the time we were rousted out on weekdays. But what I did detest was being cold; the October mornings were already chilly. During the first couple of weeks when the bell went off, I jumped out of bed, grabbed my clothes, and made a dash for the lone space heater in the washroom. Everybody else also ran to huddle in what little warmth it gave while dressing. I was gleeful about getting there first, until one morning when someone unceremoniously pushed me against the heater's hot metal grill, a not-so-subtle hint that age and size had their privilege.

As a new kid I had a lot to learn about taking care of myself; I also had to learn how to do the variety of chores from which only the very youngest of us was exempt. For the first few days Miss Clarke stood over me to make sure I washed my face, gesturing extravagantly to show me how to brush my teeth. Then she marched me back to my bed and with Ruben's help showed and explained how I was to make my bed. The other boys had by now already done this and were off starting the chores they'd been assigned. And all this before breakfast.

Like all meals, breakfast was inaugurated with a prayer. This one went:

> For this new morning, with its light,
> For rest and shelter of the night,
> For health and food and home and friends,
> For everything Thy goodness sends,
> We thank Thee Heavenly Father.
> Amen.

Miss Clarke decided Billy was too young to do any work, but not me. Probably because I was the newest arrival, the first job I got was scrubbing out the washbasins and the toilet, the most revolting of all the chores. With Ruben as my coach and though I could just see over their tops, I made quick work of the washbowls. But the commode was another thing entirely. I'd not had much to do with indoor plumbing, but I knew all about *caca* and wanted nothing to do with anything associated with it. Besides, the boys were careless about their aim (knowing, I suppose, they wouldn't have to clean up after themselves) so the toilet and the floor around it inevitably were a smelly mess. No matter how much Ruben tried to cajole me, I refused to stick my hand into the toilet bowl or touch any other part of it. When Ruben told Miss Clarke of my stubbornness, she at first exploded. But then she had Ruben explain it wouldn't be a permanent job, that I only had to do it for a week and then it would be reassigned to someone else. Then, as if to show not even she was above such things, Miss Clarke proceeded to demonstrate the finer points of cleaning the commode and the rest of the toilet, including the floor. It was impressive, but I was still not convinced it should be my job.

Until I'd done every chore at least once, one of the older boys was charged with showing me how it was to be done. They were always excellent "instructors," because they knew they'd have to do the job themselves if I didn't do it right. The matrons always checked our work, and "a lick and a promise" (as Gibsie described a job sloppily done) was never allowed to get by. If something was not done up to snuff, it had to be done over as often as necessary to satisfy Miss Clarke; the idea eventually dawned that it was easier to do it right the first time. Nor was there any escape, for if chores weren't finished by the time a kid left for school at 8:30, the job would still be there for him to do when he returned.

Except at the outset, getting me to work didn't prove to be all that hard. Of course if I refused, Miss Clarke could always resort to a slap or a swat on the rear end. But usually it only took the threat of having a privilege, like going to the movies, denied. I also didn't want to disappoint my mother or risk her disapproving eye when she was told I wasn't cooperating. Despite my continuing resentment at being left at the Home, I still tried to please my keepers and win their praise for doing a good job. Doing chores wasn't all bad. In fact, there was even a certain excitement in learning each Sunday night what the upcoming week's assignments were. There was a sense of accomplishment in doing them, too. They served as milestones, as through the years I moved up from the chores associated with the little kids to those of the big boys.

The matrons were obsessed with having everyone and everything clean and orderly. It was an attitude I didn't mind one bit and readily assimilated. I'd associated messiness, dirt, and clutter with the chaos and insecurity that had accompanied my life to that point, and now I took solace and reassurance in the order and cleanliness that was so much a part of my new life.

The rule of keeping clean applied no less to our bodies. Some of the boys didn't mind, perhaps even enjoyed, being dusty and dirty. Some actually hated bathing, but I delighted in discovering I "got" to bathe once a week. Before then I'd never been in a shower or even had a bath in anything other than a galvanized-metal laundry tub. So when bath night came around on Saturday, I was the first into the shower, staying until forcibly ejected. And with that physical washing away went some of my innocence as well.

The first time we collected in the communal washroom for our Saturday night bath, I watched, fascinated, as some of the boys, a fist clamped around an erect penis, pumped away in the shower. Though there was only one shower stall, three or four boys at a time crowded into it. The rest of us stood around bare-assed waiting our turns. All this nudity inevitably led to the comparison of individual endowments, as well as to some interesting demonstrations of what one could do with one's "equipment." It didn't take long for me and every other boy to learn at least the rudiments of "self abuse," if not its nuances.

Miss Clarke, probably embarrassed by the sight of our nakedness, preferred to leave us to manage bath night on our own. Not surprisingly it quickly turned into a frolic. It didn't take much for order to disintegrate: One boy flicking another's naked *nalgas* with a damp towel usually was enough to cause an all-out towel-snapping free-for-all. Then, like a cageful of excited monkeys, we'd all soon be leaping about the washroom, our young bodies wet and glistening, towels flying and snapping vigorously to the accompaniment of much laughter, whooping, and jeering. When the noise level reached a dull roar, the hubbub finally provoked Miss Clarke to charge into the washroom and put a stop to the proceedings, all of which I found enormously entertaining. I couldn't help but wonder what she thought about our nakedness and seeing not a few boyish erections waving in the breeze. For most of the boys—perhaps sensing a certain security in numbers—made no move to cover up.

◆

Although the four of us arrived in relatively good shape, many kids came to the Home with myriad problems. The most common seemed to be head lice—*piojos,* in Spanish. The infestation was so bad in some kids that the only way to get rid of the lice was to shave their heads. But this extreme treatment was like the mark of Cain, for a while branding a child as unclean, an undesirable. To save a girl from this embarrassment, Gibsie first resorted to a variety of homemade remedies, like dousing the creatures with ether or larkspur lotion, followed by fine combing every day to get rid of them. If that didn't do it, she escalated to using kerosene, a risky remedy besides. But when all else failed, she got out the scissors and razor and off came the hair, the *piojos* with it.

But it wasn't always new children arriving at the Home that brought on the *piojo* infestations. They sometimes started at school, the vermin quickly getting passed around from one child to the next. I was glad to know it wasn't just people like us who got them.

◆

Within days of our arrival and after she determined Billy and I had no "head problems," Miss Clarke walked us to Langley's Barbershop, located in the town's center on Kersting Court, across from the streetcar station. The shop was named for its owner who still cut hair there. She instructed him to give us the standard barbering for boys from the Home. In this stylish cut the barber removed all but a small, closely-cropped patch of hair on top of the head, leaving the rest of the scalp completely naked and very pale. Thereafter, we'd go with the rest of the boys and troop to Langley's en masse for the monthly shearing.

A group portrait of the boys at the Home, circa 1938. The author is second from the left in the second row; his brother is third from the left in the front row.

A month later, I learned another lesson about what it meant to be a new kid and one of the "little boys," when Mario introduced me to something called a "Dutch rub." He was waiting with Edwin and Ruben as I came out of the barber shop and in the friendliest of tones called me over to him. Suddenly he grabbed me around the neck in an armlock to hold my head in place, then began viciously rubbing my shorn head with the knuckles of his other hand. I gave out a startled yelp of pain as the rubbed area rapidly heated up. To their great enjoyment, Ruben and Edwin watched me struggle to free myself. They knew well that what Mario was doing could really hurt if continued for very long, so Edwin finally stepped in and made Mario release me. I ran away howling, angry, and feeling sorry for myself. Fortunately for Billy, my screams warned him about what awaited him, and he was lucky to scamper away while the bigger boys were distracted with me. From then on after our monthly cropping, Billy and I were usually able to evade the gauntlet of older boys waiting outside, dashing from the barbershop back to the Home and the relative safety of Miss Clarke. In the winter, running out of the barbershop into the cold air never failed to give an unpleasant jolt to my shorn scalp, but that was infinitely better than the heat from a Dutch rub.

I couldn't wait to grow big enough to take my revenge out on boys younger than me. That time came sooner rather than later, and of course I was every bit as merciless as Mario ever was.

The day twelve-year-old Margaret Gonzalez got her first period everybody knew it. Blabbermouth that she was, she was soon telling anyone who'd listen about her bleeding "from down there." Unfortunately, neither she nor any of the rest of us understood what it meant or why it happened. From Gibsie, Margaret learned little more than the word, "menstruation"; she learned even less from the older girls who, despite their own "monthlies," still understood next to nothing about it. Nor did Margaret fare any better when she later asked Gibsie where babies came from. "God plants a seed in a woman's stomach and a baby grows," Gibsie told her dismissively at the time. When Margaret, then fifteen, left the Home shortly afterwards to live with her father, she was still completely ignorant about such things. Then word came back she was pregnant. When her condition became obvious, her outraged father threw her out to fend for herself. Later when she visited the Home to show off her baby, she said no one had ever explained the connection between having sex and baby-making. All she learned was a new word, "*puta,*" short for *prostituta,* the name her father called her when he found out she was pregnant.

From the matrons, who were either unable or unwilling, we learned nothing about sex. But that's not to say I didn't learn about it. It was mainly the boys at school who enlarged upon my autoerotic experience. More particularly, a thirteen-year-old eighth-grader named Roger. Big for his age, he swaggered with the kind of confidence that only comes with knowing things the rest of us wanted desperately to know but couldn't seem to find out about. He was our local self-proclaimed authority on all matters like "self abuse," as well as the even more mysterious stuff involving girls. He maintained that if we overdid it, either our brains would turn to mush, or hair would grow on the palm and between the fingers of the guilty hand. Naturally there was much anxious checking in secret to see if any of these horrible consequences might be true. Roger was also the instigator of the periodic after-school contests to see whose ejaculate could spurt the farthest. This was important, he maintained, because one's manliness was supposedly directly related to how far you could "shoot." I was never a contestant in these matches because I wasn't yet old enough to achieve that wonderful something that would happen if I worked at it long enough. But that isn't to say I didn't strive mightily and often for the attainment of this goal, the achievement of which I would have to wait for until I was also thirteen.

Roger was likewise our font of knowledge about women. His claim that girls with full, firm calves really like to do "it," left me ogling girls' legs for years afterward. Then I was smug in the secret knowledge of who would and who wouldn't, should I decide to make a move. Though my intention to test his hypothesis never came to pass, I still occasionally find myself checking out a passing, well-turned leg. Then I remember Roger and chuckle.

When I was ten I discovered just how seriously the matrons considered sex. During supper one evening when beets were part of the meal, a fragment accidentally dropped through the open fly of my trousers, leaving a bright red stain on my undershorts. When they turned up in the laundry the next washday, the matron doing the sorting immediately knew whose they were, as each of us had our name stitched into the waistband. Alarmed, she took them directly to Gibsie, who directed I be brought summarily before her.

"What's this red stain on your underwear?" she demanded.

"Oh, that. I think it's from the piece of beet I dropped on my lap a few days ago during supper," I replied, my anxiety growing.

"No, it's not! You tell me right now what this is and how it got there," she demanded angrily, fixing me with her awesome, penetrating glare. Fearfully watching her jaw muscles twitch, always a bad sign, I explained again about the beet fragment, but she would have none of it. Instead, she and her sister, Mrs. Sampson, then the boys' matron, repeated the demand. I began to get an inkling of what was going on in their minds, when Mrs. Sampson suddenly blurted out, "Who's the girl you were with?"

By now I was really frightened, and replied hastily, "I wasn't with any girl. I don't know what you're talking about."

But it was clear they thought I've been doing "it" with one of the girls. The interrogation went on for some time and I sweated, certain I was in for a beating. Still, despite my predicament, I was curious and hoped they'd tell me what they thought the stain was, and how they thought I'd come by it. But no such luck, they didn't.

I stuck to my story, my only recourse, and saved myself from a thrashing. Even so, the next time my mother visited, Gibsie told her about my alleged behavior. Mother only warned me to be careful not to do anything that would get me thrown out, never saying a word about what I was supposed to have done.

But I knew the matrons were right to be concerned, because there was a lot of exploration and not-so-innocent "fooling around." And while those events were usually either ignored or hushed up, occasionally they had to be reckoned with. One time one of the older boys and a girl were accused by another child of doing what she thought was having sex. Gibsie tried to keep the matter quiet, but the rest of us eagerly passed the story around. It created such a sensation that the boy involved was temporarily evicted from the Home while Gibsie investigated. He was allowed to return when the girl involved denied the allegation and nothing could be proved. That may have been the only incident to come to light, but I knew there were others that went undetected.

All of us, girls and boys alike, seemed equally as eager to learn about the mysteries of sex. Our curiosity was boundless, and depending upon individual aggressiveness and the willingness of the kids involved, it was satisfied to one degree or another sooner rather than later. For my part, I could hardly wait for some equally curious pubescent girl to take it upon herself to enlighten me.

CHAPTER 6

Summer '89

As her personal commemoration of the Holocaust, Sherry had been planning a series of paintings of former Nazi concentration camps. In the summer of 1989, instead of making the biennial visit to see my mother, we traveled to Austria, Germany, and Poland. I'd put Mother off with the promise we'd visit her the following spring. We never got the chance. On the night of October 18, the calls from California started just before midnight. With the last one, which came on that dark divide between one day and the next, my brother solemnly told me our mother was dead. Two days later Sherry and I flew from Virginia to Colton to bury her.

Some say you're not really alone in the world until your parents die. Now, as we sped over the vast landscape far below, I couldn't shake an overwhelming sense of loss—not just of the person I'd called Mother for fifty-eight years, but of what only she could tell me, of responses to questions that would forever remain unanswered. I bitterly regretted not seeing her in the summer and punished myself with guilt.

I also dreaded what awaited me. At a few months past her seventy-eighth birthday, the woman who gave me life was gone, a fact her protracted illness had prepared me to accept. But to see her again this way, for what would be the last time, left me shaken, worried about how I'd react.

In seeming defiance of the somber occasion, it was a sparkling, sunny day in Colton, and the Church of the Immaculate Conception seemed to glow with a fresh coat of paint. Inside, the family had already gathered: Queta and her husband, two of their married sons and one of their wives, my unmarried younger sister, Connie, and my step-brother, Richard. There were few others in the pews behind us. Of those, the only people I recognized were the Pérez family, the Mexican couple I'd met a few years earlier, who lived across the street from Mother and Bill. The others, it turned out, were parish members who knew Bill from his Bible study group. I wasn't surprised at the low turnout, but saddened to realize how few friends Mother had made in the more than twenty years she lived in Colton.

It's a terrible practice, this final look at someone lying dead in a coffin. Viewing the remains, a last farewell—for some it may seem necessary, maybe even comforting in the abstract. But the fact of looking at my mother reposing deathly still in the Catholic Church that had meant so much to her sent waves of revulsion through me. It was disrespectful to look at her in this circumstance; it made me feel as though I'd seen her doing something personal without her knowledge. I was certain she would look awful after weeks of lying unconscious in an ICU, more dead than alive, a respirator jammed down her throat. My God! I didn't want to remember this once-beautiful woman that way. It was bad enough my vision of her had long since been upset by what age, cancer, and modern medicine had already done. In infinite patience she waited there now, and as the oldest male family member I would be obliged to lead the procession to her coffin to say, for the last time, *"Adios, Mamacita."*

Once strikingly beautiful, Mother, I was certain, would object to this final look at her. And she would have good reason. She was bloated almost beyond recognition, the skin stretched so tautly the deep furrows that had lined her age-tortured face were smoothed out. Her eyes were not just closed, but pressed tightly together, as if she were straining, trying not to see me or the others looking at her. Despite the mortician's efforts to give her some semblance of normal coloring, she was still jaundiced, more yellow than flesh-colored. Looking at her I couldn't cry, only shudder at the horror of her appearance. I hated the thought of being left forever with that appalling sight whenever my mother would come to mind. But that was only an overlay to the simmering anger I'd harbored about my mother for so long. Since I grew up without the presence of a father, she was the person I most needed to trust. But she had, for her own reasons, repeatedly given me cause not to.

◆

The service was mercifully short. The priest, who actually knew Mother, was appropriately solemn and it was even comforting to hear him eulogize her in a personal way. A short while later at the graveside adjacent to where Papa, my stepfather, had been buried, the priest continued with the prescribed prayers. When he was finished and before Mother was

A wedding portrait of the author's mother, Josefina Pertusatti (née Mejia) in Los Angeles, California, circa 1939.

lowered into the below-ground coolness of that final resting place, there came a moment when the solemnity took on a different tone. Anthony, Queta's son and the oldest of Mother's grandchildren, had previously informed the priest he'd composed a song he wanted to sing to honor his grandmother. We were all taken unawares. Maybe because his father is a composer and musician, Anthony thought he could carry off this final tribute. But unfortunately any composing he might have done must have been impromptu in the moments before he began his "song." Not only couldn't he carry a tune, but his song, entitled, "I Love You Grandma," consisted of repeating this phrase over and over again. The situation might have been comical to an outsider—-and even to us—except that Anthony, who's blind, had tears streaming down his face and was so touchingly sincere. What his homage underscored was that no one else had anything to say on Mother's behalf.

After the funeral, Sherry and I lunched with Bill at a cafe nearby. Our lifelong sibling antagonisms being what they were—Bill didn't get along at all with his sisters—none of the attending family members had arranged lunch for our small group of mourners. Having paid their respects, they'd all rushed off to their respective lives. Life goes on, and here we were, just the three of us, eating in a place Mother liked, where she and Bill had eaten in better days.

Sherry, who had often wondered aloud about it, now remarked again how different Bill and I look, his hair, coloring, and features strongly reflecting his part-Aztec heritage, while mine are decidedly European. Perhaps to divert our minds from the funeral for a few moments, she asked Bill what he thought about the differences.

"Well, that's because Bob had a different father than the rest of us," he said offhandedly.

Caught totally unprepared, I was stunned. I felt like the room had exploded. In mid-bite I erupted, too. "What?" I shouted, unsure I'd heard correctly, unaware I was yelling. "What did you say?" Other patrons in the place stopped eating and stared.

Looking a little startled himself, Bill repeated what he'd just said, adding apologetically, "I thought you knew."

Shaken, again I nearly screamed at him, "Hell no, I didn't know!"

Sherry looked at me and put a calming hand on my arm. Then, with a hint of triumph in her voice, she said, "I just knew you couldn't have had the same father."

For long, angry moments I looked at Bill. Then more calmly and in a softer tone I asked the question that Mother had so often avoided: "Then who was my father?"

"All I know," Bill insisted earnestly, "is your father was a young Italian Mother met in El Paso, a salesman I think, an immigrant like she was." Because I continued to look at him skeptically, he continued, "Bob, I'm not holding anything back, honestly. Mother told me about your father only a couple of years ago. That's why I assumed you knew."

"But how in hell did the subject even come up?" I asked with anxious impatience. He told me he and Mother often reminisced, and he would mostly just half listen to what she said. It was during one of those times she told him.

"Exactly what did she say?" I pressed him, my feeling of exasperation returning.

"I can't recall anything exactly. We'd been talking about her first husband, Rodolfo Batres, Queta's father. And then I asked her about ours, fully expecting her to talk about Jesús Sanábria. But instead, she just said out of the blue, 'You know your brother's father wasn't Jesús. He was Italian,' something like that. That's how it happened," he said with finality, shrugging and resuming eating.

But I couldn't let him off the hot seat yet. "I can't believe that didn't surprise you," I said.

"Yeah, sure it did," he said between chews.

"Go on," I pressed, "did you ask about him? How they met?"

Now giving up any further attempt at finishing his meal, he said, "Yeah, I did ask who he was, but all she said was he was an Italian, someone she saw only a few times."

"Did you ask her his name?" Sherry asked, preempting my next question, as eager as I was anxious to explore the mystery she'd exposed.

"Well, no. He wasn't my father, so to be honest, I never thought to ask. She didn't seem to want to say more, anyway, so I let it go. All she said was what I've told you." Still clearly uneasy and probably to deflect my continuing glare, he suggested, "Talk to Queta, she might know more about this mysterious Italian. In fact, I think Mother said Queta's known about your father since she was a girl."

That added bit of information didn't please me either, nor did having to wait until the next evening to get my sister's take on all this. One thing was clear—whoever said "maternity is a matter of fact, paternity a matter of opinion," had it right.

As we drove him home after lunch, I wondered if what Bill had told me was really, finally the truth. It seemed to fit, certainly to explain my mother's persistent evasiveness. I wanted to believe Bill, and at the same time, not to. But right then I was too angry to think straight, needed time to assimilate the full meaning of what he'd just told me. My immediate sense was that part of me had been erased, that a great swath of what up to a few minutes before I believed was my history, my sense of self, had simply been wiped out. Having grown up without a father and in an orphanage that deliberately or inadvertently taught me to hate what I was made me ambivalent about my ancestry, but it was still important. The dignity of being a link in a family line was what gave substance, a certain depth, to my being. But now the chain that connected my father's side was broken; without it part of me was left dangling. The empty place denied me part of my worthiness, my integrity. I was really mad as hell! It was this anger, I suspected, that explained why I was no longer as grief-stricken over Mother's death as I thought I'd be, a fact that had been making me feel a little guilty. An overwhelming sense of loss had welled up in me at my stepfather's funeral, but any grief I'd felt seemed to have been mostly stifled at Mother's.

Bill's revelation had another immediate effect. I'd never thought much about the fact that Queta was actually my half-sister; it never mattered before. But the assignment of my other siblings to this status gave the term new meaning; they'd all suddenly become more distant. But our estrangement from each other was hardly new. It had begun at the Home, where we were separated by gender and age; the process of becoming strangers to each other was set in motion and perpetuated. Now there was another alienating element.

Anger dominated my feeling toward Bill at that moment. But given his many eccentricities, I was being super-critical of him and knew it was unfair. Still, it was those oddities that most characterized him in my mind, just as they had in childhood, only now they were different in kind. Even at my most tolerant I'd found them somewhat repellent. They were what prevented us from ever being very brotherly. In recent years his penchant for the eccentric had turned to the occult: Bill had become, among other things, a tarot card reader for seekers coming to the Spiritualist Church of which he was president.

On the other hand, Mother's habit of holding me up as the model to which he should strive probably did a lot to make him resent me, as well. As much by design as circumstance, I'd had only sporadic contact with him since leaving home at nineteen for military service. It was hardly surprising this man I called brother was pretty much a stranger.

To give him his due, he has worked all his life, and even when he could have demanded and gotten a much higher salary he seemed to lack the ambition to do so. Yet frugal to a fault, even with such an income he bought and paid for the house he lives in and accumulated savings sufficient to allow him to live independently, if not well. Laudable, to be sure, but, suffering from a poverty of spirit, for many years he's settled for lesser furnishings and the things I've always seen as essential for a fuller life. For Mother, who had other preferences and was a fastidious housekeeper, this was a step backward. But fearful of being put out of the house and consigned to a nursing home, she was powerless to make it otherwise.

Her fears were probably groundless. As a young man, Bill began living with Mother and our stepfather and continued even on into middle age. A positive aspect of this unusual living arrangement was the deep affection Bill developed toward Mother, a devotion missing during the years we were growing up. It's what made him willing to take care of her after Papa died and she became an invalid.

◆

As we discussed my anger about the day's revelation later that evening in our motel room, Sherry suggested that Bill was really blameless, that maybe blame had no place here at all. I confessed that overriding my current feeling toward Bill was a sense of gratitude, an admiration for the dedicated way he'd taken care of Mother for so many years. At least I owed him that. And now that Mother was gone, mixed with that appreciation was a grudging sense of responsibility for him. It was not because I really thought he needed worrying over, but because of the promise to look after him Mother repeatedly extracted from me in her last years—much as she'd done with Queta at the Home. I couldn't shake it, amazed that even in death she still wielded such power over me.

◆

We had dinner with Queta and her husband, Gilbert, at their home the next evening. She's an excellent cook and for old times' sake she'd made one of Mother's favorite dishes, one we all loved. So great was my need to ask the questions troubling me that after a bite or two I couldn't eat. Mindless of the food on my plate, I said, a little more forcefully than I intended, "Queta, you must tell me about my father!"

Startled, she looked at me and then at Gilbert, as if for help. Gilbert, who'd been at the Home with us, had labored as a steel worker to support his family—and his music. This wasn't his gig; he had no help to offer.

But before she could answer, I said, "Yesterday Bill told me that you've known for years my father was not Jesús Sanábria, but an Italian she met in El Paso."

"Yes, that's right," she said, a hint of shame in her voice. After taking a moment to collect herself she added, "But I'm sorry to say I don't know any more than that, really."

I looked at her accusingly, my anger barely hidden.

"Do you know his name?" Sherry asked, momentarily relieving the tension. Queta shook her head, no.

Far from satisfied, I asked, my tone sour, "Do you know anything at all about him?"

"No, nothing, I'm afraid," she said, shaking her head as she looked at her hands.

"Okay, let's back up a minute," I said with a sigh of exasperation. "How long have you known about this?"

"I don't remember exactly, but maybe Mother told me just after we came to California."

"You've known that long and you never thought that I might like to know?"

"Well, of course I did," she said, flushing. "But I felt it was Mother's place to tell you, not mine. I just never thought more about it."

"Well, now you know that she never did," I said bitterly. "What was she hiding? A one-night stand? The circumstances of her affair with this Italian?"

"Bob, really," she pleaded, her face reddening, "all I can say is it was not something Mother was particularly proud of, mainly because her family made her feel she had shamed them. But beyond that, I can't answer your questions. You know how Mother was. She did things for her own reasons and never explained herself. I know it wasn't fair to you, but I can't change that. If I knew anything else I'd tell you, please believe me."

I looked at her, skepticism written on my face. I felt a great need to blame someone, and with the person responsible being beyond reach, I attacked my sister. Leaning toward her, chin jutting, I said, "Queta, I'm very upset about this. It's bad enough she never told me, but I feel doubly angered because she told you and Bill."

"I know, I know, and I can't blame you. I'm really very sorry," she said with what sounded like sincere contrition.

I backed off. So much for that.

◆

Anger and mistrust flooded my mind, and my feelings toward Queta at the moment were anything but brotherly. Again this was not unusual; our relationship had always been an on-again-off-again thing. Her relationship with Mother had been closer than mine; Mother confided in her in a way she never did with me. Though I remained silent about it, I'd always resented being made to feel left out.

The three years difference in our ages did their part to minimize whatever closeness we'd had at the Home. She also left there before I did, and even after I came to live with her and Mother, we were together for only four years. But those were years in which she worked full time and was often away. She suffered from an anguish that surfaced with periods of violent verbal and physical attacks she sometimes directed at me, but more often at Papa. All of us were convinced the Home was to blame, that somehow she'd been damaged by being there. I remained unsympathetic even after learning her problems had required a brief hospitalization and were more severe that I'd imagined. I left home feeling I never wanted to see her again.

As a young woman Queta was exceptionally beautiful, her fair face brightened a pair of charming dimples and copies of Mother's large brown eyes and dark wavy hair. Her beauty was such that schoolboys fought bare-knuckled for the privilege of being regarded as her boyfriend, a status she might or might not agree with no matter who won. She's still very pretty and, at about five feet, only as tall as Mother was, though heavier. Gilbert had begun pursuing Queta when they were young teenagers at the Home and continued after they'd both left it. His persistence finally won him the prize; they were married in 1950. When Queta moved out I rarely saw her again. Shortly after she moved I left to go into the service. During the succeeding twenty-two years we saw each other only sporadically. I was determined to live a mainstream American life, while it appeared she was living, by choice or not, one more ethnically oriented; that put further distance between us.

The combination of Papa's death, Mother's becoming an invalid, and the breakup of my marriage had the effect of drawing me back to my family to begin the process of reconciliation. Yet, what I'd now discovered about my father made me wonder whether I wanted to have any more contact with them.

Queta had six children and, by my estimation, turned out to be a better mother than ours was. And despite many marital and personal hardships, she's also stayed married to the same man. As for the person she is, I'm still learning. But one thing I now knew: Queta is as secretive as Mother was. I resented her for keeping the fact of my father's identity from me all these years. That resentment was only slightly lessened by the realization that Mother, in her usual fashion, had probably sworn her to secrecy; Queta's loyalty to Mother came at the expense of her sisterly loyalty to me.

Queta was right—Mother reveled in being secretive. Through the years we were growing up, she seemed to get a perverse pleasure out of telling each of us something, usually only half true, if at all, and then swearing us to secrecy. Of course, the secrets were never good ones: "I may need an operation," she might whisper, "but don't tell the others." Or, "The business is losing money every day, but keep it to yourself." So, instead of being able to talk it out among ourselves and maybe feel better as a result, we had to swallow it and worry ourselves sick. In time I learned to disregard her secrets and came to look on this propensity as an amusing quirk of her personality. But this—swearing my sister to secrecy about my father's identity—was only infuriating.

Later, when I began to ponder why Mother felt she couldn't tell me, I couldn't help but imagine a damning scenario. If it were only a case of her being lonely and falling in love, so what? I wouldn't have thought badly of her. I might even have enjoyed knowing about a romantic encounter. But because she'd kept my father's identity from me all her life, I couldn't believe it was as simple as that. There had to be more to it. It tormented me. From the earliest days of my childhood and throughout the short time I lived with her, I would often look up to see her gazing intently at me. I always found it unsettling and, when I'd question her, she would only respond with a sad smile and a shake of her head, before looking away. Now I wonder if what she saw in my face was the reflection of her absent lover of so long ago. Rather than showing interest in me, perhaps she was indulging in fantasies of a time past.

I seem to have felt ambivalent about my mother all my life, at least beginning when she left me at the orphanage, something for which I've never quite forgiven her. Even so, I'd still regarded her as a hero of sorts; in spite of the many hardships she endured, she never actually deserted us. My love for her undermined my anger at her now.

This new revelation only reinforced both of those feelings and made me realize I never really knew the person I'd called Mother. The dark truth about my birth and heritage was extremely disturbing and had the effect of unearthing long-buried memories of the childhood I'd tried to forget. It was bad enough being tormented by a childhood that left me with such awful feelings of shame and self-loathing. Life at the Home had also left me struggling for identity: a view of myself that was confused, on one hand, by a contest between the culture I'd arrived with, and that with which the Methodist Church was determined to replace it. That experience engendered a quest to know who I was and where I belonged, if anywhere.

And now there was this.

CHAPTER 7

Prologue to the Past

The sky above the city was a nearly clear, limitless blue, the air actually fresh-smelling, good signs for all living things in Los Angeles. Our landing at LAX on that October day in 1993 was so smooth that our plane's passengers spontaneously broke into applause when we touched down.

Sherry and I had flown to California this time to visit my son and his wife and to return to Sierra Madre for a reunion of former Home kids, one of many held since the Home closed in 1954. During the past forty years, Regina Rivera, a former Home girl who still lived in the town, had been the moving force behind these efforts to keep the memories alive. All I'd ever wanted to do with those memories was forget them, so I'd avoided the reunions; this would be my first, and I looked forward to it with mixed feelings.

Delving into the past was something I'd studiously avoided. But continuing to run away had not been possible since learning the truth about my father. In the four years since that revelation, my anguish about the past not only persisted, but grew worse. Like a pot boiling over, those memories had come to the surface and spilled out, refusing to stay where I'd put them. The cliché "you can run, but you can't hide" certainly applied in my case. I'd come to realize that trying to flee from my past had been misguided and had done little for my peace of mind. The change hadn't come easily.

When I left the Home in the summer of 1945, on the cusp of completing my fourteenth year, I thought I was leaving my life there behind. But five years later, when I left California for military service, I realized I'd only begun to run. I saw the military as my chance to escape from where I felt persecuted to someplace where I could be regarded and treated as an individual, rather than a member of a group, reviled or not. In many respects it worked. The army, really a community unto itself, slowly helped to change how I saw myself. But even there I was never quite able to dispel the feeling I was one of "the other," always on the outside.

Coming to the reunion was an important first step in facing the past. I wanted to exhume it to find out all I could about what really happened at the Home, about who was responsible. Two years before I'd started this search by calling Regina Rivera—Re, as we all knew her—because she not only grew up at the Home, but stayed on as a matron until it closed. When I explained what I wanted to do, she at first was very helpful, even excited, and gave me the names and addresses of many other former Home kids with whom she'd stayed in touch. Some of those I wrote to added still other names to the list. But as soon as I began to ask Re about her own recollections, she clammed up and became hostile, evidently fearful about what I might write.

In anticipation of attending the reunion, I'd written to all the former Home kids whose names and addresses I'd collected. To my disappointment, of the more than thirty I contacted, only a few were able or willing to provide anything meaningful about their experiences. I wasn't surprised, given my own reluctance to relive my past and the fact that after more than forty-five years we were virtual strangers. Yet my efforts hadn't been entirely fruitless. Before she became uncooperative, Re sent me a number of copies of *The Plazagram*, the periodic newsletter of the Plaza Community Center, the organization that founded the Children's Home. Rachel Parra Quick, another former Home girl, had sent me photographs as well as many of the monthly reports Gibsie sent to the Center through the years. Most exciting of all was the copy of Gibsie's personal diary Margaret Gonzalez Trejo had promised to give me. It was the prospect of reading the diary that made attending the reunion most enticing.

The documents I'd read so far about the Home had already made me see it in a light much different from the narrow vantage of my misty child's memory. If nothing else, they'd helped to order the bits and snatches of memories my former Home-mates and I could recall and had begun to answer questions that bubbled up into my mind the deeper I probed. I'd also located the Plaza Community Center itself, much diminished from its former scope and removed from its origins in the heart of Old Los Angeles to a site on the fringe of the East L.A. barrio. Its executive director had promised I could mine the Center's archives, which I determined to do before we left California.

On Saturday, the day before the reunion, Sherry, my daughter-in-law, Anne, and I visited the home of Elwood Williams, a grandnephew of Katherine Higgins, the woman most directly responsible for establishing the Home. The director of the Plaza Community Center had given me his address and I'd been corresponding with him in preparation for this meeting. Purely by chance, Elwood had come to live on part of what was once the site of the Big House. The boys' building, now remodeled into a complete private residence, was nearby. He was waiting as we arrived and came out to greet us in what was once the Home's terraced garden area which we called the East Yard. As we returned to the house, he pointed out the remnants of the brick stairs that once led to the white-pillared portico in front of the Big House.

Inside, we met Elwood's wife Pat, who'd graciously prepared coffee and pastries. Conversation came easily; there was little of the awkwardness I'd anticipated. Elwood told me that as boys he and his younger brother often came to the Home with their great-aunt and played with the children while she took care of business with Gibsie. Although Elwood and I are of the same generation, he's somewhat younger, so I doubted I was still at the Home when he and his brother visited. If I was, I don't remember them. But children often came with their parents to see the Home, and my recollection is that they came not to play, but gawk, to be shown the strange people called Mexicans. Elwood and his brother were exceptions in that regard.

Elwood was a gracious host and generous with his time. He'd already laid out for my benefit a number of photographs, clippings, and other documents about his much-admired great-aunt. I barely remembered Miss Higgins and knew nothing at all about her as a person, so everything he showed me was a revelation. He was eager to talk about her and began by telling me she was born Katherine Banfield Higgins in Billston, Stratfordshire, England, the youngest of seven children. She emigrated to the United States in the early 1880s with her widowed mother, brothers, and sisters, and the family settled in Pittsburgh, Pennsylvania, where Katherine attended public school. She then went on to secretarial college in Indianapolis, later moving to Elwood, Indiana, where she had secured a secretarial job at a steel company. She was evidently very successful during the next nineteen years in Elwood, eventually becoming head bookkeeper for a larger company.

Elwood (who was quick to point out that there was no connection between the town of Elwood and his given name) was very knowledgeable about his great-aunt's career. What Katherine had really wanted, he said, was to be a Methodist missionary. As I learned more about her, it became obvious that Katherine Higgins was more ambitious than the average woman of her time, and may have regarded missionary work as a way to realize a larger, more personally meaningful role for herself. In any event, she eventually resigned her job and returned to Pittsburgh to work among the tenement poor.

According to an obituary Elwood showed me, Katherine came to Los Angeles in the spring of 1915. She'd answered an "appeal for a Christian Social Worker and Stenographer" to work among the Spanish-speaking, and was hired as the assistant secretary for something called the Methodist Board of Latin American Missions, only recently formed. Her main job, at least at first and probably always, was raising money.

Elwood had collected and preserved these mementos about his great-aunt with evident care, so I was surprised when he offered to let me take whatever I thought might be useful for my project. I was moved by his interest and trust and promised to return whatever I took when I was finished. While we talked I was gratified to detect no sign of condescension or patronization, attitudes I almost subconsciously check for I when I meet new people. It's an old habit, one I was barely aware of until the early 1980s, when I agreed to be a Veterans Administration peer counselor for a group of Vietnam vets suffering from post-traumatic stress syndrome. After one of the sessions, I told the supervising psychologist about an ethnic remark one of the participants had made, though not one directed at Latinos. He suggested that I try not to be so sensitive and pointed out how I seemed to "range," as he put it, for any evidence of personal slight. He was probably right, but my sensitivity hadn't developed in a vacuum or without ample cause. Elwood was not only innocent of this, but one of the most sincere people I'd ever met. I felt a twinge of shame for being suspicious.

Elwood Williams no doubt developed his accepting attitude at the knee of his great-aunt. But it was not until much later that I learned just how fortuitous it was that someone like Katherine Higgins answered that "appeal" to work among the Spanish-speaking. When she arrived, Los Angeles was teeming with immigrants, the majority of them Mexicans uprooted by the revolution. Most of these *peones* were fleeing the brutal life on the haciendas. They were not only impoverished and completely unschooled, but lived among Americans who looked down on them and seemed determined to limit their opportunities to work and advance. Mexicans of any economic or social class were completely new to Katherine, but her efforts on their behalf soon gained her a reputation as "The Good Angel of the Plaza." Bright, ambitious lady that she was, she quickly advanced to the position of secretary of the Latin American Missions, renamed the Plaza Community Center in 1918.

In light of the work the Center was doing, it was probably inevitable that a place like the Home would be created. From one of the early *Plazagrams* I learned that it was the abandonment of a seven-year-old Mexican girl on the Center's doorstep in the early summer of 1923 that presented Katherine the opportunity she needed to found such a place. The Plaza Community Center Children's Home became a reality when she rented a house in Eagle Rock, a suburb north of Los Angeles, and set up housekeeping for herself and that first child.

Each time we returned to Sierra Madre my awareness of its charms increased. I knew this had only been possible because Sherry kept pointing them out; she saw the town and its environs unfettered by the cloud of negative feelings about the place I still carried. I was grateful for her eyes. My interest in this "hometown" I'd been so reluctant to claim had also grown: in the process I discovered it had quite a history.

The area the city occupies lies at the foot of 5,700-foot-high Mount Wilson, in the foothills of the San Gabriel Mountains northeast of Los Angeles. Originally it was part of a Mexican land grant named the Rancho Santa Anita after Jesus' maternal grandmother, St. Ann. Those who settled it in the late nineteenth century sought a healthful climate, fair weather, and a good water system, and to one degree or another, they found all three. Artists also found the relative isolation of the small town inspirational and created an early art colony in it. Even as we walked around it, the town still had a village atmosphere, with barely more than 10,000 inhabitants.

A Sierra Madre Chamber of Commerce pamphlet describes the city as a sort of Shangri-la, "a distinctly separate town, next to—but not part of—its neighbors, Pasadena and Arcadia." It has always been a place one went *to,* rather than *through,* on the way to somewhere else. When I lived there, Sierra Madre Boulevard was the only primary road connecting the town to greater Los Angeles, though there was also the Pacific Electric streetcar line, which ended in the heart of town. The townspeople used the streetcar at least as much as they used automobiles, if not more. But for us kids, who really had nowhere to go, it was useful mainly for flattening pennies on the tracks, when we felt affluent enough to sacrifice a coin that in those days could actually buy something.

Sherry is a city girl, and though we now live in the Virginia countryside a few miles outside of a small town, she still couldn't imagine what it was like to live in this one. At the risk of sounding trite, I told her about its typically small-town outlook. Indeed, it was a place where everyone knew just about everyone else—and of course their business, too. I suppose this was a good thing, because I could find a familiar if not necessarily a friendly face wherever I went; in a way, this seemed to create an enfolding sense of security. Knowing there were watchful eyes everywhere also had the effect of keeping us in line; reports of any mischief could reach the Home well before any of us returned there.

I could see now that in many respects Sierra Madre really was a splendid place in which to grow up. As quiet as it was, I was never bored or at a loss for something to do. Of course that was partly because we were kept busy with chores and after-school and weekend jobs. But when there was free time there were canyons to explore, where it was easy to find treasures like garnet and pyrite crystals; and mountain trails to hike, especially when the peaks were snow-capped. In the summer there was Heasley's Swimming Pool in one of the canyons; as a kid from the Home I sometimes got to swim for free, but other times I had to raise the dime it cost to enter. The town's small size meant that all the important and interesting places in it could be reached on foot. And the steep and straight north-south streets were tailor-made for skating, scootering, or racing homemade "soapbox racers." The general absence of automobiles then also meant we weren't likely to collide with anything significant on the way down, and if we took a spill usually nothing more serious than a scraped knee or bloodied elbow would result.

Of course the town had other attractions, like the huge Wisteria Gardens that brought tourists. But for us, a favorite was the jail at the rear of the City Hall, which I never failed to check out when I had the chance. It had a lone, barred window that was low enough to peer into, if one could get a lift up from a companion. The jail's usual occupant was the town drunk, a man we knew simply as "Blackie," though he wasn't actually a black man. When he was sober, he was friendly, gentle, and harmless. Though his demeanor didn't change much when he was drunk, he was jailed mainly to get him off the sidewalk, the place he was most likely to be found sleeping the morning after a binge.

Strangely, none of the former Home kids I wrote to remembered Blackie and I'd begun to wonder if he was just a figment of my imagination. Later I heard from Helen Obazawa, a woman who'd also grown up in the town. Her letter mentioned Blackie, confirming his existence. Memory is clearly selective, and I think I've figured out why I remembered Blackie. Despite his innocuous nature, I felt a tremor of unease whenever I saw him, drunk or sober. It was not that I thought he might hurt me; I was more disturbed by his child-like vulnerability and the sense that he was one of those whom society had discarded. I could relate to being abandoned—it was my worst fear.

◆

How the townspeople felt about having a place like the Home in its midst is something I'd always wondered about. The Center was obviously pleased with Sierra Madre's scenic, somewhat-secluded, small-town atmosphere. But among the documents I'd collected was evidence that not all of the town's citizens found the Home's presence appealing. Within a few months after the Center set up its Children's Home in a rented house on Baldwin Avenue in 1924, there were complaints. I can't say I was surprised. Not only was the idea of a group home foreign to the community, but this one housed two dozen or so poor Mexican and other Latino children, aliens in a town that previously had few if any such folk. Besides, we had parents, relatives, and friends who visited regularly, used the city's park for picnics, ate in its few cafes, and shopped in its stores. Given the prevailing hostile attitude toward Mexicans in the Southwest, it was even less surprising that some of the townspeople might have viewed our presence unkindly.

No overt opposition surfaced until three years later at a meeting of the town planning commission, one of whose members wrote to Gibsie about it:

> "Someone wanting a change in [zoning] on a lot across the street from you appeared before us. In the general discussion that followed, it was remarked that property in that neighborhood was lowered in value by [the presence of] the Children's Home. Mr. Thomas Reynolds, the City Attorney, spoke up and said he had lived next door to you for many years, that not even one child had ever been a nuisance, that they were the best behaved children he knew, and that anyone who lived next door or across the street could ever say they were disturbed in any way by the children in your home. In a world full of harsh words and hatreds, I feel it a privilege to pass on to you that spontaneous tribute to your work and your charges."

Bless you, Tom Reynolds.

A few years later when the Great Depression had grimly set in and put millions of Americans out of work, immigrants soon were being blamed for many of the country's ills, but specifically for taking jobs from Americans and then for overwhelming what little welfare aid was available. It wasn't long before the country, especially Southern California, was aflame with rabid, anti-immigrant and particularly anti-Mexican sentiment. In response to this xenophobic clamor, federal, state, and local governments organized the wholesale, unlawful deportation of Mexicans, Mexican Americans often among them.

It was in the midst of this turbulent climate in 1930 that the Center made known its plans to buy a permanent site for the Children's Home in Sierra Madre. Feelings about the Home had been generally good up to that time, but it appears the City Council felt constrained to test the winds before approving the purchase of the property the Center had in mind. At least one resident, George E. Hapgood, another of the Home's neighbors who'd heard of the council's concern, wrote an earnest, unsolicited testimonial to the planning commission:

> "I wish to state that in the four years that I was next door resident to the Home, I cannot recall one instance when the children were troublesome, noisy or made it disagreeable . . . . Instead, it was quite the reverse. As Mrs. Hapgood was ill all the time we lived there, she often said how wonderful the children were. I can honestly say that I have seen families with only two or three children that caused much more noise and damage to property than those children would ever do.
>
> "I also feel that the Home is rather an asset to my own property . . . the yard at the Home always looks cozy, they have always taken pains to keep it cleaned up and flowers growing, and that is a great deal more than a good share of the residents of the city do to keep up their own property."

Bless you, too, George.

If there was any opposition, it wasn't sufficient to prevent the Center's purchase, financed by the local bank, of the property at 72 West Alegria Street, which the City Council approved the following year. In fact, there was substantial support for the Home from the town's merchants, who stood to gain from its presence, and also from the city government, the school administration, the local Congregational Church, and many townspeople, all of whom supported it at least on humanitarian grounds. My own recollection of the town residents' attitudes toward us is that they ranged from tolerant indifference at one extreme, to active involvement with us on the other. It's true that as Home kids we were looked upon as different, but we were usually treated respectfully and indeed there were even times, especially in the early years, when we were regarded as the town's mascots: The City of Sierra Madre always enters a float in the Tournament of Roses parade on New Year's Day in Pasadena. One year its entry featured a scene from Longfellow's Hiawatha and included three kids from the Home, dressed as Indians. But that demeaning attitude was not typical; that type of incident only happened once. Whatever prejudice or active dislike that was directed toward us was sufficiently hidden that we were largely unaware of it.

CHAPTER 8

Keeping the Faith

My meeting with Elwood Williams had gone much better than I'd anticipated. I was excited by the material he'd loaned me and had to restrain an impulse to go through it then and there. That would have to wait until I got back to Virginia. Returning to the town center, we lunched at a small cafe and afterwards embarked on more exploration. It was a Saturday afternoon and there were preparations for a wedding under way at the Congregational Church, but the participants didn't seem to mind our intrusion. The main building hadn't changed in the least from the way I remembered it, nor had the feelings it evoked as we walked through the sanctuary. I had no difficulty recalling Sunday School, singing in the choir, and especially two of its ministers.

We'd arrived at the Home on a Thursday and just three days later I had my initial taste of Sunday School. Of course in the beginning I had no idea what it was about. But I knew it must be important, not only because we got dressed up—in our case in borrowed clothes—but because Gibsie was in the middle of it. She particularly loved to teach the Bible and really seemed more alive, almost another person, when she was teaching than at any other time. Billy and I both started out in her class; later, when I learned English, I was moved to another group taught by one of the women from the town, the mother of one of our classmates. Sunday School seemed to be about having miraculous stories read, praying, and learning to sing songs about Jesus. It wasn't bad.

I understood nothing of the church service afterwards. It seemed interminable, though the singing, led by the choir, which included Fuller and a few of the older Home kids, was enjoyable. When I was old enough I also joined it, singing first in the junior choir and later with the adults. But on Christmas, Easter, and Children's Day, all of us had to sing. For those occasions the Center's superintendent often showed up at the Home to rehearse us in a number of standard Protestant hymns or Christmas carols in Spanish, so that the Home kids would have "something special" to offer.

I had a hard time believing the stories told at Sunday School, but that didn't seem to matter. When I was nine, I was advanced, like my classmates, from Intermediate to Junior level on Promotion Day and received a personal Bible. A few of our girls were so moved by the presentation they not only read their Bibles regularly, but later formally "joined" the church. I lacked the girls' zeal, and regarded going to Sunday School as just another imposition I had to endure. When my turn came, I failed to appreciate the significance of the advancement.

All this happened at the Sierra Madre Congregational Church, where we seemed to spend lots of time. Besides Sunday School and the service following, there was a Wednesday evening prayer meeting at which a group of us kids often sang, preceded or followed by others performing on the piano. On Friday evenings there was a church social and supper. When Gibsie could manage the fee for the supper, or one of the townspeople came up with the ante, we all attended. Sometimes instead of paying we sang for our supper, performing in the program that followed.

At one of those Friday evening programs we put on an elaborate vignette. Too young to take part, I didn't mind missing the rehearsals and other preparations it entailed. Gibsie and Fuller helped the older girls make peasant blouses and skirts, Miss Clarke made sashes for the boys, and together they even decorated the stage with serapes and large, flashy sombreros. The show began with a few of the kids singing in Spanish. Then others did a Mexican dance or two, accompanied by Victoria or Berta at the piano. The finale was a diorama of all the performers, including two girls patting corn dough between their small hands, as if making tortillas. The audience loved the show and applauded enthusiastically. Strangely, at any other time we were reprimanded for speaking Spanish, but for the performance and others like it we were turned into exotics; we sang in Spanish, dressed up like *peones*, made tortillas, and performed Mexican dances. And most of what we presented was as foreign to us as it was to our audience.

The person responsible for all this activity was Dr. Arthur O. Pritchard, minister at the church and among the first of the townspeople I came to know. A big, florid man with hair already turning white, he was kind, sympathetic and, when he introduced himself, quick to say he was from "back East." Actually he was from Rhode Island and arrived in town in 1925 to fill the church's pulpit. If I was seeing him often at church, I saw him almost as much at the Home, in which he took great interest. He often stayed for lunch or supper, and I soon got to know and like him, as did the other kids. It was he who gave me—and every new boy—the books to get started collecting stamps and coins, hobbies he pursued himself. And to keep our interest alive, he came once a month just to look over our collections, relate collecting lore, and give advice. I found stamps too insubstantial to bother with, preferring the solidity of Indianhead pennies and shield, liberty head, and buffalo nickels, all of which I eagerly collected.

Dr. Pritchard knew most of us had been baptized Catholic, and that his and Gibsie's main work was getting and keeping us on the straight-and-narrow Protestant road. That made them both wary of St. Rita's Catholic Church, located on Baldwin Avenue less than a half-block away at the east end of our street. I was absorbing the notion that there was something bad about Catholics and their church. But in time, like everybody else, I nonetheless become curious about it. I never thought about venturing inside St. Rita's until one day when three of our girls sneaked into a service. When he heard about their adventure, Dr. Pritchard became alarmed and had words with Gibsie. This was serious business. She quietly admonished the girls not to go near the church or play on the grounds of the adjacent parochial school. But when the word about what they'd done filtered to the rest of us, everybody was suddenly intrigued. Inevitably other kids sneaked in, too.

To one degree or another, all of us were aware that the Catholic Church had been significant in our lives, and that it continued to be for our families; I knew my mother regularly went to Mass and often carried her rosary. Everybody—the matrons, our minister, and even some of the parishioners—was determined that, except when supervised, we should have nothing at all to do with the Catholics in the town or their church. When the Catholics were spoken about—they were sometimes referred to as "catlickers" (from the Spanish *católicos*) by some of us—rumor had it St. Rita's was involved in something bordering on witchcraft. But that kind of talk just had the effect of keeping curiosity bubbling in the back of our minds.

It was really impossible to avoid St. Rita's, anyway, since we often played on the street close by, and it wasn't unusual to see the parish priest or the parochial-school nuns walking around the grounds. We looked at them with curiosity, and I don't doubt they wondered about us, too. They probably lamented their inability to bring us back into the fold, certain that our families were Catholic.

No one ever specifically forbade me to go into St. Rita's, but I knew it was forbidden territory and that made it enticing. So when two other boys dared me to go there with them, my curiosity was too great to resist. We ventured to St. Rita's and tremulously peeked inside the heavy wooden main door, certain we were about to be abducted, before running away, laughing and congratulating ourselves on our daring. But my curiosity had only been whetted, and I returned again, alone. It was easy enough, since the church was close by, and though there was usually activity at the school, for much of the time the church seemed deserted. Though nervous as a cat, I was bold enough to risk going into the dimly lit nave and forced myself to stay until my eyes adjusted to the half light. Alert for any noise and ready to dart out should the need arise, I peered around the amazing high-ceilinged chamber. After that, I returned from time to time and stood pressed against a wall in the semidarkness, wondering at the statues, the paintings on the walls, the flickering votive candles, and the faint, sweetish odors that permeated the place. All of this was both disturbingly familiar and strangely comforting.

When I began reading through some of Gibsie's monthly reports, I discovered Dr. Pritchard did much more than start us on hobbies and involve us in the activities of his church. He was part of the Children's Home Advisory Committee, the body that advised the Plaza Community Center about the Home's functioning. Shrewdly, he also got other members of his church to serve on the board, people like Mrs. Gossard, who arranged to get her physician husband to look after our health, often at no charge. And in the depths of the Depression, when the Center found itself unable to make its mortgage payments, Dr. Pritchard, who evidently could be very persuasive, got the bank to renegotiate the loan and even to forgive $400 of the principal, the amount then in arrears.

Even as a child I was aware food was scarce. Now I saw that Dr. Pritchard was deeply involved in keeping us fed through appeals to churches in other communities for money, food, and clothing for the

Home, apparently with great success. During the years of the Great Depression, he arranged for government-supplied bulk food like butter or margarine, salt pork, beans, and dried apples to be sent to us.

He didn't just acquire food for us. He arranged for Kiwanis Club sponsors to send some of us to summer camp, though more often it was to the no-frills camp that Mexican boys from East L.A. went to, rather than the more comfortable, expensive YMCA camp. And he got the Women's Society for Christian Service at his church to spend one morning each week mending and darning for us. That's what kept us from looking ragged and from the embarrassment of holes in our socks. The good ladies kept it up even after Dr. Pritchard resigned his pastorship in 1940. The goodness in the people of Sierra Madre was never lacking, but it often took Dr. Pritchard to bring it out.

It didn't take long to get to know the people in the town, since we were hardly kept isolated. And of all the ones I met, the merchants were the most accepting, no doubt because we spent money in their shops. I'd met the barber, Mr. Langley, within days of my arrival in town. The next was Mr. Olsen, a big, patient man and one of the last real cobblers who could actually make a pair of shoes from scratch—or so the other kids liked to say, though none of us ever saw him do it. Olsen's, located on Baldwin Avenue near the town center, was the only shoe store in town. That's where we bought our one good pair of shoes for church and other dress-up occasions and where our everyday, hand-me-downs were repaired. Although his real name was Martin, everybody called Mr. Olsen "Heine"—everybody, that is, except us kids, who only did so among ourselves. He spoke with a slight accent I later learned was Norwegian. By the time I first met him in his store, Mr. Olsen was already an old man, an immigrant who'd arrived in Sierra Madre in 1887, well before the city government was established.

Spending money was always special, it happened so rarely, and buying our shoes just before school started in the fall was a festive occasion. Besides the process of buying the shoes, which included having my feet measured, I liked going to Olsen's for another reason: Mr. Olsen had a kind of X-ray machine through which you were supposed to be able to see the bones of your feet. While Mr. Olsen was fitting one of us, the rest took turns at the machine, marveling at our podiatric anatomy. But after a few turns, I became suspicious of the bony, white image displayed in the pale, greenish light that came on when a foot was inserted. It was the same one no matter whose foot was in it, and as I looked through the eyepiece, I never saw any movement when I wiggled my toes. We didn't care whether it was authentic or not, and there was always a lot of pushing and elbowing so each of us got his fair share of looking before the buying spree was over.

Mr. Olsen became the first dead person I ever saw, and that for me was his most memorable aspect. He was a member of our church and it was there we paraded by his coffin to view his body while it lay in state. It was impossible to believe he was dead; a pale Scandinavian who probably rarely saw the sun, he looked more lifelike in death than when he was alive, thanks to the mortician's expert makeup.

After Heine Olsen died, his son, Henry, worked the shoe store until he closed it later in the 1940s.

The most important of the town's merchants, for the Home and probably everyone else, were Harold and Leila Roberts, owners of Roberts' Market, located a few blocks downhill from the Home at the corner of Baldwin Street and Sierra Madre Boulevard. It was identified by its trademark, a large green frog. Both the Roberts were very friendly and even took the trouble to learn our names. They extended the same courtesy to all their customers, which gave real meaning to their slogan, "Large enough to serve you; small enough to know you."

When I was a little older, I learned the Home and Roberts' Market arrived in Sierra Madre at about the same time in 1924 and, so to speak, grew up together. Gibsie seemed to have some sort of special arrangement with Mr. Roberts and bought all our groceries from him. Even I knew Mr. Roberts let Gibsie continue to get our supplies there when she ran short of money and couldn't pay on time. And, as he had for years, Mr. Roberts gave us the still-edible culls from the market's stock of fruits and vegetables, deemed too unattractive or that had become too ripe to sell. The Roberts were more than friendly, they were generous, providing the Home a turkey or other groceries at Thanksgiving and Christmas when they could.

Mr. Roberts could even be understanding when he caught some of us shoplifting. But once, when he caught six of the Home kids stealing fruit, he thought things had gone too far. He could have called Police Chief

McMillan and put a real scare into them, but that would have blemished the Home's reputation. Instead, he called an embarrassed Gibsie, who assured him it wouldn't happen again. Maybe because there were so many children involved and she realized the exhausting physical effort whipping them would have entailed, she tried talking to them rather than take a strap to their behinds, her usual form of discipline. But that seemed to have been enough, because not only did the culprits confess, but they kept their sticky fingers off the goods at Roberts' Market and the other stores in town—at least as far as she knew.

When I was seven, I began doing odd jobs for town residents to earn money, as every boy my age or older was required to do. The way we preferred to make money was by taking turns selling an afternoon daily, the *Los Angeles Herald Express.* Besides selling the newspapers on the street, we also delivered them to a small group of merchants whose shops were clustered around the town center. Saturday was collection day, and in addition to the thirty cents they paid for the week's worth of newspapers, most of them included a tip of some sort. Mr. Roberts never failed to tip a nickel. With that I could buy a candy bar or a soda. But what I preferred and always got was a bottle of fiery, pickled chili peppers, which came in an elongated bottle that slipped conveniently into a pocket of my trousers. From Cy Young, the butcher at Roberts' Market, I got a big, juicy dill pickle as a tip, which he let me choose myself from a large glass jar perched on top of the meat counter. Thoughtfully, he always wrapped it in a large square of waxed paper so I could eat it without getting myself and my newspapers wet. I ate the pickle as soon as I got it so I'd have a hand free, and reserved the chilis for later.

Mr. Decker, the owner of the bakery that supplied the Home with bread and an occasional cake, as well as "Old Bill," the owner of the candy store up the street from Roberts' Market, were also weekly customers. For my tip at each of their shops I was allowed to fill a small bag with as many cookies or as much peanut brittle, respectively, as I could stuff into them, a knack I quickly honed to high art. This disparate combination of food became the staple of my regular Saturday post-luncheon menu; I spent the rest of the afternoon alternately munching on my peppers and sweets. At some point near the end of the day my stomach invariably rebelled, forcing me to the facilities at the gas station across the street from Roberts', or, if those were in use, to make a hurried, anxious trip to the public rest rooms at the city park a few blocks away.

But to us kids, probably the best known of the town's merchants was the one we competed with in selling newspapers. He was the owner of Emil's Malt and Candy Store. He had a last name, too, of course, but I don't think any of us ever knew it. His store was easily the most popular place in Sierra Madre for all the town's children, if not its adults, and one of the few places where we could buy some of those forbidden things that only cost a penny, the amount of money we were most likely to have at any given time. The most strategic place for selling our newspapers, twenty or so each day, was a spot just to the left of the entrance to Emil's and next door to Hart's Jewelry Store. Both were also directly across the street from the streetcar station. Many, if not most, passengers alighting from an incoming streetcar would head directly for Emil's, making our chosen location the ideal site on which to intercept customers. And although Emil offered the same newspaper, he never seemed to mind our stationing ourselves close to his front door. He well knew most of our tips were immediately spent on candy or the pinball machines inside.

This favored spot also provided another small benefit, one that helped break the monotony of the long hours spent hawking papers. Some 1930s-vintage Fords and Chevys were built so the front doors were hinged on a post midway along the sides of the car body, rather than at the front of the car near the windshield, which meant the door opened from front to rear. This feature, coupled with the head-in parking in front of Emil's, provided a continuous exposition of female anatomy, as unsuspecting women drivers alighted from cars so designed. The possibility of catching a flash of inner thigh above the edge of gartered silk stockings kept me alert; I learned to observe without appearing to stare. That possibility often provided me the company of other boys, who were willing to stand beside me for prolonged periods in hopes of catching such a glimpse; but unlike Tom Sawyer, I couldn't also get them to do my work for me.

While most of our weekly customers could be counted on for a tip, Mr. Hart, the jeweler, took a more active interest in us. Delivering the newspaper to him each afternoon involved a little question-and-answer period, with Mr. Hart doing the interrogating. It wasn't exactly the "third degree," because he seemed genuinely interested in what was going on in my life. As we were all decidedly thin, he usually inquired whether we were getting enough to eat. I always answered yes, but wondered what he'd say or do if I were to answer that I was hungry, which I often was. My progress at school was also a regular item on his list of questions, and was followed by a lecture on the merits of good study habits. Maybe because he well knew of our frequent trips into Emil's, he would end with a lecture on saving money and the magic of compound interest, a subject that went right over my head. I might have taken more interest in his advice if he'd seen fit to punctuate it with a tip, which he never did.

We especially prized weekly customers, not only because making money was more assured, but having them meant spending less time hawking newspapers on the street. We were always on the lookout for new ones, and during one of my turns at selling the *Herald,* I managed to find two, Mr. Jones, a realtor whose office was around the corner near Olsen's Shoe Store, and "Doc," the pharmacist whose drugstore was a few doors west of Emil's. Mr. Jones's office was a cubbyhole at the end of a long hallway, always overheated and filled with a haze of smelly cigar smoke. But those weren't the only reasons I disliked going there. At my knock, this rotund little man would tell me to enter, tilt back his chair, stretch, and blow another smoky billow into the haze already polluting the cramped space. After greeting him and handing him his newspaper I'd be obliged to stand there while he quizzed me on the day's news, because, as he said, if you sell something you should know your product. He was probably doing me a favor in that regard, my recitation doubly worthwhile because he also tipped a dime.

"Doc" never tipped, apparently believing, like the jeweler, it was enough to buy the newspaper. But I swear it wasn't resentment at his no-tip policy that moved me to steal from him. In any case, one Saturday while I was waiting for him to get the week's payment, I spied a slightly mashed nickel candy bar on one of his displays. I quickly decided he'd never be able to sell it and I'd be doing him a favor to take it. The display was at the front of the store, and he had to go to the pharmacy in the rear to get my money. While he was back there I felt certain he couldn't see me, ignoring the small voice in the back of my mind that suggested he wouldn't have such a display out front if he couldn't watch it. So I deftly plucked the candy bar from the display and cradled it in my fingertips behind the newspapers I was holding in my left hand.

But when "Doc" returned he had exasperation written all over his face. "What are you hiding behind your newspapers?" he asked darkly.

"Oh, you mean this?" I replied, sheepish, flushing as I showed him the candy bar. "I was going to pay for it," I added, summoning as much as earnestness as I could.

"I'm sure you are," he said, his voice dripping with sarcasm, as he held out his hand.

I was quick to put a nickel in it.

Then looking over my head, he continued, “Thank you. Here’s the money for the week’s newspapers.” And with finality, he added, “Don’t come back.”

It was only on the way out that I spied the convex mirror that had betrayed me.

I was ashamed of myself both for stealing and for being caught, crestfallen at having lost a customer, as well as frightened that he might call Gibsie, who was certain to give me one of her terrible whippings. No one questioned my story that the druggist had simply decided to take a morning newspaper at his home, but for days afterward I lived in fear that he’d call the Home and expose me. Thankfully, he never did. But getting caught red-handed was the best thing that could have happened to me, the experience bringing to an early end any thoughts about the benefits of thievery.

The combination of Sierra Madre’s small size, its somewhat removed location, and the fact that everyone was suffering through the Depression seemed to draw the community closer together. That’s probably why the city fathers showed movies in the open air at the city park on Saturday nights during the summer. They were still doing it when I arrived and continued for a few years after, until some enterprising soul brought a real movie theater to town.

The park originally had been part of John Hart’s vineyard and winery, which he established there in 1884. Although he continued to grow grapes for years on part of the property, he closed the winery in 1918 and donated the land to the city, leaving the adobe winery building on the northern half. It was on this structure that a white sheet would be draped as a movie screen. The movies were mostly silent comedies featuring stars of that era like Charley Chaplin and Max Sennett. Newsreels, travelogues, and a variety of other so-called short subjects were often included in the evening’s program.

Those open-air movies provided one of the few pleasant memories I have of Sierra Madre. It wasn’t the movies themselves that mattered, but the fact that we and the rest of the townspeople were gathering for a community event, one that—maybe because there was no entrance fee we couldn’t afford—made us feel like we belonged. When a movie theater was finally opened in the late 1930s and the movie evenings in the park came to an end, that feeling of community was gone, too.

CHAPTER 9

Reunion

In past years, some of the Home reunions had been held at Sierra Madre's city park. But the one Sherry and I returned to Southern California to attend was at the home of Edwin Beach, the boy with the glass eye I'd known as Edwin Ortiz. A successful career as an attorney and judge behind him, he was retired and living on a small avocado ranch in Santa Clara. The drive there on that splendid Sunday morning reminded me why so many people choose to live in California. Briefly, I thought of moving back.

Except for my siblings and brother-in-law, Gilbert Martinez (he and my sister were the only Home kids ever to marry each other), I'd be seeing others from the Home for the first time in some four decades. I wondered whether I'd recognize anyone. But as we drove up to the house and Edwin and his wife came out to greet us, I recognized him instantly. He was grayer, but still slim and fit, simply an older version of the boy I remembered. Our greeting was warm, though there was some reticence between us, probably heightened by the presence of our wives.

Like mine, Edwin's wife, Janet, was not Latina, something I already knew. Later, as others arrived, I found it interesting so many—at least half—of these former Home children I'd been in contact with had also intermarried. I could only guess at their reasons, but I had long since known that one of mine, in my first marriage at least, was to make me more acceptable in American society. That subconscious thought process was the result of being taught, deliberately or inadvertently, to detest myself and others like me. As a consequence, and to my mother's chagrin, I had a problem even dating Latino women, much less considering marrying one. It was not a subject I planned bring up with anyone that afternoon.

When we were still on speaking terms, Re told me the turnout for past reunions was always substantial, that she and the former kids who attended were " . . . close, very close." True or not, only fifteen of my former Home mates showed up this time, everyone bringing food of some sort for the picnic the Beaches had set up on garden tables on their shaded back lawn. With spouses and a few children, the number of guests swelled to more than thirty. Whatever hopes I had for mutual recognition, it was immediately clear that I was in a group of strangers. And disappointingly, though I'd been corresponding with most of them before the event, no one was particularly eager to talk about our mutual past. Inexplicably, Re actually shunned me. Something more than her fear of what I might write about her was there, but I had little time to find out what it might be. The matriarchal role she'd assumed for herself struck me as a little comical. Now I could understand why over the years she'd repeatedly called the group together; she saw these people as her family and her years at the Home as her best. She was not unlike some Vietnam veterans I've known, who hang on to their wartime memories, even occasionally donning their uniforms and going to reunions to relive the experience that may have been the most significant of their lives.

I was determined not to be thwarted by the indifference of my former mates, and I assumed the role of reporter, talking to each person in turn to learn what I could. From most it wasn't much, mainly platitudes about how much they'd enjoyed life at the Home. But from Edwin I learned his family had come from Peru when the Depression destroyed the family business. For reasons he didn't explain, years ago he changed his surname to his mother's maiden name. I suspected it was done when his parents became U.S. citizens and they, like all newly naturalized Americans, had the option of taking any name they wished. A name like Beach would be more acceptable than Ortiz in the mainstream of American society.

One of my more interesting companions at the Home was Frank Flores, the second-oldest of three brothers and a year younger than I. I'd been hoping he'd show up so we could have a good talk. But Frank, a natural athlete as a boy, was a show-off when I knew him, and now back in this group, he reverted to the part. He was so busy performing I couldn't pin him down. We planned for a visit with him at his home later in the week.

Mario Uriarte was also present, retired from a career with the California Highway Patrol. He'd brought with him an attractive, youngish Latina, who turned out to be his latest girlfriend. He took a good ribbing from Frank about robbing the cradle. Mario was even less forthcoming than Frank; my attempts to talk with him were repeatedly brushed off.

A number of the others, the oldest members of the group, were people who were at the Home and left it before I arrived. If they'd come here to reminisce, it wasn't apparent in their conversation or in their responses to my questions. All in all they had little to say of any substance, either to me or, it seemed, to each other.

Of those at the reunion, the most forthcoming and interested in what I was trying to do was Rachel Parra Quick. I didn't have much to do with her when we were at the Home, but now I found her warm, sincere, and eager to help. She'd brought me more documents about the Home as well as photographs of some of the other children who lived there. Among the latter was a group photo of the Mendoza sisters. Adela, the second oldest, was for a brief time my partner in lust. It was a shock to see what she actually looked like, as opposed to how I remembered her. I was almost sorry to have that image replaced by this reality.

Rachel told me she was seven when she was placed in the Home early in 1939, along with her brother and four sisters, of which she is third oldest. Her mother's advanced case of tuberculosis—she died that December—had made caring for Rachel and her siblings impossible for their father, an army enlisted man. The L.A. County Welfare Department arranged for them to be sent to the Home. As I listened to the story of how she and her siblings made their journey to the Home, I could see it was just a variant of mine and that of all our former Home mates.

It was about Gibsie that Rachel really wanted to talk. While she lived at the Home and long afterwards, she grew to love Gibsie, whom she considered a composite of her mother and father and later even a sister. Other than Re, Rachel was one of the few girls allowed to remain at the Home until she was eighteen; she worked in the town and went to high school in Pasadena. After that, when there was room for her, Gibsie let her live at the Home periodically. During those years, she and Gibsie vacationed together, even visited Gibsie's brothers at their family farm in Upland. They became increasingly close, frequently shopping and traveling together on excursions to places as far away as San Francisco. Indeed, their relationship continued for the rest of Gibsie's life. In later years, she told me, whenever she was in a quandary she would ask herself, "What would Gibsie do or advise me to do?" Their relationship gave Rachel the love and attention denied her by a mother who had died too soon. And for Gibsie, I suspect, there was a child's adoration and later devotion to relieve the loneliness of her life as manager.

Rachel's heartfelt expressions about Gibsie came as a surprise, as did her perception of this woman we both knew so well. I suppose it was entirely reasonable that Gibsie's relationships with us would have been as varied as the children themselves. I can't speak to how she actually felt about us boys, but it was clear even to me that she treated the girls differently than she did us. When I told Rachel I remembered Gibsie mainly as a stern disciplinarian, she couldn't believe we were talking about the same person.

Gibsie was a remote figure I saw mainly at meals and on those occasions when she substituted as the boys' matron. In all matters she was the final arbiter, especially in matters of discipline. Her punishments were the stuff of fable, and every boy had at least one story to tell about a terrifying encounter with her. Whether true or not, it was only after I got whipped by her myself that I learned all those tales contained some grain of truth. From the outset she inspired awe and trepidation whenever I was in her presence and with good reason: my behavior was all too often reproachable. I dreaded the times she'd call me in—sometimes with my mother—for an unpleasant conference. I was no longer fooled by the trace of a smile Gibsie wore, and I learned it was a bad sign if her eyes weren't also smiling. And if her prominent jaw muscles were flexing under that steely gaze of hers, I knew for sure I was in trouble. Standing under her scrutiny made me scroll desperately through the list of my recent transgressions for the one she might be about to name and punish me for.

The matrons had a whole catalogue of ways to control our behavior. On the positive end were rewards and reasoning. When these failed, action quickly escalated from scolding to more impressive, physical, punishment. There was a menu of means ranging up to a vigorous old-fashioned whipping. If the rod was spared, they believed, the child would be spoiled.

It was far better to have one's problems resolved by Miss Clarke or whoever the boys' matron happened to be, than to involve Gibsie. Miss Clarke limited herself to pinching, ear-pulling, or slapping. If those persuaders didn't do the trick, a threatened trip to the Big House to see Gibsie could usually get any of us to knuckle under. Gibsie, the High Disciplinarian, was to be avoided at all costs. Once she determined you had it coming, she was unrelenting and energetic, wielding a strong arm with a strap of some sort at the other end.

I never believed she took joy in whipping any of us; more likely, she disliked doing it. But that distaste never interfered with her vigor in wielding her variety of straps, including a cat-o'-nine-tails, to buttocks and the backs of thighs bared to receive their sting. Even though being sent to her meant a beating would likely follow, she often gave a culprit a final chance to explain himself. If a boy could create a reasonable doubt in her mind, he might get off with a stern "talking to." That didn't happen often.

During my first four years at the Home I'd somehow managed to avoid any of those whips. But given my proclivity for mischief, my turn was inevitable. When I was eight or so, it was my obsession with those jams and jellies that did me in. Seeing one or the other spread on a piece of toast, and then scraped to leave only the barest traces in the crevices, was very frustrating. Those sweet concoctions in the basement pantry, whose contents could be clearly seen through the chicken wire that made up one of the walls, were just too tantalizing to children who were on the edge of hunger every day. So the time inevitably came for my foray into the storeroom. The idea was not original with me; I knew it had been assaulted successfully before and would be again. I cased it carefully and, with two accomplices, planned a raid in detail.

The chicken wire was nailed to a wooden framework that made up the open side of the storeroom. Inside, like prizes in a carnival shooting gallery, were row upon row of glass jars, pints and quarts, of canned fruits and vegetables, as well as the jams and preserves I craved. They were stacked on shelves that covered three walls from floor to ceiling. I was sure a jar or two wouldn't be missed. But without the key to the padlocked door, the only way in was to make an opening in the chicken wire. And that's exactly what we'd planned, afterwards to restore the chicken wire to its original state, with no one the wiser.

With my partners in crime stationed at two of the three approaches to the storeroom, I managed to pull the wire free at one edge, creating an opening large enough to squeeze my small body through. But just as I was about to pass out the first jar, we could hear footfalls on the steps leading down from the floor above. "Somebody's coming," the boy nearest the steps whispered, and without a backward glance both lookouts fled, leaving me to be caught. Hastily returning the jar to the shelf and with no place to hide, I flattened myself against the shelves and froze, hoping against hope the intruder would turn out to be another kid, whose silence I could buy by sharing the booty.

No such luck. It was Fuller, who was coming to the storeroom. She unlocked the door, stepped inside, and let out a startled yelp when she saw me. The surprise on her face immediately turned to an angry frown, and I knew I'd get no sympathy from her. There was no need to ask what I was doing. "You wait right there," she said, ordering me out. Dejected and fearful, I stood where she'd directed while she closed and snapped shut the padlock on the door and re-fastened the chicken wire as best she could. Then, ignoring my howls of pain, she pulled me along by an ear up the stairs to the south porch where she delivered me to Gibsie, who was ironing clothes there.

When Fuller told her where she'd found me, Gibsie sighed tiredly and for a long moment just stared at me, jaw muscles flexing rapidly. There was no trace of a smile now, as she shook her head with disgust. "Are you hungry?" she finally asked, her voice calm. Fearing the worst and unable to meet her glare, I shook my head, no.

Then she asked menacingly, this time a little louder, "What were you after?"

Still not looking at her, I mumbled, "Nothing," one of my standard replies whenever I was in the wrong.

"Bobby, look at me!" she hissed, glaring at me with anger-widened eyes, and arms akimbo. Waggling a finger, her voice rising, she said, "Do you think I'm a fool? You tell me what you were after, right now!"

"I just wanted some jam," I blurted, still unable to look her in the eye.

For a few moments she said nothing while she struggled to calm herself. Then in a more patient, lowered voice tinged with sadness, she lifted my chin with a finger so she could see my face and said, "You know the food in the storeroom is for all of us to share, and it has to last us through the year. I don't think you realize how difficult it is to get food, and if everyone did as you just tried to do, we soon would have nothing left to eat."

Now peering up at her through my eyelashes and trying to look as contrite as I could, I was beginning to think I might get off with just a tongue lashing. But when she told me how seriously she considered what I'd done, and that she couldn't allow stealing to go unpunished, I knew I was in for it. By then Fuller had returned with the infamous whip, and Gibsie told me to drop my pants and bend over a nearby chair. Placing a hand on my back to hold me in place, she delivered an uncounted series of hard, swift blows, the shock of the pain so sudden and intense at first I could only suck air in one long gasp. And it was over none too quickly. When she finally stopped, I was left screaming, fighting for breath, all the while hopping about the room trying to hold up my trousers while gingerly massaging my burning backside barely aware of the crowd of kids who'd gathered—some somberly, others gleefully—to watch. Gibsie, meanwhile, no longer interested in me, had handed the whip to Fuller and was leaning on the ironing board for support, her face flushed, huffing from the exertion. She, too, was struggling to regain her composure, but only managed to look disheveled, so much carefully finger-waved hair had flown free of her ever-present hairnet.

The experience left an indelible mark. After that I hesitated anytime I thought of mischief-making. There was no doubt I deserved the beating, and I only briefly held a grudge against Fuller for turning me in. But I still wanted the jam, not necessarily a whole jar of it, just more on my bread. That never came to pass, nor did the yearning subside. Some deprivations are never satisfied and I vowed when grown I'd take pleasure each morning in slathering an extra-thick layer of preserves on my breakfast toast.

Before we left the reunion, Margaret Gonzalez Trejo showed me a photocopy of Gibsie's personal diary. I was only able to scan a few of the pages, which were hard to read because of its author's small, cramped handwriting style, but I knew it could answer many of my burning questions. It was a document I had to have, but despite my promise to return it, Margaret refused to let me take the diary with me. She finally agreed to let me have a photocopy if my sister would make it in Margaret's presence and I would pay the cost. Of course I agreed and, thankfully, so did my sister.

West Covina is another of those nondescript, suburban communities that surround Los Angeles, a conglomeration of wood-frame and stucco houses, typical Southern California tract homes. In one of them we talked with Frank Flores over a beer in his back-garden patio.

Frank reminded me that he and his brothers, Margarito and Arthur, arrived at the Home during the summer of '38, after their mother died and their father could no longer care for them. Frank was six, Margarito, seven, and Arthur, five. We laughed over how Margarito hated his name and tried to get us to call him "Rags." But instead, when one of the girls started calling him "Maggie," the name stuck. For a while after, he fought anyone who called him Maggie in his presence, then resigned himself to the inevitable. I remembered Frank as the quickest of the three, both intellectually and physically, though he wasn't so bright that he could steal from the merchants in town without repeatedly getting caught. He said it took a few sessions with Gibsie and her cat-o'-nine-tails before he finally realized he was better off keeping his sticky fingers in his pockets.

Frank and I fought a lot, usually in defense of our younger brothers. When the Flores brothers arrived, Arthur was the youngest boy at the Home and he became fair game for all the others. Arthur was determined to involve himself in Billy's peculiar practices. Billy, equally determined to keep Arthur at bay, discovered to his delight that Arthur was a kid he could easily beat up. But whenever he did, he set off a chain reaction: Frank would beat up Billy; I would come to Billy's defense and pound on Frank, who would call Maggie to take me on. For a time, the matrons were beside themselves, breaking up one fight after another.

Later Frank and I got to be reasonably good friends, mainly because we seemed to have the same proclivity for mischief. It was with him that I got dizzily sick from smoking a cigarette he'd lifted from his father and later seared my throat trying to smoke a homemade stogie he'd fashioned out of toilet paper and crushed sycamore and eucalyptus leaves. And when he got hold of a bottle of hydrogen peroxide, we both became flaming redheads for a time, then got rid of most of it by cutting each others' hair in the Mohawk style.

Since I'd left the Home before Frank, I never knew that he and his brothers, with no family to go to, had gone to live at the Spanish American Institute, another Methodist-sponsored home for teenage and young adult men, located in Gardena, California. There, besides continuing their education, Frank and Arthur learned to be printers, a livelihood they later pursued as adults. When he was seventeen, Margarito enlisted in the U.S. Army, intending to make it a career. He did very well, rapidly attaining the rank of sergeant, but later suffered an early death from cancer. The surviving brothers remained close all their lives; even now Arthur and his family live just across the street from Frank and his.

Frank was articulate and animated and seemed to be enjoying the visit as much as we were. What he liked most to talk about were what he remembered as his athletic glories, and he was soon recounting how he got on Sierra Madre School's tennis team. The school normally had no organized athletic programs, but now and then sports teams were organized and matched against those of other schools, like St. Rita's. One of those was a tennis team. This sport had become popular in the town during the 1940s. Pancho Gonzalez was then a popular Mexican American international tennis star and inspired some of the Home boys to try and make the team; Frank was certain he was already good enough. Gibsie did her best to help him, but only managed to find an old tennis racquet and a worn-out ball for him to practice with. He had no other equipment, not even a pair of tennis shoes, so Frank played barefoot, his leather-soled shoes being too slippery.

Buddy, another boy at school, was also an acknowledged athlete. When he decided to take up tennis and try for the team, his parents outfitted him with all the cans of tennis balls he might need, top-of-the-line brand-name racquets and tennis shoes, and all the other "right" accouterments. A match between Frank and Buddy was inevitable.

According to Frank, it took place on one of the waning days of the school year during the physical education hour, which everyone thought would be more than enough time for Frank to be trounced. As Frank enthusiastically told it, the volleys were long and fast-paced, and the hour quickly passing with the contest far from decided. Although the players were evenly matched, it was evident Frank might not last. His bare feet were blistering from the hot asphalt court, and he was noticeably hurting. But no one watching, not even the teachers, returned to class, so eager were they all to see the outcome of the grudge-match between Frank and Buddy. Buddy was conceited and roundly disliked, and many hoped against hope that lightning might strike and Frank would win.

Of course we knew the outcome before Frank revealed it—why else would he relate this tale? We indulged him and the pleasure he took in the telling. He did win, and limped back to class a hero. Frank said he was so fixated on his game he hardly remembered any pain in his feet until the match was over. And for a week after, as if they were badges of honor, he showed off his blistered feet to anyone who would look.

I read about this exploit of Frank's later in one of Gibsie's reports to the Center. She, too, reported that back at the Home, Frank was hailed as a conquering hero, though it was nearly intolerable living with him for a while afterwards.

As our mutual reticence declined—maybe it was the beer—and we warmed to recounting our experiences, Sherry developed a bit of a smirk on her face when the conversation drifted to our dalliances with some of the Home girls. That was when I discovered my erotic encounter with Adela Mendoza, one I'd treasured for years because it was my first, was not exclusive. It came as no small disappointment to learn I was only one among many of Adela's consorts, that the excitement of mutual discovery had probably been little more than a passing titillation for her. Frank told me she'd "tried out" most of the boys who were anywhere near the age of puberty. He was only nine when she got around to him, and rather than being excited, he was so confused and frightened by Adela's aggressiveness he'd run away crying.

I didn't.

Adela was the second-oldest of the troublesome quartet of Mendoza sisters who'd arrived three years earlier. At thirteen in mid-summer of '41, she was nearly three years older than I and somewhat taller, a slim girl with breasts budding. None of the sisters was particularly pretty, and of the lot, Adela's strong Indian ancestry was most pronounced in her straight black hair, light olive-colored skin, and high cheekbones. Of the four, she was also the most self-engrossed, tending to pick and choose what and with whom she associated or played, often preferring to sit on the sidelines to watch rather than participate.

It was a hot afternoon in July when a group of us were cooling off in the East Yard, cavorting in the former fish pond that had been converted to a wading pool. It was constructed of stone with a smooth cement bottom, and though not much deeper than a foot, it was still possible to launch a sort of shallow dive into it without hurting yourself. The East Yard was the prettiest of the grounds, the pool surrounded by a stand of bamboo, papyrus fronds, and mature shrubs, all of which made the pool area somewhat secluded.

All the kids, me included, were wearing hand-me-down woolen bathing suits, the kind that stretch and sag when wet, which they also did because for most of us they were a size too large. The ones the girls wore were the one-piece, "Roaring Twenties" variety, which regularly slipped from their shoulders. And that was part of the fun of playing in the pool: checking the girls' physical development.

On that hot July day, the pool was crowded, and I didn't notice when Adela entered it. But suddenly she was right in front of me, a dripping, glistening Venus, just rising from a shallow dive. We were both on hands and knees and she made no effort to move as my eyes left hers and deliberately shifted to the now-exposed mounds of her small breasts. After what seemed like minutes, she smiled ever so slightly, rose and adjusted her suit to cover herself. Glancing seductively over her shoulder, she stepped from the pool and walked toward the brick stairs leading to the usually deserted portico in front of the Big House. When she looked back again at me, the unspoken invitation to follow her was unmistakable. None of the other kids seemed to notice the little drama unfolding in their midst.

Before starting after her, I looked around for the matron who usually kept an eye on things. Seeing no one, I followed. We'd not spoken, and when I caught up with Adela at the empty portico, remained wordless. Still dripping wet, she was resting her back against the wall with both hands behind her, and at my approach, she shrugged the strap of her bathing suit from a shoulder, exposing a breast. I stared at it, a small pink mound, in heart-thumping wonder. I was content to do nothing more than look, but she wasn't. Reaching for my hand, she raised it to her bosom, which I touched gingerly with my fingertips. Apparently unsatisfied with my tentative caresses, she pulled my head to her chest, where I needed no further coaxing to encompass the firm prominence with my lips. She said nothing, only sighed and held my head lightly, even tenderly, to her as I continued my oral and tactile explorations.

She allowed this until I suggested a fuller exposition of our respective anatomies. Instead, she suggested we do so after supper in the relative privacy of the tall grass in the empty field across the street from the Big House.

Mealtime seemed to last forever. I could hardly eat, I was so excited by what I hoped was to come. I was also fearful that, after a more sober consideration of what she'd committed herself to, she'd change her mind. On the contrary, she was already lying hidden in the waist-high grass when I arrived, and this time with little hesitation we showed and fondled each other at length. I was sure I was a lucky boy.

For the rest of the summer Adela and I were inseparable. We met regularly for petting, going for long walks together after dark and stopping at intervals in the more deeply shadowed places to caress our respective centers of pleasure. When fall arrived and the nights chilled, we met in the basement furnace room, where our groping became more adventuresome. But events came to a climax, so to speak, when I tried to penetrate her. The pain it caused frightened us both and she decided it was time to end the affair. Soon afterwards she made it clear we were finished. I didn't understand the sudden rejection and moped around for days with hurt feelings. I'd really gotten to like her and depended on the apparent affection she showed me. A few months later she was gone for good.

CHAPTER 10

Supper for a Song

"This is where we'd very likely have grown up, if mother hadn't found the Home," I said, a tremor passing through me at the prospect. "The Home at least spared us that misfortune." Sherry and I were in the East L.A. barrio, the traditional home for most of the city's Mexican Americans.

"You mean if you'd grown up here you'd be a different person?" Sherry asked. I was sure she already knew the answer, just wanted to hear me say it. I didn't disappoint her.

"No doubt about it. I'd probably speak English with an accent. The schools here being what they were and maybe still are, I'd probably not be as well educated, if at all, maybe even have become a gang member or be in prison."

"But not everybody who grows up here is in a gang, or a criminal. Would it necessarily have been all bad?"

"Maybe not. Who knows? But we arrived in L.A. during the depths of the Depression, and things had to have been worse here than in most other places." I hadn't grown up here, but my beginnings in an El Paso slum had been as bad.

As we drove through the barrio looking for the Plaza Community Center, I wondered if East L.A. was really much improved since that time. Indiana Avenue, where the Center was located just off The 5, lay near the barrio's western boundary. The neighborhood was rough, the streets trash-strewn and walls graffiti-covered, though in this latter aspect it looked pretty much like the rest of the city. The iron grills barring windows and doors of homes and public buildings lent an air of danger, an expectation of break-ins. The Center had added a double-entry vestibule, its steel doors controlled by buzzer from the inside. Seeing these precautions made me realize Sherry and I had been too long in the relative safety of middle-class

America; we'd driven through the area with the car doors locked. I worried about leaving our shiny rental car on the street.

Before coming to California for the reunion we'd had the good fortune to meet and have dinner in Washington, D.C., with the Plaza Community Center's executive director, Geraldine Zapata. She'd come the preceding June to attend a conference. By the time I showed up at the Center in L.A., she'd cleared the way for me to look through its archives. There was a lot of material, but surprisingly little about the Home itself. Still, I was hopeful of getting my questions answered.

One thing I wanted to understand was the interest of the Methodist Church that led it to create a place like the Home. For the years I was nominally a Methodist, I had no idea what the church was about. So it was a revelation to learn that it, and all the other American Protestant denominations for that matter, had set out to make "real Americans" of immigrants and their children, from wherever they came in the world, and to create new adherents to the faith. The converted in turn were to go out and "work among their own people." In this the churches were deadly serious. Theirs was not just a mission to save souls, but a determined crusade to save America from the Pope! That campaign led them not only to build houses of worship, but schools, colleges, and universities.

Along with the Irish and Italians, Latinos must have represented a prime opportunity, since virtually all were Catholic. To turn such immigrants into "real Americans" meant replacing their original culture with one the church deemed to be American, whatever that was. And however well-intentioned, this was bound to create confusion for the immigrants about who they were. That kind of confusion created my own limbo of identity, and I wasn't alone. Indeed, problems with identity seem to affect everyone, as if it's not enough to be only American. These days it's common to hear people refer to themselves with their racial or ethnic origins prefixed to their American nationality.

During the eighteenth and nineteenth centuries, it was common for Protestant churches to establish orphanages for the whole range of ethnic groups. By the turn of the twentieth century, the Methodist Church had already begun its ministry in Southern California for what it called "Latin Americans"—a grouping of all the Spanish-speaking, plus Italians and Portuguese—during the next decade preaching to small congregations of this group. Even so, the Methodist Church still might never have established the Home had it not been for the vectors of three lives converging at a particular place and time, and the fact of a revolution in Mexico.

In 1911, a young minister named Vernon M. McCombs arrived in Los Angeles. In the preceding four years he'd been stationed in Peru, plagued by an illness that eventually forced him to return to New York. His doctor then recommended he go west to regain his health. Vernon McCombs was young, ambitious, and aware that the revolution begun the year before in Mexico had turned the Southwestern United States into a haven for Mexican refugees. Fluent in Spanish, he saw his rest-cure as an opportunity, one in which he might realize the aspirations his illness had thwarted in Peru.

He told a charming story (related in a biography published by the Council of Women for Home Missions) about how, on his first Sunday in Los Angeles, he visited a small Sunday School in which a woman was teaching to a class of rather listless Mexican children. When a child asked a question that the woman hesitated to answer, the missionary asked if he might reply. But instead of continuing in English, he answered in Spanish, the effect electrifying both the children and the enthused teacher, who invited him to continue. "I fell into heaven today," the exhilarated young minister told his wife when he returned home. The experience of that day had "captivated his soul," he said, and he took it as a sign from God.

Visionary and energetic despite his physical condition, McCombs approached the local Methodist hierarchy with a plan to provide a church and relief services to the Latin Americans. Within the space of five years, he'd put together a Mexican Methodist Episcopal Church and the organization that became known as the Plaza Community Center. But he couldn't do it alone. It was his appeal for a "Christian social worker and stenographer to work among the Spanish-speaking" that Katherine Higgins had answered.

In addition to McCombs's vision and organizing, it took Miss Higgins's compassion, energy, and insight to propose an orphanage for Latin American children. When in 1923 a seven-year-old Mexican girl was abandoned on the Center's front steps, her arrival put an end to discussion and set in motion the train of events that led to the founding of the Home. The requirements for entry were few and straightforward. The first was that a child have an apparent need and pass rigid physical and mental examinations. The other, predictably, required the parent or guardian to be willing to have the child receive instruction in the evangelical Christian faith.

But to make the Home a functioning, thriving institution, one more person, the right manager, was still needed. After two years of false starts, Katherine Higgins hired Elsie Nora Gibson, the Irish-American woman we would come to know as Gibsie, to be the Home's manager. She was the person who made the enterprise work, guiding it through the Great Depression and the other travails that beset the Home during the thirty-one years it existed. During those three decades, superintendents at the Center—all men—came and went, but for the most part it was the constancy of the Misses Higgins and Gibson that provided the stability and continuity the Home itself needed.

In its heyday, the Center had provided extensive social and welfare services for Latinos. This brief history, gleaned from its files, sadly showed the existing Center to be only a vestige of its former self. Now it struggled to provide minimal health care for impoverished women and children of any origin.

Among the documents I was allowed to take from the Center were a number of black-and-white photographs, pictures of children involved in many activities at the Home: boys and girls reading in the living room, children eating in the dining room, girls in the backyard hanging clothes on the lines of rope zigzagged across it, among other scenes. In all of them the children were stiffly posed, frozen in the photographer's attempt to depict life there, their rigidity an attitude not too far removed from the Home's atmosphere and a reflection of its manager. I recognized the rooms, buildings and grounds, of course, but there was no sense of déjà vu until I came across one photo of a decorated Christmas tree with smiling children arrayed around it. In the background I recognized my own unsmiling face. As I gazed at the photograph I was suddenly projected back in time, and not happily.

Even after almost two years at the Home I couldn't seem to settle into life with any sort of comfort. It wasn't necessarily the strictness with which every activity was scheduled and carried out that bothered me; there was actually a kind of security in having some predictability about the future. It was more my resentment, my own misery at being left there.

But however badly things seemed to be going for me, they weren't going well for the Home, either. And despite my removed state of mind, I was aware there were problems about feeding, clothing, and sheltering us. Matrons spent their days with worried expressions, reminding us not to waste anything. At mealtimes we seemed to eat much the same thing day after day; never very large, meals were skimpier than ever as the Depression went on. Even the Sunday dinner was more often chicken than roast beef or ham. Some of the older kids, the lucky ones, got to eat lunch at the school cafeteria; many of our suppers were provided by the Red Cross.

The situation at the Home was no secret in Sierra Madre, either. Many of the townspeople were genuinely concerned about us. Teachers at school and people at our church seemed to look at us with doleful eyes and mutter expressions of concern and sympathy. I got patted on the head a lot. Mr. Roberts, of Roberts' Market, learning the Home might be closed, had even written asking the Center to wait until the town had a chance to see what it could do to help keep it open.

Then Eleanor Miller, one of the town's better-known artists, had the idea for a "Mexican Fiesta" to raise money for us. It was held in the lovely gardens of her home on a sunny April afternoon. The kids from the Home performed, of course, and she arranged for Elena Rico of the Los Angeles Opera Company and the Lizarraga family's Sonora Quintet to entertain. People came from Pasadena and Los Angeles as well as the town. The music was excellent, as was the food, and everybody seemed to have a good time. It must have raised some money, too, because the Home wasn't closed.

The "fiesta" was another of a growing number of events in which we found ourselves singing for our supper. They were put on mainly before the religious and charitable groups Gibsie went to for help. Having us perform wasn't new, but now it happened more often and before a greater variety of people. We even traveled to churches and organizations in other towns with our acts.

Long before I arrived, Miss Higgins had arranged for the loan of a piano and engaged Freda Foss, her young niece, to teach the kids to play it. Those who learned well enough gave recitals or just played because they liked to. But now, with the need for donations growing, they performed in earnest. Those of us who neither played nor sang learned to recite poetry or passages from the Bible, so we could all participate. In one way or another, and whether we wanted to or not, we were all drafted into the fund-raising effort. Even those of us who spoke little English could at least sing in Spanish, and the very youngest kids who were otherwise exempt, like my baby sister Connie, were still brought along for their sympathy value.

When they decided I should also be a performer, Gibsie and Fuller auditioned me. Sitting beside her at the piano, Fuller had me sing scales to see what my voice was like; we both discovered I could sing like the proverbial bird. Soon afterwards I was singing with the other children.

Then as my English improved, Gibsie had me recite poems, though I didn't always understand what I was saying. One that went over especially well was "The Rocking Horse."

I climbed up to the attic
    to see what I could see,
And there I found a rocking horse
    as pretty as could be.
I ran to find my grandmama,
    and tell her what I'd found.
I thought I saw a teardrop fall
    and heard a funny sound.
With a wistful smile she picked me up
    and set me on her knee.
That was your daddy's rocking horse,
    when he was only three.

Until it was explained to me, I'd no idea what an attic was, or for that matter a rocking horse. Nonetheless, each time it was my turn, I'd walk out to center stage, and as I recited, stiffly mime the actions described in the poem. The audiences were for the most part older women, and they loved it, though I never understood their hand-to-bosom, pained smiles accompanied by the breathy "Oh's!" the recitation usually drew from them. But Gibsie knew very well such a poem delivered by a dimpled seven-year-old would touch hearts and open pocketbooks every time. I was made to repeat it endlessly.

The following year, Gibsie drilled me and others on reciting Bible passages. I recited "The Christmas Story" so often I was sure I'd never forget it. Other children recited, sang, or played screechy renditions of "Over the Waves" or "Goldenrod" on violins they could barely hold.

Most of our performances took place in the Big House, in the large foyer whose floor was two steps above the level of the living room, where the audience sat. Curtained off from the living room, the foyer became a stage permitting us, as our "numbers" came up, to enter and exit "stage left"—that is, from the south porch. We were always well-rehearsed, our get-ups appropriate for our acts. Costumes ranged from Sunday best for music and poetry recitations, to cut up sheets for "angels" reciting the "Christmas Story" and the like, to Gibsie's idea of traditional Mexican costumes for those of us who sang, in Spanish, songs like "*Allá En El Rancho Grande,*" a standard of our repertoire. Those were the only times we were allowed to use our first language; when I learned English—forgetting Spanish in the process—the words to these songs were the only Spanish I retained.

We also danced "*El Jarabe Tapatío,*" the "Mexican Hat Dance," dressed in sombreros, colored waistbands, and brightly-hued serapes. A wind-up Victrola provided the music when Berta, Regina, or Victoria—our best piano players—weren't available to pound it out on the piano.

We performed all through the year, but most often from Thanksgiving through New Year's Day. Indeed, Miss Higgins considered the performances so important she visited early in the fall to plan with Gibsie their scheduling at the Home and away from it. Meanwhile, Gibsie and Fuller had already begun assigning us poems, instrumentals, and songs. Fuller's main effort was with the singers, who rehearsed Christmas and other songs in Spanish so they'd have the "flavor expected of them." We practiced both afternoon and evening so we could put on a show at a moment's notice.

By Thanksgiving Day, we were thoroughly rehearsed and presenting shows regularly. When December rolled around, our performances, and the Christmas parties that usually followed, were in full sway. Many of the groups we performed for were well-established donors, and as the holiday season progressed, we tried to get around to all of them. The pace became hectic. By mid-December our travels began. Typically we went first to Alhambra, where we gave our annual Christmas program. Later, back at the Home, we entertained a group from Glendale. Then some of our older girls were guests of a group in Monrovia, where they performed, and others went back to Glendale to play and sing for a men's Christmas luncheon. One of the regular groups we performed for at the Home usually brought a Christmas tree and the makings for a party, one of their number playing Santa Claus and passing out gifts.

For at least a week before Christmas, people bearing a variety of gifts dropped in at all hours. And within a day or two of Christmas Eve, the Sierra Madre Fire Department showed up with Santa in a fire truck to bring rebuilt toys and sometimes a tricycle or skates. The Center's superintendent also brought donated supplies, which always included sacks of coal for our furnace. Of course we had to entertain whoever showed up.

◆

At first I liked performing, but doing it so often and on demand quickly took the fun out of it, turning it into a chore; that we were being used to earn our keep was not lost on us either. The parties that often followed softened my resentment, but the feeling of being second-class was always there. We were reminded always to "be grateful," a state of mind my child's brain didn't easily take to or find pleasant. Worst of all were the looks on the gracious, smiling faces of many of our benefactors—sometimes pity, sometimes self-righteousness. Some were better than others at masking those attitudes, but they were always present and left me feeling demeaned in their eyes and, more importantly, in mine. I wondered if Gibsie realized we could resent those who were so generous.

The performances we gave during the holidays brought in a great variety of donations, but usually no Christmas gifts for individual kids. As many of the children were orphans, there was a great disparity in the presents. To equalize matters and avoid a lot of hurt feelings when the gifts were passed out on Christmas Eve, Gibsie prepared lists, assigning each child to a donor group or individual giver. Thus every child was likely to get at least one good gift, like a coat, a sweater, or shoes.

But this presented the possibility of having to endure something far worse than performing: receiving a gift personally from one or another of our benefactors, especially when they got their children to make the presentation. No matter how much I might have craved the gift being offered, the show of gratitude expected of me as I accepted it soured any pleasure. "People like to be appreciated; you be sure to say thank you," Miss Clarke or Gibsie would prompt. It didn't take long to master appearing to be pleased, humble, and even a little fawning while thanking the person. I learned to do this with downcast eyes, a dimpled smile on my face. I wasn't really ungrateful, I just so disliked feeling inferior it overrode any feeling of real gratitude I might have had. I couldn't help disliking the giver and myself.

We opened gifts on Christmas Eve, and I knew Gibsie and the other matrons did their best to make this joyful. A few parents and even some donors showed up. After supper, everyone gathered in the living room to sing carols and hear a reading of "A Christmas Carol." Santa Claus, played by a visiting father, a donor, or even one of the older boys, hid in the fireplace behind the blanket-draped fireplace screen. At the appointed time, a matron and one or two of the older kids would begin stamping on the deck above the living room to simulate the "prancing and pawing of eight tiny reindeer." We didn't realize until we were older that thirty-two feet would have made a lot more noise. Then Santa would pop from the fireplace to the delight—and sometimes terror—of the younger children. The donated tree, already decorated a few nights before, usually had a pile of gifts—impressive for their number if not their contents—around its base. These would be passed out by Santa, who'd then finish up by passing out apples and candy from within his bag.

No matter how often I experienced it, Christmas Eve was always an event mixed with unreal expectations and very real disappointment. Parents made an effort not to miss it, but many of them, my mother included, were often working and couldn't come. Others didn't care enough to show up, and some children had no one of their own to share the evening with. Unhappiness and resentment toward the festivities were inevitable. Despite all the efforts to make the evening a happy one, for me there was always an undercurrent of melancholy. What I wanted most was not to be where I was. This feeling—the sense of being "one of those who was needy"—suffused the entire holiday period. All of this made Christmas a time of dejection to be gotten through as quickly as possible.

◆

At noon following church services on Christmas Day, we all walked to the beautiful home of Mr. and Mrs. Joseph P. Nash, located on Alta Vista Drive, higher up in the foothills overlooking the town, for a big Christmas dinner. The Nashes were the wealthy owners of a large department store in Pasadena, and one of Sierra Madre's most prominent families. They began entertaining the Home's children in 1932 and continued what became a Christmas Day tradition. By the time I first knew him, Mr. Nash was already elderly, short and white-haired, with crippled arthritic hands he used as prods to move us from one part of his spacious house to another. He was gruff to the point of seeming angry, and the prodding in our backs and ribs by his rigid fingers actually hurt. One experience was enough to make us scurry when we saw him coming.

The Christmas program at their home hardly ever varied from year to year. First we'd gather in their commodious living room to listen to their son play the accordion. He was accomplished, it seemed, on only one piece, which he played loudly and repeatedly for his captive audience. "Tango of the Roses" we derisively dubbed "Tangle of the Noses." Then, prodded on by Mr. Nash, we adjourned to the dining room to a sumptuous dinner, most memorable for its aspic and green-tomato pie. Both were always on the menu and none of us cared for either one. The pie, which looked unappetizing but didn't really taste that bad was Mrs. Nash's specialty, her way, I supposed, of using up unripened tomatoes left over from the summer's crop. Instructed before our arrival to eat everything on our plates, we had to down every bit of it, a small price to pay for such generosity.

After dinner, while Mr. Nash herded us around the grounds, one of the matrons and a few older girls washed dishes. Then we were corralled back into the living room around an enormous, ceiling-high Christmas tree, drenched in a stupendous array of tinsel, ornaments, and colored electric lights, to receive our gifts. We invariably came home loaded with fruit, cookies, and candies; polo shirts for us boys and similar tops for the girls; and—always—soap. Except for the fruit, these items, plus pencils and writing pads, all came from Nash's Department Store. Other town residents were often present at the Christmas Day dinners at the Nash's home, and some were inspired to give similar dinners for us, too. Their inclusion at these events curiously had the effect of making me feel more like a guest than a charity case, and not having to sing, or do anything else in return but be there, made it more enjoyable.

The holiday season was almost always capped off with a trip to Pasadena on New Year's Day to watch the Tournament of Roses Parade. All of us who wanted to go would be bundled up and herded to Pasadena on the streetcar under the watchful eyes of one or more matrons and the older children. But New Year's Day wasn't quite the end of the holiday season. Another holiday, I was delighted to discover, was observed at the Home and for a few years after I arrived: *La Fiesta de los Reyes Magos,* the Festival of the Three Wise Men. For Mexicans, it's the Three Wise Men, the Magi of the Christmas story, who deliver gifts, and families traditionally exchange gifts on January 6, the Feast of the Epiphany. So for a while we had the best of both worlds and received gifts on this occasion as well. I understood very little about either day, but put my shoes on the landing outside the dormitory like the rest of the boys, and we marveled the next morning when we found small toys or pieces of candy had magically appeared in them.

CHAPTER 11

Better Times

When the matrons got salary increases at the start of 1937, it was but one sign that times were improving. But that wasn't enough to keep Melissa Clarke, a matron for more than a decade, from leaving. When she left in early spring, I wasn't sorry to see her go. In her place came Miss Melton, a young woman who seemed promising, mainly because she couldn't stand to discipline us. But she only stayed until March, when she was replaced, one after the other, by two more young women, who also made hasty exits for unexplained reasons. But then came Ester, a young woman, pretty, voluptuous, and vivacious. Although she was only with us for the summer, that was long enough for us to remember her vividly and fondly after she was gone.

Ester, who seemed not much older than the oldest boy, had an easygoing, even careless way about her, and we were quick to respond to it. One afternoon, when we'd just returned from the Canyon Plunge where she'd taken us, I saw the two oldest boys, Mario and Ruben, peering through the partially open door of her room. Curious to see what they were up to, I found them intently watching Ester in the process of changing into her clothes. She seemed oblivious to the fact that from our vantage point we could see her every movement reflected in the full-length mirror mounted inside the door of the walk-in closet.

I arrived in time to see her strip off her bathing suit and begin redressing. My sudden intake of breath at the glimpse of her naked body quickly resulted in a hand clamped over my mouth so I wouldn't give away our position and put an end to the show. I'd never seen a woman undressed before, and seeing her nude, though only partially, left me awestruck. I'd seen no other woman against whom to compare her charms, but I was still sure she must be perfection itself. For days afterward my head was filled with images of the vision I'd had the good fortune to see.

Naturally I wanted to see it again. And the next week when she announced she was taking us swimming, I was lucky to be in the dormitory at the time. As soon as she entered her room, I made a rush with other boys to get a good spot outside her door to watch her change. But this time and others that summer, I was disappointed. The older boys insisted I was too young for such things, and wouldn't let me get close enough to see, no matter how much I protested. Not even my threats to tell Gibsie moved them. When Ester left at summer's end, we were really sorry she was gone; we were certain her departure was because of the displays, intentional or otherwise, she'd been putting on for us.

The next boys' matron, a Miss Mallard, proved to be not only more modest, but rather unattractive. We hardly missed her when she left just before Christmas. Then, with no boys' matron, Gibsie inducted nineteen-year-old Re, who served until Gladys Black arrived in February '38. Gladys showed up just in time to help clean up the mess from one of the most destructive windstorms in Southern California's history, which fortunately did no real injury either to us or the buildings; and to oversee our move from the old boys' dormitory to the basement of the Big House, which we made later that month.

The demolition of the old dormitory began in March, and that was when we nearly lost Rico, our canine mascot. Rico's arrival was unrecorded in the annals of the Home, but it must have been in the early thirties; he was a gift, no doubt, from someone in town with an unwanted litter on his hands. No one seemed to know who named him, either, but Rico, Spanish for "rich," undoubtedly referred to the treasure he represented to the children. He was a much-loved mutt, medium-size, with short black hair, who took the attentions of nearly thirty children in stride. Despite his even temper, probably every child had either been snapped at, if not bitten, at one time or another for the mistake of petting him while he slept or patting him encouragingly while he ate, exceeding the limits of his doggy tolerance.

Except for being housebroken, whatever Rico knew he learned on his own. Friendly, but aloof, he enjoyed his freedom, and that included digging up flower gardens or barking in the night when he cornered a cat or some other nocturnal creature. That was perhaps his only undesirable feature, for then Gibsie or someone she sent had "to round him up in the dead of night and quiet him." In addition to an agreeable nature, Rico had a lore all his own. That he was particularly modest, and did his business in out-of-the-way places, was appreciated by everyone. That meant not having to clean up after him or inadvertently stepping in something unwelcome.

Because he came and went pretty much as he pleased, Rico was well known by the whole town. His preferred place of residence was upstairs in the Big House with the girls, which he doubtless selected because the kitchen, the site he associated with being fed, was located just downstairs. And Rico was always remembered at Christmas; at some point during the festivities, everything stopped while we delightedly watched him devour his standard gifts: a stocking full of dog biscuits and wieners.

When the old boys' dormitory was about to be torn down and replaced with a new one, Rico explored the crawl space under the building's main floor. A lot of lumber had been stored there in years past, and we were in the process of hauling it out and chopping it up to burn in the incinerator. Rico, who was every bit as curious as a cat, used the opportunity to explore the crawl space in detail. Probably because it was cool and dark, on the last day of this effort he napped there while we worked. When we left, closing the door behind us, he was trapped. For reasons known only to him, he never barked. And because we'd all moved to the basement of the Big House in anticipation of the dormitory's demolition, no one heard his pathetic whining.

He wasn't missed until he should have shown up to eat, an immediate cause for worry given his usual punctuality at mealtimes. When the two days of the weekend had elapsed with no sign of him, the word was passed around town and everyone began searching for him. But finally on Monday morning, one of the carpenters working on demolishing the dormitory finally heard his weakening whimpers and released him before he suffered any lasting damage. A hungry and dehydrated Rico, somewhat thinner and enfeebled, was welcomed back to the land of the living and showered with affection—for at least a few minutes. Then having eaten and drunk his fill, he resumed his place in society with his usual élan.

The new Boys' Building was the gift of Mrs. Edgar Adamson of Pasadena, who we were told was one of our biggest donors. When construction was completed in June, the gleaming, off-white stucco structure was dedicated in a ceremony to which Mrs. Adamson, Katherine Higgins, and others from the Center, as well as many townspeople, were invited. The building, which had room for as many as fourteen boys and quarters for a matron, was named "Bradley Hall" in memory of Mrs. Adamson's two brothers. Besides creating a memorial, Mrs. Adamson explained in her remarks she'd given the money for the building "to do something for someone else, to make friends with folks of lowly degree, to grow in grace."

While the Center's former superintendent, the Reverend Dr. Gilliland, made the main dedicatory speech, we of "lowly degree," dressed in our Sunday best and for once really trying to behave, listened patiently, if not attentively. He assured Mrs. Adamson her reward in the next life was secure. She was apparently so pleased at hearing this from such an ecclesial authority she gave no hint of annoyance when he upstaged her by presenting Gibsie with a portrait photo of Mrs. Bultman, the benefactor who had provided the large down payment for the purchase of the Alegria Street property in 1931. He concluded by proclaiming the Big House would thereafter be known as "Bultman Hall" in her honor.

For a time afterwards, Gibsie tried to get us to observe the reverend's proclamation, but we seemed unable to break a long-established habit and continued calling it the Big House. Eventually she, too, gave up. Similarly, in our lexicon, "Bradley Hall" remained the Boys' Building.

The new dormitory was extravagant by comparison to our former quarters. At its north end was a suite with private bath for the matron and a library across the hall, though as yet lacking books. The hallway divided the rest of the building along its north-south axis. On the east side, separated by a utility closet, were two large dormitories, one for six younger boys and the other for six older boys. Both had built-in closets and chests-of-drawers. Arranged along the other side of the hall were a room for the two oldest boys, a large linen closet, and next to that, what seemed like an immense washroom with two multiple-head shower stalls. It included a row of washbasins and a waist-high tub, to make it easier for the matron to bathe very young boys. And instead of all the boys using one commode, there were now three to dirty and clean up.

Our accommodations had taken a remarkable leap for the better; we were living in comparative luxury. All of the interior walls were a bright cream-colored plaster, a sharp contrast to the dark-brown and the sickly pea-green paneled walls of the old dormitory. Though covered with a deep-brown linoleum, the floors were smooth, eliminating the worry of splinters in our feet. The exterior was a light, salmon-colored stucco instead of the painted wood siding we'd been used to. To outfit the dormitory further, a church group had donated fourteen new beds with mattresses, and two tables for the library. The chairs came later, along with a crank-up Victrola and a stock of old classical music recordings.

Other improvements were taking place outside. The local Kiwanis Club first installed a large sandbox under the arbor in the backyard and filled it with beach sand, something Gibsie had wanted to have there since she'd arrived fifteen years before. The sandbox was such a novelty that even the older kids, who would ordinarily have regarded it as beneath them, played in it. For its next project the club decided it was time to clean out the fish pond in the East Yard and turn it into a wading pool, which they completed in time for us to begin using when summer arrived.

The great expectations of summer were usually fulfilled, because they were so few and simple. Not only was school out, but the daily schedule at the Home was more relaxed, and we could go barefoot, one of the immense joys of a child living in a temperate climate. Except at church on Sunday, the first warm day in June was the signal to take off our shoes for the rest of the summer. The announcement came down at the end of the school day and everyone walked home carrying his shoes and socks. Anyone who wanted to could go to school barefoot for the few remaining school days, and everybody did. There were still our daily chores to do, of course, but when I was not selling newspapers or doing outside jobs to earn money, I could spend most of the summer doing mostly nothing.

But in June of '38, something called Vacation Bible School started on the Monday after school let out for the summer. New in Sierra Madre, it was held at the Bethel Church on Baldwin Avenue. The Center was always pressing Gibsie to get us more deeply involved in our newfound religion, and she wasted no time taking advantage of this opportunity. When told we had to attend, we were disappointed at losing so much of our vacation time, but thankful it only lasted four weeks. In a newly constructed building adjacent to the church, we attended classes for three hours each weekday morning, helping to set up the austere classrooms when we arrived and cleaning up afterwards. The part I liked was making things—beaded belts, birdhouses, and other crafts. But religion lessons were the main purpose. Generally they were a reiteration and expansion of Bible stories taught at Sunday School, and at the beginning of each day's session we learned a number of songs expressing our love for Jesus.

Some of the lessons were graphic, as when we were instructed to cut out a series of five heart shapes from white construction paper. After we colored four of them with crayons, one in each of the primary colors and black, the object of the lesson was revealed: Our hearts start out pure and white when we're born, and as we grow but don't live good lives, our hearts gradually assume the darker colors. If we're really bad, we end up with a black heart. But even then there was still hope, because if we asked for forgiveness and turned to Jesus, we could regain the white heart we started with.

At week's end we discovered we had the opportunity either to retain or regain, as the case might be, that white heart sooner rather than later. On the first of the Fridays, classes were cut short and we were led next door to attend a church service. After leading the congregation in a few hymns and prayers, the preacher gave a sermon. Facing the congregation, arms raised, and with a beatific expression on his face, he asked, "Is there anyone who would like to come forward and accept Christ as his personal savior?" Looking meaningfully at the group of us he explained, "This is what we call 'being saved'."

He repeated his question again and again, with long drawn-out pauses in between, and this had the effect of raising the tension in the room. He continued his coaxing and prodding, and we soon got the impression that nobody would be leaving until somebody got saved. Finally, the pressure reached the point where someone, no longer able to take the tension or resist the preacher's cajoling, hurried to the front of the church, fervently announced his acceptance of Christ, and was declared "saved!" Once the first person had broken the ice, others followed.

We all looked at each other in wonder, thinking this behavior strange, certain the preacher wasn't talking to us. Surely we weren't expected to accept this unusual invitation. But to our astonishment, during the service at the end of the second week, Billy rose from his seat at the rear of the room and slowly, step after hesitant step, walked to the altar, where, after being asked if he accepted Jesus and nodding assent, he was pronounced "saved!" Having done it once and to the obvious satisfaction of the preacher and the regular congregants, on each of the succeeding Fridays he got himself "saved" again. But every time, as he returned triumphantly to his seat, the sly, crooked grin on his face left little doubt he was in anything but a state of grace.

◆

At some point during the summer, kids who had a parent or guardian might spend a week or two "at home." That time finally arrived for Henrietta and me, when Gibsie told us we were to spend a week in Los Angeles with my mother, who lived in a court apartment. The court manager, a woman named Tillie, agreed to look after us while she was at work. It was the first significant amount of time I'd spent with Mother—and away from the Home—since I went to live there. I was very happy, even hopeful she'd keep us when she saw how little trouble we were. To ensure this outcome, I was scrupulous about minding Tillie and did my best to ingratiate myself to her so she'd give Mother a good report on my behavior. Mother seemed unusually cheerful, which I attributed to our being with her. But Henrietta suspected it was probably because mother had a man in her life, something I was sure couldn't be true. When he failed to materialize, I dismissed the thought from my mind, not wanting anything like that to dilute my pleasure at being "home." The visit seemed to end before it had begun, and I was despondent after we returned to Sierra Madre. I was so miserable about having to leave Mother, it might have been better not to have gone at all.

◆

A number of kids left the Home during the summer of '38 and were replaced by newcomers, the largest turnover ever. Almost all the new kids were orphans coming from bad situations with the County Welfare Department. They were rougher than any I'd known before, and many didn't speak English. Suddenly the tone of life at the Home got worse; the newcomers wouldn't cooperate, and it was especially tough getting them in line and teaching them the ropes.

The first group, the Flores brothers, Margarito, Frank, and Arthur, arrived in July. Later in the summer, an older sister brought the Martinez boys, Gilbert and Rudy. Others trickled in through the end of the year; the Mendoza girls, Josephine, Adela, Angela, and Gloria, completed the turnover.

The Flores boys were the most disruptive, stealing and getting into fights with the rest of us. The Mendoza sisters created their own special brand of problems. Of the four, seven-year-old Angela was especially angry and combative. Though she rarely actually hurt anyone, she was intimidating. Everybody shunned her, which made her angrier still. The two older sisters had other mischief in mind and soon introduced some of us to the exciting game of "you show me yours and I'll show you mine." Gibsie was petrified when she discovered what they were up to. She could only guess what lasciviousness the sisters engaged in with the rest of us.

It was at school that many of these new kids who spoke little English really had trouble. None of the teachers spoke Spanish, or if they did, chose not to. Getting the new kids to learn English and catch up in other subjects was tough on everybody. If only one or two children were in this predicament, Gibsie or one of the other matrons could have somehow found the time to tutor them while they progressed. But with so many newcomers at once, the problems were overwhelming. Gibsie knew that children who didn't speak English well were put in "dunce classes"; for a time she regularly showed up at school to talk with teachers so this wouldn't happen to our kids.

Confused and silent in classes, some of these children acted out their anger and frustration. Angela, with whom I shared classes, quickly gained a particular reputation for pugnacious unruliness at school as well as at home. Afraid I'd be stigmatized by associating with her, I began to avoid her, and my unwillingness to help only made her more furious.

Even if I'd wanted to help Angela I couldn't do much, because I was having my own problems. Mine no longer had to do with speaking English, which by the time I finished the third grade I'd learned to speak, read, and write at least as well as my classmates. I was angry for other reasons, and fighting seemed to be the only way to express my frustration. It was a big problem, one with which my third-grade teacher had little patience. She frequently had to drag me to see the principal, Mrs. Steinberger, which in turn brought an angry Gibsie to school more often than usual. When the year finally ended, I was advanced to the next grade and away from Angela, who wasn't.

◆

The right teacher could make such a difference, and for the next couple of years, still a difficult time for me, I was headed for encounters with three of the best. The fourth grade had the same teacher for all classes except music and art, and my new teacher was a wonderful woman named Yerda Adams. I was with her all day, every day; we got to know each other very well.

She was an attractive, fortyish woman, starting to gray, who seemed to sense my need for mothering, and more importantly, was willing to provide it. She was extremely tolerant of me and skilled at curbing my tendency to cut up in class. Thanks to her great patience and understanding I did well enough, in spite of my bullying. Though she didn't condone my beating up on other boys, Mrs. Adams also didn't condemn me for doing so, vigorously defending me in my inevitable conferences with Mrs. Steinberger. Mrs. Adams seemed to understand why I fought, though I was at a loss to explain myself when I did. Her policy was "give the kid a break," and I loved her for it. With someone so accepting, how could I not love her? My feelings even carried over into childish erotic fantasies about her.

All I really wanted was not to be looked upon as different, to be regarded as just another student, but I couldn't seem to shake that self-perception or control the resulting rebelliousness. Ironically, Mrs. Adams' special treatment implied permissiveness and probably perpetuated my disruptive behavior. During my year with her, she always gave me the benefit of the doubt. There was a lurking feeling, too, that she was giving me a satisfactory grade whether I deserved it or not.

Three other teachers, two who taught music and one art teacher, also helped calm or otherwise channel the rage I took out on other boys. Mary Fowler, my first music teacher, tolerated my behavior because I could sing. Singing had a calming effect on me, and I gave her little trouble in class. She also favored clingy knit dresses that hugged and showed off a luscious, curvaceous body, which had a different, though also pleasant effect on me. When she was later replaced by Wanda Weihs, that attention and reassurance continued. Mrs. Weihs was taken with my ability to harmonize and made no secret of liking me, even to the extent of including me in the small groups of children she took to hear professional orchestras in Pasadena and Los Angeles.

Saramae Butler, the art teacher during my later years at Sierra Madre School, also became a favorite of mine, mainly because she seemed so impressed with me. Together we discovered my natural ability in drawing, painting, and ceramics. She often held me up as an exemplar to my classmates, a view I sensed few of them shared, and she further expanded my notoriety by pulling me out of other classes to create posters for school events. Her genuine appreciation of my emerging talents was affirmation I sorely needed. Being different in that way I didn't mind at all.

◆

There was one time of year when being different was the only way to be, and that was at Halloween, always treated as a major event at Sierra Madre School. The start of the school day was delayed until noon so the town's children would have time to prepare. Getting myself ready for the event brought with it the discovery that there was something liberating about hiding behind a mask and pretending to be someone else.

Without money we were limited when it came to costumes. Some kids simply put on pajamas or long winter underwear over their clothes and called it a costume. But if we wanted to be more creative, Gibsie turned us loose on the boxes of old, worn-out clothes stored in the basement. The

Great Depression had created the hobo as a sort of poor man's hero, and turning ourselves out as one seemed a natural for us boys. We made ourselves fairly convincing by stitching patches on our clothes, smudging charcoal on our faces to simulate a growth of beard, and shouldering a short pole with a rag bag tied on one end. Though I enjoyed dressing as a hobo, some of the disparaging looks I got at school could make me regret my choice.

The girls made themselves up as ladies. Rushing to the basement a few days before Halloween, they'd fight over the matrons' discarded dresses, hats, hosiery, and high-heeled shoes. Garishly applied lipstick and rouge completed their ensembles. Wearing our get-ups to school for the rest of the day was great fun, even though we were outclassed by our schoolmates, many of whom had more elaborate, store-bought disguises. I was grateful no prizes were handed out for the best costume in the parade held at the end of the school day. For a number of years, the Roberts hosted Halloween evening festivities at their market in the town's center.

It happened that Halloween comes just a day before *El Día de los Muertos*, the Day of the Dead, celebrated with much exuberance in Mexico during the first two days of November. If her visit coincided with these days, or on the weekend following, Mother might bring candy skulls, skeletons, and other delicacies associated with remembering the dear departed. Because this event came so close to Halloween, I grew up thinking they were one and the same.

Contributing to my confusion was the legend of *La Llorona,* the Crying Woman, whose name always came up at Halloween. One version of her story was that she drowned her children in a lake and went mad searching for them forever after. Among ourselves we whispered with mock dread, "Better watch out, *La Llorona* is coming to get you tonight." If we were out after dark on Halloween or any other time, all someone needed to cry was, *"La Llorona!"* and everyone would run, the mere mention of her name shooting a rush of adrenaline into blood. *La Llorona* is uniquely Mexican, and we shivered, fear mixed with pleasure, at the thought of her.

I found the story really frightening. No one seemed to know why *La Llorona* drowned her children, or much else about her. If she knew, Gibsie wasn't saying. She had no interest in perpetuating Mexican myth. When I asked my mother about *La Llorona* she either claimed ignorance, or brushed me off with a wave of a hand, saying it was just a foolish story.

◆

Departures and arrivals of kids at the Home were pretty routine, but a new boys' matron was always serious stuff. In September 1938, Kathleen Sampson, Gibsie's widowed sister (she'd been married to a Methodist minister) showed up. Kathleen was older but, like her sister, tall and thin. There the resemblance ended. Mrs. Sampson projected a warmer, less-stern feeling, which may have been an illusion created by the looser hairstyle she favored and a longer face of softer features. At age fifty-two, she'd already grayed and wrinkled considerably, but I could see that at one time she might have been quite attractive. She dressed more colorfully than her sister, too. And she appeared genuinely interested in each boy as a person, a quality I'd rarely if ever detected in other matrons we'd had.

Kathleen's arrival had a noticeable effect on Gibsie, who clearly liked her sister and was happy to have someone she could depend on. Having the use of Kathleen's automobile also solved the problem of getting us to the doctor and dentist, something she usually had to ask neighbors to do.

Mrs. Sampson lost no time making herself comfortable, furnishing her room with items from her former home in Huntington Park. The relative luxury of her newly furnished quarters was remarkable. Not only was there a deep pile rug nearly covering the entire floor, but fancy curtains on the room's two windows, paintings on the walls, a double bed that looked like it must be wonderful to sleep on, and even a big easy chair with an ottoman. There were many other items to make her feel cozy. One of these was a radio, which we'd never had in the dormitory before. Suddenly there were music and radio programs to listen to in the evening, the latter especially captivating to young, inquisitive ears.

Mrs. Sampson was addicted to certain programs, which we could hear from our bedrooms. I often drifted off to sleep distantly listening to the Richfield News, which came on each night at nine o'clock. If we'd earned her favor, the older ones among us were allowed to stay up for a while and listen to some programs with her. Her favorite was "One Man's Family," on Sunday nights, and I soon became a fan. The life of this make-believe family was as alien to me as the lives of rich people I saw in movies. Though it seemed an impossibility, that family had exactly the home life I yearned for: easygoing parents, no worries about food or money—or being accepted—and all problems solved in fifteen minutes.

Like her sister, Mrs. Sampson was a former schoolteacher and enjoyed reading to us, which she usually did at bedtime. She also set aside time for us to read on our own, arranging for books to be sent from her late husband's former parishioners in Huntington Park. After her arrival, gifts for birthdays and Christmas were more often than not books; I learned to love reading.

We never addressed her other than as "Mrs. Sampson" and discovered she was every bit as strict as her sister. From the outset she made it clear she'd never have to send an unmanageable boy to Gibsie for punishment, being perfectly capable of meting it out herself. But her prowess in this regard was put to its stiffest test when she encountered Danny Meza.

Six-year-old Danny had been a troublemaker since arriving two years earlier. When he wanted something another child had, he fought furiously to get it, no matter the size of the other kid. He was hyperactive, incorrigible, without honor that could be appealed to, a chronic and unrepentant thief. Most of us really had nothing worth stealing, but treasured what little we did have just the same, and this last aspect of Danny's behavior was especially disruptive. When Danny discovered Frank Flores had money and other things he saw as worth stealing, he became the little thief's most frequent victim, and it was mainly with Frank he got into fights.

Danny's temperament made him virtually uncontrollable, and on more than one occasion Gibsie lost patience and tried to have him expelled. But the County Welfare Department—whose policy on orphans was to give, not to receive—hadn't wanted him back either. In the two years Danny had been with us, he'd already won the distinction of receiving more whippings than any other boy who'd ever been at the Home. Until Mrs. Sampson arrived, most of these beatings were delivered by Gibsie herself, the boys' matrons lacking the stomach. Regardless of who administered them, none of the whippings subdued Danny or changed his behavior in the least.

When she first met him, Mrs. Sampson was convinced she could straighten Danny out by reasoning. She soon gave up talking in favor of the beatings. She discovered to her chagrin that whipping him had little or no effect. Danny seemed to have *nalgas* that were completely insensitive, and though he screamed and feigned agony while being whipped on his naked buttocks, he did so with a wicked grin on his face. Those almost-nightly beatings, which Danny seemed so obviously to enjoy and which I suspected Mrs. Sampson did as well, were spectacles of consuming, if sadistic, interest to the rest of us. The image of a furious, disheveled Mrs. Sampson, a hand firmly gripping one of Danny's skinny arms, the other flailing away with a belt on his bare, brown behind, were unforgettable.

Like many of us, Danny was starved for affection and seemed to cause trouble deliberately so someone would just acknowledge his existence, even if that meant getting beaten regularly. At least then he had gotten someone's attention. The rest of us found less dramatic and usually more positive ways of doing so.

CHAPTER 12

Days of My Fathers

On a July Sunday in 1939, Mother told us she was going to marry again. Henrietta claimed she'd known it all along. Though suspicious and feeling betrayed, I tried to console myself with the thought I might at least get to leave the Home sooner. Henrietta made no effort to hide her anger from me; she saw any man in Mother's life as competition for her affections. But as with me, the possibility of leaving the Home sooner kept her from being overtly hostile.

Mother's new husband-to-be was Giuseppi Pertusatti, an Italian immigrant who'd come to America as a young man. Thin and of medium height, he was pale as parmesan, hollow-cheeked, and no longer young; his light-brown, curly hair, starting to gray, softened the sharp, angular features of his face and faded blue eyes. He was a butcher; his shop, part of the large wholesale market in Los Angeles that opened in the early morning hours, was appropriately called *La Luz del Día*, "The Light of Day." Mother, then working as a cashier at the Club Zarape, met Joe through another man, Felipe Cerrillo, the club's maitre d', who also doubled as its purchasing agent. From the moment Giuseppi saw Mother he was smitten.

Giuseppi was a U.S. Army veteran of the First World War, a fact of which he was very proud. His stint in the service made him eligible for American citizenship, and with the prospect of marriage, he wanted to take advantage of his eligibility. He had for some time been studying diligently.

Two weeks after Mother's announcement, Henrietta and I took the streetcar to Los Angeles to spend what had become an annual weeklong vacation with Mother in her garden apartment. That evening we met Giuseppi, who proudly drove us to see the home he'd bought for his wife-to-be, himself, and—we hoped—for us. The neighborhood of nearly identical, white-stucco Spanish-style houses, all of which had red-tiled roofs and neatly trimmed lawns, was impressive. When I saw the house had enough bedrooms so I could have one for myself, I decided the new arrangement might not be so bad after all. To get things started off on the right foot, Mother suggested we begin getting used to calling Giuseppi "Papa" right away. We could only manage "Joe," the name he planned to adopt when he became a citizen.

Soon after meeting Joe, it became clear he had little interest in Henrietta or me, but tolerated us because we were part of the package. But his regard for me perked up when Mother suggested I could help him learn the Pledge of Allegiance. For the rest of the week I spent part of every evening drilling him so he could pronounce the words clearly. It seemed next to impossible, his accent was so thick. When she saw how much difficulty Joe was having, Mother told him not to worry about how he said the pledge, since no one would notice him among the few dozen other people who'd likely be taking it at the same time. But saying the pledge was a point of honor with Joe, and he wanted desperately to deliver it perfectly. To my chagrin, he ignored Mother's counsel and continued his labors—and mine. After hours of struggle, he could get through almost the entire pledge so it was understandable, all except the word "allegiance," whose pronunciation continued to elude him. The closest he could come was something akin to *ah-lee-EN-ses*; we agreed that was close enough.

Though we knew he would rather we weren't around, Joe was nice enough to us and the love-eyes he laid on Mother made it obvious he really cared for her. I was no judge of amorous relationships, but it seemed to me she wasn't smitten by him, though she enjoyed being wooed and went around singing a popular song, something about a butcher boy. Henrietta and I suspected and hoped Mother was marrying Joe so she could finally have a home and get her children back with her. In any event they were married a short time later.

On the weekends when Mother came to see us, she and Joe drove out in his car and we could count on going for a drive, a real treat, particularly when it was to the Monrovia Airport where stunt flyers and parachutists often did their stuff. But it wasn't long before Mother began showing up alone. At first she explained away Joe's absence by saying he had to work. But we kept asking for him, not so much because we'd really grown to like him, but because we missed the outings in his car. The day came when Mother finally confessed neither she nor we would be living with Joe after all. Only Henrietta seemed to know what had really happened between Mother and Joe, and while that also interested me, what really mattered was I wouldn't be leaving the Home any time soon.

Even while Mother was still involved with Joe Pertusatti, the man who'd introduced them began to show up in their company on visiting day—he was interested in getting his own son admitted to the Home. Felipe Villareal Cerrillo was a Mexican immigrant who'd come to the United States right after World War I when he was barely twenty. There was a sincerity behind his easy smile that projected a sense of warmth and made him likable. More than that, he seemed to have a genuine interest in me and my sisters and brother. To go with his small size and wiry frame, Felipe was full of energy and had a sharp mind to match. His features were arranged over a longish face with high cheekbones, slightly bulging eyes, and a thin-lipped, off-center mouth.

He was also a good storyteller, and I loved hearing about his exploits as he made his way in America. But laboring in factories, fields, or on railroads, as so many others did in response to wartime labor shortages, was never on his list of things to do, he said. For him, America was an opportunity to make some real money. With only four years of formal education, he nonetheless could easily master the math needed to make money from the many and varied deals in which he was involved.

One of his best stories was about how he distilled and sold bootleg whiskey during Prohibition. Renting basement space in a Paso Robles, California, hotel, he went into business with another of his *paisanos* and made large and early profits. But he was soon muscled out by the local mob who discovered his operation and shut him down. He tried parlaying some of those boozy profits into greater returns in the floating craps and poker games he organized. Unfortunately, his love of gaming too often exceeded his luck, But he was shrewd enough to rein in that compulsion before it ruined him.

Felipe had a longer-lived and profitable operation trading in automobiles and trucks. With an Italian immigrant as partner, he secured the necessary papers allowing them to buy used vehicles in the United States and sell them in revolution-devastated Mexico. For a couple of years they were riding high, enjoying the success that accompanies an idea whose time is right. But their business, along with many others, foundered in America's 1920 recession. Felipe tried his hand at a variety of other schemes, but after an initial run of luck, Dame Fortune abandoned him, seemingly for good. And when the Great Depression soured everything, he was finally reduced to working for wages.

The author's mother and stepfather, Felipe V. Cerrillo, at the Club Zarape in Los Angeles, circa 1942.

He was a practical man and reasoned that even during a Depression people ate. He became first a cook and then a waiter. With his natural talent as an organizer and manager, it wasn't long before he had worked his way up to headwaiter and then maitre d' at the Club Zarape, one of Los Angeles' largest and most popular Latin-oriented night clubs. His path crossed Mother's in early 1939.

Felipe was thirteen years older than Mother, and their interest in each other at first centered on their respective children. Felipe's seven-year-old son, Ricardo, had been living with his alcoholic mother, from whom Felipe was divorced. With my mother's help, Felipe was finally able to get Ricardo admitted to the Home in May, 1940. Afterwards, he and Mother sometimes arrived for Sunday visits in Felipe's car, which we of course liked. When Joe Pertusatti dropped from the picture, we all spent our Sundays together, picnicking in the mountains or the parks of neighboring towns. Felipe's and Mother's affection for each other was obvious. More than their children's welfare was involved. It was no real surprise when they married two years later.

Life in Sierra Madre had kept us pretty well insulated from scornful attitudes toward Mexicans, though the older I got the more aware of them I'd become. I came face-to-face with this prejudice on one of our Sunday picnics at Monrovia's public park. Before we left the Home, Mother told us to bring swimsuits, as the park had a swimming pool. After lunch Felipe gave Richard, Billy, and me each a dime and, with swimsuits in hand, we attempted to enter the swimming pool. We were stopped short by a sign at the entrance that read "No Negroes or Mexicans Allowed." I'd never seen such a sign before, and having it glare so boldly in my face made me feel like I'd been hit in the stomach. We looked at each other and then returned to tell Mother and Felipe about it. At first all Mother could do was exclaim, *"Ay, dios mío!"* She and Felipe exchanged hurt, angry looks, but I could see they felt powerless, as much so as I was. Felipe was so furious he wanted to leave the park immediately, but Mother refused and said, "Go back there, and if they try to stop you from going in, say you're Italian." Fortunately, the woman at the entrance didn't seem to have her heart in keeping out us undesirables, and despite her skepticism about Richard's and Billy's darker skin color, she let us in.

We all thought Mother was pretty clever in figuring how to get around the restriction at the pool. But what I really wanted was for her or Felipe to storm up to the window and challenge the right of the authorities there to keep us out, and especially to make them take down that sign. To my hurt and anger were added disappointment and confusion about why they didn't.

◆

While giving us physical exams ordered by the Center in late August of '41, Dr. Gossard fingered eight of us, including Billy and me, for tonsillectomies. During the checkup, he decided some boys also needed to be circumcised. Danny and Billy, both seven, were among the unlucky ones. Not only weren't they told they were slated for both operations, but they didn't learn about the surgery on their privates until the morning we arrived at the hospital where Dr. Gossard was to operate.

We changed into hospital gowns and anxiously awaited our turns in the operating room. A nurse tried to calm our anxiety by explaining how simple the operations would be. "You won't feel a thing, once you're under the ether," she assured us, failing to mention the agony that awaited our reawakening. Then she made the mistake of mentioning circumcision, directing her remark pointedly at Billy and Danny. We still had vivid, gruesome images of Rudy Martinez's circumcision, the results of which he'd shown to anyone who cared to look, and the suffering he'd loudly endured afterwards. Alarmed that the same was about to happen to them, the boys took one look at each other and, as soon as the nurse left, fled the room in terror.

Though they were unfamiliar with their surroundings, they managed to hide, succeeding for a time in delaying the inevitable. But they were eventually hunted down, discovered cowering in one of the bathrooms, and returned struggling to the operating room, where they were physically restrained and anesthetized.

Afterwards, Billy reveled in repeating his ordeal in excruciating detail. "It's the worst thing that has ever happened to me," he declared. When he woke up, he said he was sure he was going to die. He claimed Gibsie said he'd hemorrhaged twice and lost a lot of blood—from the tonsillectomy. No one doubted it. All I remembered was going under the ether and the terrible pain in my throat when I woke up and tried to swallow. Through the fog of our pain, the rest of us who'd only had our tonsils removed took some small comfort in having gone through the trial together, especially grateful to have been spared Billy's and Danny's double agony.

Before we could tell anyone at the Home about our hospital ordeal, another far more devastating event occurred. Gentle fifteen-year-old Mario, who'd left the Home to live with his mother only a few months before, had shot his stepfather as he tried to wrestle a gun from the man to protect his mother. Gibsie tried to keep the news from us, but that was impossible. We knew something was up when we weren't allowed to sell our newspapers for two days. But someone had seen the write-up in the neighbor's copy of the *L.A. Times* and the news spread among us like a wind-blown brush fire. The details we got from other kids in town. Whether they had known Mario or not, for days everybody seemed consumed by the tragedy. To us it came as a great shock, and for a time we were fearful Mario might be put in jail. But his act was deemed self-defense and he wasn't. At the Home, we were in awe of Mario and regarded him as something of a hero, but Gibsie was mainly upset over the publicity.

CHAPTER 13

"Gibsie"

Here at last was Gibsie's diary. It had taken a year of cajoling to get Margaret Gonzalez Trejo to relinquish it long enough to make a photocopy. For her, she said, it was a very personal memento of her life with Gibsie. Though it was obvious she treasured the diary as an archeologist would a Dead Sea scroll, she told me she hadn't actually taken the time to read it herself. As it would be for an archeologist, the diary was research material for me.

Unfortunately, the diary only included entries for seven years ending in 1938, after which, for some reason, Gibsie had stopped keeping it. Nonetheless, the diary contained enough for me to learn more about who this woman really was. The handwriting, small and cramped, was hard to decipher, and the unusual organization of the entries made them even more difficult to read. What surprised me as I plowed into these pages was my growing sense of embarrassment. I realized I was learning things about Gibsie she never intended for me or anyone else to know. She surely would have been appalled, even incensed, to know that I, on whom she'd never looked with much favor, was reading about her thoughts and feelings. If she were still alive, she certainly would have recoiled at being so exposed. Yet I had to wonder how it was that Margaret came to possess the diary in the first place, since presumably she got it with Gibsie's knowledge and approval, just as other mementos were given to former residents when the Home was shut down. That was a question I doubted would ever be answered. I put aside my unease and read on.

My perception of Gibsie had changed little from reading the monthly reports she sent to the Center over the nearly thirty years she was manager.

The person they portrayed was in keeping with the woman I remembered; a strong, capable manager, one firmly in control of things and confident about her ability to overcome the daily problems she encountered. But those reports also read as though she fully expected them to be quoted—as they often were in the *Plazagram*—and therefore showed a public face. They revealed little about herself.

As I'd hoped, the diary entries offered more. The pages divulged a more human, often lonely person who had her share of disappointments and worries. I found it impossible to reconcile the person I knew as a child with the one now being revealed. As I read, I began to detach this other Gibsie, this newer woman, from my lifelong sense of her. She became more an abstraction, an object for study and evaluation. My original feelings about her, though blurred by the passage of years, remained stored away in their time lock, undisturbed by the voice speaking to me from the diary.

At the reunion, Rachel Parra Quick told me about how lovingly she thought of Gibsie, what a wonderful person she was. Despite all that, when I thought about her at all it was mainly as a disciplinarian. I now knew it was my fear of her that pushed aside any possibility of seeing her otherwise, clouded any awareness of her compassion and dedication to the children placed in her trust. These latter aspects were very evident in the diary entries, and I could begin to see why she was loved by many of the girls, as well as admired by so many others outside the Home. Although I lived with her for ten years, I had missed all that.

Among other roles, it was evident Gibsie saw herself as that of a surrogate mother, especially to girls who didn't have one of their own. She was both an employee and an official of the Plaza Community Center in Los Angeles, so there was much in the diary about writing reports and attending meetings. She also wrote of her dealings with the merchants and the town's officials, as well as with civic and church organizations. Because of the sympathy and admiration she evoked, these latter groups were often important sources of the money and supplies she depended upon to operate the Home. But of her many public roles, she especially liked attending PTA meetings and conferences with teachers, showing up for performances in which the Home kids participated, and otherwise doing all those things that would be expected of any conscientious mother with a child in school. It wasn't hard to see she lamented not actually being a mother herself.

By her own admission she was often uncompromising, even tough, dealing with the children's parents, especially when a child's interest was at stake. She wrote of occasionally having to calm a parent or relative who might have arrived drunk in order to keep them from taking a child away from the Home. And when there were attempts by divorced parents to kidnap a child, or children, by snatching them from school or the Home itself, she handled these serious situations with a natural finesse and considerable ingenuity, in the process preventing a calamity.

With only a few lapses, in which she confessed discouragement, there was little sign that her enthusiasm ever flagged during her nearly thirty-year tenure. Nor did her devotion have anything at all to do with how much she was paid. The paychecks, which were sometimes late in coming and which remained unchanged through almost all the years of the Great Depression, were modest at best: $22.50 per month for her and $15 per month for each of her two assistants. For this salary and their room and board, she and her matrons were expected to parent the children, see to their secular and religious education, minister to their illnesses, as well as feed and clothe them, often with clothes they made themselves or which they helped the older girls make. Our clothing had to be kept washed, ironed, and mended, and when they got too old or ragged to be used, the remaining serviceable cloth was cut up and transformed into quilts for the children's beds. Gibsie hated to throw anything out that still had any apparent utility; she took to heart the popular adage of the time, "Use it up, wear it out, make it do, or do without"; we did every one of those, especially the last. During the Depression, after her mother had shown her and the older girls how, she even went to the extent of making braided throw rugs out of our discarded polo shirts. It wasn't long before multicolored throw rugs began to show up everywhere around the houses, some areas beginning to resemble the prayer-rug-covered floor of a mosque.

◆

In an era when a young woman was expected to marry by the time she reached her twenty-fifth birthday, Elsie Nora Gibson was already well past her "prime" when she became the Home's manager. That may partly explain why she was content to remain in that role indefinitely. She was a complex personality, friendly and sympathetic, but also stern and somewhat humorless; a woman who made up in intelligence, sincerity, and dogged persistence what she lacked in warmth and charm. Her farming background had imbued her with a practical view of life, and although she was conscious of changing styles, hers was a no-nonsense approach to dress and fashion. I remember her favoring simple print dresses; I didn't know, but could have guessed, she made many of them herself. Over

The Plaza Community Center's executive secretary, Katherine B. Higgins, right rear; the Home's manager, Elsie N. Gibson, left front; and girls' matrons, Regina Rivera, left rear, and Eloisa Garcia, right front, circa 1947.

these, she habitually wore a duster-type smock to protect them from the soiling that was inevitable in dealing with us children and the variety of daily activities in which she was likely to find herself. It was this costume of dress and smock, along with sensible shoes, that she was most likely to be seen wearing around the house and grounds any day except Sunday.

Seeing pictures of her now reinforced my memories of how she looked, with rarely any rouge, lipstick, or other cosmetics to relieve the pallor of her complexion. Because she was thin and wiry, I remembered her as taller than the average height she actually was. The illusion was enhanced by her near-military bearing, and her hair-netted finger waves, cut close at the neck, did nothing to soften her image. It was obviously a style she preferred for its practicality, and one she continued to use so long after it was out of vogue it became her trademark. On especially difficult days, wisps of that hair would escape the net, and the effect was oddly humanizing, a break in the stern aura that seemed to surround her. Her hair was also prematurely gray, eventually completely silver; combined with the rest of her demeanor it made her seem much older than she was. Lighthearted she was not, and around us children at least, she was rarely heard to laugh, doing so only when the occasion seemed absolutely to demand it. Otherwise, she wore an enigmatic Mona Lisa smile on her face, probably the result of being trained as a girl to keep the corners of her mouth upturned so as to appear pleasant.

Her choice of attire, along with the prominence of a square jaw, thin-lipped countenance, and her rimless eyeglasses all gave her a magisterial severity that may have been unintentional, but I could imagine was discouraging to potential suitors. She was not known to have had offers of marriage, though her diary mentions one unidentified man who might be construed as an admirer. In any event she remained a maiden lady all her life. Whether this was by design or circumstantial, her lack of experience in affairs of the heart seemed to have left her unwilling or unable to discuss matters of sex with the girls, much less with us boys. When Tallulah Bankhead said, "It's the good girls who keep diaries, the bad ones never have time," she knew of what she spoke.

For most of us Gibsie was not only a powerful, towering figure, but enigmatic as well, and only a few of the girls ever came to know her as a person. To her diary she might occasionally mention she was tired or not feeling well physically, but only rarely did she record any expression of emotion. Just once, in early 1935, she confided to her diary that she was experiencing periods of depression. But ever the good soldier, she followed up on this confession with a declaration of her firm resolve not to let them get in the way of doing her job. If she was given to deep introspection, she kept it to herself, and there was little evidence of it in her writing.

Far from it. Her diary entries usually recorded the weather condition for the day, and because she loved gardening, the status of plants in the Home's gardens. Curiously, the entry for every Monday included whether the washday was a great, just good, or a bad one, which depended on how quickly the washing and clothes-hanging could be done. I knew keeping our clothes clean was a major concern—along with other kids I spent enough time cutting up bars of Fels Napha Soap and turning the hand-wringer on the washing machine—but I could only guess at why it loomed so large a subject in her diary.

There were usually brief mentions of news events, including some that took place in the town; for example, August 31, 1932, reports, "[The] Sierra Madre bank was robbed at 1:30 in the afternoon—[they took] about $800.00. Miss Sealy [a teller] was taken a few blocks [before being released by the robbers]." She also recorded her chagrin at certain national events, like Franklin D. Roosevelt's election to the presidency in November 1932, a disappointment she shared with most of the members of the Congregational Church. Their displeasure, it seemed, had less to do with their being Republicans than with the fact that Herbert Hoover as the president would no longer be visiting his son, who lived in Sierra Madre.

Natural calamities also deserved mention, like periodic destructive windstorms and the major earthquake of March 1933, that destroyed much of the town of Costa Mesa. That happened while she was visiting her married sister in Huntington Park. And in July 1934 she noted the notorious gangster John Dillinger had been killed.

Although she usually mentioned visits by parents and other guests, she rarely said anything else about them—unless, of course, they were contributors to the Home's coffers or pantry. Then her notations might list the gifts in some detail. On the other hand, she always included events involving the children, which she referred to as "her family." Their illnesses, especially epidemics of childhood diseases; birthdays; arrivals of new children and departures of others; as well as events involving them at school and church all deserved noting. If she was particularly fond of a child, and invariably it was a girl, there was a running account of the small drama surrounding that child's life, and it was clear she derived vicarious, motherly satisfaction from watching and shaping the child as she grew up.

From her college records I'd learned Gibsie moved to the relative isolation of Sierra Madre from her parents' home near Santa Maria, California. That may explain why she had few personal friends or the social life they might have provided. Except for occasional visits from the two or three women she knew from her days at the University of Southern California, and periodic visits to her family members, she had a rather lonely personal existence, a loneliness she occasionally confessed to her diary. She was friendly with the other two matrons, especially Fuller, but she was, after all, the boss. Their genial interaction was more the type designed to assure cooperation and the smooth running of daily life at the Home than a true friendship. Of necessity, her contacts with the town's merchants, school officials, and church members were many, but none appeared to have been of a warm, personal nature, either.

Nonetheless, her position as manager afforded her considerable satisfaction. Rather than being regarded as just another "old maid," her post elevated her to a somewhat exalted status in the community. She was a person, as one local newspaper reporter put it, "doing God's work," and certainly someone to be admired. Surely there were few other jobs then available to women that would have provided the same degree of social recognition and spiritual if not economic compensation. To many who knew her, and perhaps for good reason, she was a paragon of virtue, industry, and dedication to religious principles. With the possible exception of Regina Rivera, few if any of us ever really knew the person behind that idealized façade.

CHAPTER 14

Gibsie's Girls

Having kept a journal myself, I knew the subjects of the daily entries could be about anything and were unlikely to be consecutive. Gibsie's diary was no different. It took a number of readings to piece together the stories the entries related to. The more charming tales were about her relationships with the children she especially favored, as well as those who gave her problems. Also told, perhaps unintentionally, was a more important story about herself, one that made her much more human.

When I lived with her I assumed Gibsie regarded us all as pretty much the same. But what I discovered in her writings was her relationships with us wasn't that way at all. There was no doubt she favored the girls. I never knew her to be close to any of us boys. Yet her diary showed there were exceptions. She was clearly partial to the orphaned Carlos Hauffen, who regarded Gibsie as his mother. For years after he left the Home, Carlos wrote regularly and never failed to send a card on Mother's Day.

That Gibsie would have her own need for love and companionship was something that never occurred to me. She did, of course, and the diary showed she apparently derived both by getting very close to some of the girls. In particular she seemed to be drawn to girls who were motherless, though the resulting attachments differed markedly depending on whether the child was very young or older.

Gibsie's mothering instinct showed up strongly in her writings when Rosita Reyes came on the scene. Only two years and eight months old when she arrived in February, 1933, Rosita had already been the center of controversy. With her mother dead, and apparently deserted by her father, Rosita was slated to go to the Home with her cousins, the four Gonzalez children. But the Center required that all children be raised as Protestants, and their admittance was being delayed until the County got approval from Rosita's absent father in this regard. When Mr. Gonzalez assured the Center that

Rosita's father wouldn't object to this condition, Rosita and the Gonzalez children were finally allowed in.

Gibsie made a makeshift crib for Rosita in her room so she could more directly look after her. Rosita quickly became the center of attention. As Gibsie noted in her diary, ". . . all the children are crazy about little Rosa," and some of the older girls helped make her a set of clothing. Rosita soon adapted to the routine, and within a week Gibsie wrote, ". . . she is a busy, happy child and likes it here, *'mucho, mucho.'*"

By late spring Rosita had become an important part of life at the Home. So it was a shock when in late May Gibsie was informed that the little girl might have to leave. "We are sick about our little papoose. The [county] caseworker has dug up the father [in Arizona], and he wants [Rosita] raised as a Catholic." A few days later she wrote that the Center's superintendent, Dr. Gilliland, and [his wife] came to bring us [the] bad news . . . . We will [definitely] have to let our little Rosita go; the case worker is putting her into a Catholic [foster] home!" When the Gillilands left, Gibsie wrote, "I bathed my little papoose and felt like [I was] doing it in [my own] salt tears."

The timing was unfortunate, for the next day the children celebrated Rosita's third birthday. As Gibsie described it, "We feel like we are staging a party and a funeral at the same time . . . I seem to be walking around in a daze . . . . [and] the children are all heartbroken." Three days later she wrote, "We went about our usual Saturday work and little Rosita [took her nap] as usual, but about 1:30 P.M. the caseworker came for her. [When] Fuller had dressed Rosita, [and taken] her downstairs, I shut myself in the bathroom . . . to enjoy a good cry by myself, [but it was not to be as] all the girls raised their voices and wailed, and I went out to quiet them. The case-worker came hurrying back, too, but they were not to be comforted. [When the caseworker drove away with Rosita, the crying children] all stood in a huddle by the gate to watch the car pass by."

During Rosita's three and a half months at the Home, Gibsie and the girls had grown to love her. Gibsie was also outraged that the father had the child summarily removed from the Home without ever taking the trouble to see how Rosita was being cared for. Losing one to the Catholics was also a bitter pill to swallow for the Center, which saw the small drama revolving around Rosita Reyes as as example of the continuing struggle between the Protestant and Catholic churches for the souls of Latino immigrants.

Eighteen months later, Gibsie had another child on whom to unleash her pent-up affections and to give the kind of intimate care she reserved for the children she regarded as special. The object of her attention this time was my younger sister, Connie, who, at only ten months when she arrived, was the youngest child ever at the Home. Gibsie was overjoyed to have an infant to care for, and not only set up a crib in her own bedroom, but showered Connie with all the attention she might have given a baby of her own. The other girls were also encouraged to share in Connie's care and feeding, which at first they did enthusiastically. Connie basked in the pampering.

Foolishly, I believed that because Gibsie liked Connie so much, somehow I might also benefit, that some of that affection would rub off on me. But it never did. The rest of us, Henrietta, Billy, and I, might as well have been completely unrelated.

It would be no exaggeration to say Gibsie loved Connie. So it was not surprising that Connie came to treat Gibsie very much as her mother, and did everything short of addressing her that way. If our mother minded, she never let on then, even when Henrietta reported to her what was going on. Predictably, as she grew older Connie was spoiled by Gibsie's favoritism and came to regard her special status as her due. That fact was not lost on the other girls, whose resentment would certainly have been taken out on Connie had it not been for Gibsie's and Henrietta's vigilance and intervention. When it came time for her to leave, Connie probably suffered more than other kids did; for weeks afterward she was inconsolable. Gibsie had mothered her in the way her own mother had not, and the lack of closeness between mother and daughter during the rest of their lives, while unfortunate, was perhaps predictable.

Connie's lack of closeness to Mother extended to the rest of us, too. Though we got together when Mother visited, the way life was arranged at the Home did much to keep us from seeing ourselves as a family. I hardly ever saw Connie or had anything to do with her while we were there, and that was also true for Billy. Living as they did in the same house, Connie was closer to Henrietta, but the six years difference in their ages automatically kept them apart in most situations. In any event, whatever closeness they might have had at the Home never carried over afterward. Our estrangement as siblings continued thereafter, and it was most pronounced between Connie and the rest of us, with her the odd person out.

My younger sister's experience at the Home had other consequences as well. The attention Gibsie lavished on Connie stopped abruptly when she came to live with us, and the loss left her desolate. When it came to Connie's schooling and other aspects of her life, Mother, preoccupied with a new husband and a business, provided little care or guidance, showing concern only when notices of delinquency or Connie's repeated truancies came from school. Like a boat cut adrift from its mooring, she was floundering helplessly. When she reached ninth grade she was failing all subjects. She soon dropped out entirely, staying home or working in our family restaurant.

Life has continued to be difficult for Connie. How much her early dependence on Gibsie contributed to this outcome is anybody's guess. Whatever the cause, Connie has paid a lamentable price.

The intimate involvements Gibsie had with older girls were equally fascinating, for it was they who were better able to alleviate her loneliness. In a few instances she and they became more like friends, their lives so entwined that when the girl departed, Gibsie was truly heartsick. There were four in particular who as young women enjoyed the pleasure of being one of "Gibsie's Girls," as I've dubbed them. But those who were not among the chosen often suffered, the sting of exclusion being especially sharp when sisters were involved and one was shown more attention than the other.

So it was with the orphaned Najera sisters, Ruby and Rosa, who were two of the first eight children at the Home when it opened in 1923. They had arrived in October of that year, when Ruby was ten and Rosa five. Gibsie arrived in 1926 and her relationship with neither girl was particularly close, until it came time for Ruby to leave a year later. Leaving was traumatic for most children and especially so for orphans, and Gibsie was sympathetic when Ruby pleaded to be allowed to return. During the next five years, Ruby lived at the Home intermittently and finally returned for an extended period in 1931, after the Home had moved to its permanent, larger location on Alegria Street. Then the relationship between Gibsie and Ruby blossomed.

Ruby was the oldest girl in the Home at that time, and Gibsie wrote about being drawn increasingly into Ruby's life and activities. Since there was no extra space in the dormitory, Gibsie shared her room and bed with Ruby, the physical closeness allowing them time to talk, often late into the night. For a time while Ruby attended school, Gibsie got her a job in nearby Monrovia working as a mother's helper for the dentist the Home was then using. When that arrangement ended and Ruby returned, they again shared Gibsie's room until space could be made elsewhere. Despite her scant experience in matters of the heart, Gibsie became Ruby's confidant and advisor in the latter's widening circle of relationships at school and in the community. She shared Ruby's excitement at the prospect of dating men, something Gibsie had done little herself. That lack didn't stop her from acting as a sounding board, counseling Ruby when she expressed a reluctance to date the "Spanish" men she met at school. Ruby left the Home for the last time in January 1934. By then the two women's fondness for each other far exceeded friendship, and the sadness of their parting was hardly softened by Ruby's promise to return often, a promise she kept.

In contrast, Gibsie treated Ruby's much younger sister, Rosa, with virtual indifference. Rosa seemed lost among the other little girls, and she was troubled all through her elementary and junior high school years. Nor were her endless difficulties helped by the absence of the affection she saw her sister and a few other girls receive from Gibsie. Not surprisingly, she got some of the attention she wanted by getting into trouble. By the time Rosa was seventeen, any mention of her in Gibsie's diary had only to do with her skipping school, having difficulty keeping a job, and "running with the wrong crowd." When she finally left the Home to live with her sister, it was none too soon for Gibsie. While her sister's departure years before was tearful, Rosa left dry-eyed and with little intention of ever returning to Sierra Madre. Yet however relieved each was to be rid of the other, this wasn't the end of Rosa's and Gibsie's relationship. Ten years later, in one of Fate's twists, it would be Rosa on whom a grateful Gibsie would depend.

◆

The chemistry that draws human beings to each other is as natural, necessary, and irresistible as breathing. This was never more apparent in Gibsie's writings than it was in her accounts of her relationship with Ester Hauffen. When Ruby Najera left the Home, Gibsie transferred her interest and more personal attentions to Ester, an orphan who had by then already passed her twelfth birthday. Ester had also arrived at the Home before Gibsie became its manager. She was a pretty, fair-complexioned, and talented nine-year-old when she arrived in the late spring of 1924 with her older sister, Sara, and younger brother, Carlos; upon meeting Ester, one prospective donor remarked, "I would gladly give if they were all like her." Sara, who was already nearly twelve when she entered, left two years later at age fourteen, as would Carlos, when he reached that age. Following her fourteenth birthday, Ester had also tried to leave the Home to live with her sister, but soon asked to come back. Her beauty, pleasant disposition, and musical ability had early made her a favorite of Gibsie's, who quickly got Dr. Gilliland's approval for her return. Ester resumed her life in Sierra Madre and began attending junior high school in Pasadena. As Ester matured, her relationship with Gibsie intensified.

When Ester was seventeen, despite Gibsie's reluctance she found her a position as a mother's helper at the home of the Greenstreets, a prominent Pasadena family, where she was to live while she finished high school. By this time the women had developed a deep mother-daughter-type bond, and neither looked forward to the coming separation. On the eve of Ester's departure for the Greenstreet's home, they shared Gibsie's bed. When Ester left, Gibsie was distraught, and in a rare expression of emotion the next night, confessed to her diary she felt "like the bottom had dropped out of life."

By the time Ester graduated from high school in the late spring of 1932, she'd fallen in love with Dilworth Deushane, the son of another Pasadena family, and everyone in their respective communities was watching the romance develop with great interest. Both young people were active in the youth groups of their churches, Dilworth in the First Methodist Episcopal Church of Pasadena, and Ester in Sierra Madre's Congregational Church, where she was a popular member of the choir.

When Ester entered Pasadena Junior College that fall, the often-tempestuous love affair had blossomed. Her position as a mother's helper had not turned out well, however, and once again she returned to live at the Home. Gibsie was delighted to have her back, and initially they shared the same bed for a few weeks until Gibsie could make space for her in Fuller's room. By then Dilworth was asking Ester out every evening, and Gibsie watched the courtship with growing concern that Ester's schoolwork would suffer.

As each day passed, Gibsie found herself a passenger on Ester's emotional roller coaster. If Ester's evening out with Dilworth went well, Gibsie could expect to have a night's sleep, though not a long one; if not, she could expect to hear all about Ester's troubles well into the early morning hours. These nightly sessions drew them closer together. In addition to her growing role as confidant, Gibsie became Ester's tutor and her nurse when she was sick; they set each other's hair, went shopping together, made clothes for each other, and in general carried on like mother and daughter, if not sisters.

By Ester's eighteenth birthday in March, Dilworth had already proposed marriage and presented her with an engagement ring. A few days later, Gibsie wrote in her diary, "In the evening Ester, Fuller and I discussed weddings, clothes, etc. We made out a list of necessary clothing; [Ester] plans to make her own [wedding] dress and a [going-away] suit at school. I told Fuller that I thought the old maids were more excited than the bride to be."

But Ester's special treatment was not sitting well with the other girls at the Home. The older ones, Regina Rivera in particular, were disgruntled that

Ester did little work at the Home and could come and go as she pleased. Nor did they make any effort to hide their jealousy about her fiancé. The younger girls took their cue from the older ones, and one night when Dilworth arrived to pick up Ester, they made such a fuss that to quiet them Gibsie was finally forced to reveal Ester was soon to be a bride. When she told the younger girls they would also be attending the wedding, their attitude changed to delight. But the older girls, again led by Regina, remained unmoved and acted out their jealousy each time Dilworth showed up. Things eventually got so bad that for a time Dilworth and Ester were forced to meet in town.

When the semester ended, Ester's friends gave bridal showers and garden parties in her honor. Meanwhile, detailed plans were made for the wedding and reception, which were to be held in the Sierra Madre Congregational Church with its minister, Dr. Pritchard, presiding. Money was donated to cover expenses, and Mrs. Hill, a local music teacher, began rehearsing the selections she and some of her students would play. Mrs. Bacon, another town resident and a member of the Home's Advisory Committee, was in charge of decorations and met frequently with Gibsie to go over the details. The Church Women's Society, which met to help with the Home's darning and mending once a week, was now also making a comforter for the couple. In early June the Home kids gave Ester a surprise bridal shower. A few of the parents also got caught up in the event and sent gifts, some of them actually quite valuable, like the authentic Spanish-lace veil given by the mother of Edwin and Betty Ortiz.

By mid-June, most wedding decisions had been made, but a few days later Gibsie noted, "[Everything and everyone] is set but the bridegroom!" Dilworth had already postponed the date once, but reset it for July 7. The invitations were mailed and preparations for the event assumed a feverish pace, particularly within the congregations of respective churches. Gibsie was preoccupied with the approaching wedding; there were entries in her diary about it almost every night.

Although there would be at least one other, this was the first instance in which a Mexican American girl from the Home was to marry a local boy, and the prospective event captured everyone's imagination, including and especially that of the people at the Plaza Community Center. Dr. Gilliland monitored developments closely and counseled the young couple. He also saw to it that the Center's Board provided a waffle iron as a wedding gift. Joy seemed to abound as enthralled observers in Sierra Madre, Pasadena, and Los Angeles saw what Christian love had wrought.

But as June came and went, Ester began bringing home disturbing tales of Dilworth's dithering. Despite his protests of undying love, she said, he kept finding excuses for not buying the marriage license. On Monday morning, July 3, the last day he could obtain the license for a July 7 wedding, Dilworth neither called nor showed up at the Home. Gibsie tried to console a fretting Ester, who was now certain he had gotten cold feet. When he finally showed up at 2:30 that afternoon, her worst fears were realized. Dilworth confessed he still hadn't bought the license, and during the next two hours, tried unsuccessfully to explain himself. Disgusted, Gibsie tried to make Ester give him an ultimatum—that it was "now or never"—but Ester was too torn to heed.

That evening and a good part of the July 4th holiday was spent relaying the bad news to everyone involved. The respective communities were thrown into an uproar, and the name of Dilworth Deushane was roundly defamed.

To get the distraught Ester away for a while, Gibsie arranged through Dr. Pritchard to use the East Long Beach vacation home of one of his parishioners. But when Ester returned three weeks later and learned Dilworth had tried to reach her every day she was gone, she was overjoyed, promptly forgot her anger and hurt, and called him. They met excitedly at the Home that evening, and their tearful and repeated embraces made it abundantly apparent that Ester wanted to salvage the engagement. Gibsie was furious and wrote that night, "I told [Dilworth] he would have to face an investigation—that I wanted him to see Dr. Gilliland . . . and also to track down and face some of the things that had been said about him" for backing out of the wedding, which had upset and inconvenienced so many people. "I went to bed tired and with a terrible headache. I would this had never started up again."

Dilworth promised to do as she directed, and true to his word, began making the rounds to apologize to the people he had disappointed and put out. His first visit, with Dr. Pritchard, was harrowing. The minister expressed his complete disgust with Dilworth's behavior and sent him on his way "embarrassed and sweating." Ester, meanwhile, was having problems with her friends, who, she was afraid, would hate her for not giving Dilworth "the gate." Dilworth next met with Dr. Gilliland at the Center in Los Angeles, who, as Ester said, "Told him what he thought of him, but in a nice way." He also made it clear he expected Dilworth "to make things right with the Sierra Madre folks." Most of those "Sierra Madre folks" were forgiving and even understanding, but when Dilworth emerged from his meeting with Mrs. Hill, the music teacher, he was "red-faced and perspiring."

The chastening effect of having to apologize to so many people also seemed to stiffen Dilworth's spine. On August 7, he and Ester went to Los Angeles to get the marriage license. Four days later, despite a temperature hovering near 112 degrees, they were quietly married in the back garden at the Greenstreet's home in Pasadena. Sara and Carlos were there, as were the Deushanes, and looking every bit the proud mother, so was Gibsie. Dr. Gilliland performed the ceremony, Mrs. Hill, sufficiently calmed down from Dilworth's affront, provided the music, and Dilworth's nieces served punch and cake. In her diary that night Gibsie wrote, "Ester was a lovely bride and very natural . . . I feel real happy over the wedding tonight, and I even kissed the groom."

The episode had a happy ending, but Gibsie continued to pine for Ester, her sense of loss especially acute in the weeks that followed. There were frequent entries in her diary attesting to how much she " . . . was lonesome for Ester." In her entry for August 25, Gibsie recorded, "I'd give a farm to see her tonight," and there were similar entries well into the fall. Nonetheless in subsequent years, they continued to be close, Ester returning to spend the day and sometimes overnight with Gibsie, and occasionally meeting in Pasadena for lunch and shopping. When Ester's daughter was born two years later, an anxious Gibsie was present. She considered and referred to herself as "the grandma," regularly sitting with the baby Diane during the months that followed. In later years there would be other girls on whom she would dote, but Gibsie would never love any of them the way she had Ester.

◆

Among Gibsie's Girls was Regina Rivera, whose relationship with the Home manager was even more extended, but of a different sort. "Re," as everyone called her, was a coppery-skinned girl whose jet-black hair, high cheek bones, and other facial features reflected her Indian-Spanish heritage. She had been born in Mexico and emigrated with her father, who had fled the aftermath of the Mexican Revolution for what he hoped would be a better life in the United States. Like so many others, he found life north of the border extremely difficult. Jobs were scarce, and without a wife, he was unable to care for his young daughter, whom he finally placed in the Home in late 1927, when she was nine.

The Great Depression arrived three years later, and as it continued to deepen in the years that followed, thousands of Mexicans and Mexican Americans were forcibly and often illegally expelled from the United States. Because he was unable to locate documents proving he was in the country legally, Re's father was among them. Although he lived and worked in Los Angeles, he had ignored Re for years, rarely visiting her as she was growing up. Then in early April of 1934, within days of being deported, he suddenly appeared at the Home and asked her to return to Mexico with him. Tearfully, Re told him she wanted to stay at the Home and would only go with him if she were forced to. She was terrified she might be made to go anyway, especially after Gibsie explained that her father not only had the legal right to take her with him, but since she was also lacking the necessary immigration documents, technically she was in the country illegally herself.

Despite her own feelings of helplessness in the matter, Gibsie assured Re she would do her best to protect her, and turned to Dr. Gilliland. Privately, he confessed there was little he or the Center could do if Mr. Rivera insisted on his rights, or worse, if the immigration authorities discovered Re's presence and decided to deport her as well. They were all fearful that someone from the immigration department would be the next to show up and compel her to go with her father. But the day of her father's departure passed quietly, and Re stayed. She was certain Gibsie had protected her, as promised, and she never forgot it.

A bright and musically talented girl, Re's attachment to Gibsie continued to grow. As Re matured, Gibsie increasingly confided in her, frequently including her on shopping trips and affording her special treatment. When Ester left to live and work at the Greenstreet's home, Gibsie chose Re to share her two-week summer vacation at what was then her parents' home in Creston, California, a small farming settlement inland from the coastal town of San Luis Obispo. With evident pride and pleasure, Gibsie introduced Re to her friends, who found her warm, gregarious nature appealing. On one evening during their stay, they attended a dinner and missionary meeting at the local church, where Re delighted the group by playing the piano. In the ensuing days they went sightseeing, swam, and sunbathed together at Pismo Beach, a few miles away.

When she reached her fourteenth birthday, Re ordinarily would have left the Home, but having no parent or home to go to, asked and was allowed to continue living there. Although Re had been jealous and resentful of Gibsie's special treatment of Ester, she had no problem accepting similar attentions when Ester was gone, and basked in her newfound status. As time passed, Gibsie relied increasingly on Re, more often treating her as a matron than a resident child. And Re responded to this greater responsibility and trust by doing everything she could to be worthy of it.

By the time she was sixteen, Re was exceptionally mature for her age, completely familiar with the routine and increasingly took on the role of matron. Not long after, she became a paid staff member, assigned as a matron for the girls and sometimes a substitute matron for the boys. Re worked at the Home until it closed its doors in 1954. Through all the years they worked together, she and Gibsie remained close, though their relationship lacked the quality of love and intimacy Gibsie and Ester had shared.

Rachel Parra Quick was the fourth older child who could be considered one of "Gibsie's Girls." When I met Rachel at the reunion, she told me in some detail how close she and Gibsie were. I have no way of knowing how the other three girls really felt about Gibsie, but Rachel told me she loved Gibsie and considered her, as she put it, "a composite of a mother, father, and sister."

That Gibsie played favorites is most evident in her treatment of the other Parra girls, toward whom she was all but indifferent. Angelita, a year older than Rachel, could not even get a sympathetic consoling from Gibsie on the day her mother died. Word of Mrs. Parra's death reached the Home on a Sunday. Instead of calling the family together to tell and console them, Gibsie asked my mother, who was visiting us that day, to do it. I was startled to learn that, despite the great compassion of which she was otherwise capable, in matters requiring expressions of deep personal sympathy, Gibsie was somehow wanting.

The contrast between the way she treated Rachel and her sisters was most stark when Angelita asked to return to the Home after leaving in December, 1947, to live with her father. She quickly discovered life with him was not only difficult, but actually "foreign." In February, she called Gibsie to see if she could return. Although in the past she had been unhesitating when Rachel had asked for help, this time Gibsie was disinclined. She just allowed Angelita to come out "to talk it over." Only a county caseworker's intercession persuaded a reluctant Gibsie to let her return until summer, when Angelita was again forced to leave.

Just as there were some favorites who were "Gibsie's Girls," there were others who decidedly were not. The standout among these was my older sister, Henrietta. She, not the diary, revealed that her relationship with Gibsie bordered on antagonism. As much if not more than I, Henrietta hated going to the Home in the first place. She felt betrayed and was deeply resentful that Mother put her there. When she entered it in the fall of 1935 at the age of seven, she and Mother had developed the kind of bond that only comes from living through many difficulties together. To Gibsie, who was ignorant of all that, Henrietta was just another little girl; she treated my sister like the child she was, creating dissension between them that was never really overcome.

Henrietta's rage wasn't the only reason that the seven years she lived at the Home were turbulent ones. As she left us that first day, Mother charged her with looking out for the rest of us. And though she didn't much care for the role, the mission reinforced her feelings of independence and satisfied a sense of importance she was reluctant to give up. Carrying out her charge unavoidably brought her into confrontations not only with most of the other children but with the matrons, with whom she vied to see to our welfare. She had a violent temper, which could seethe to boiling and could be quite intimidating. There were many times she showed up in the middle of an argument I was having with another boy and glowered at him until he backed down. How she knew she might be needed at those times was a mystery to me. It attested to her vigilance, and I was always grateful for it.

Henrietta was equally watchful at school. Once in the fall of 1940 as Connie and Alicia Lopez, both six, were walking to school, Alicia taunted Connie about being pigeon-toed. By the time they reached school, Connie was on the verge of tears. Henrietta overheard Alicia's ridiculing in the school hallway, but she did nothing then; back home that evening she suddenly flew at Alicia and began pummeling her. Alicia, who by then had probably forgotten the matter, ran crying to her older sister, Mariana. She, of course, felt honor-bound to defend Alicia, and the fray that ensued in the girls' dormitory became legendary. The fighting, screaming, hair-pulling pair battled their way from one end of the Blue Room to the other and continued even as they tumbled and rolled down the long staircase to the main floor below. There it finally ended with Gibsie sitting on a still-furious Henrietta until she stopped struggling. Miraculously, only feelings were injured. Instead of reprimanding both girls, Gibsie blamed Henrietta, who was outraged; afterward she never forgave Gibsie for what she saw as a gross injustice.

The incident only enhanced Henrietta's reputation as our defender, and there were many, both boys and girls, who declined a showdown with her when she would show up to champion our cause. Her bravado, however, often masked the frightened little girl, who hoped and prayed that her image would be sufficient to forestall anyone actually testing her courage and combat-worthiness.

I don't doubt that Gibsie and the succession of other matrons knew it was important to treat us with an even hand. But I was surprised to learn how often they didn't. From the diary pages and other documents it was clear the matrons were open about their favorites among the children. Some of my sharpest recollections are about being resentful when one kid was favored and I wasn't. Any display of partiality compounded our other petty jealousies. We hungered for individual attention, which was always in short supply. Though the effects might not be catastrophic, partiality nonetheless reinforced feelings of rejection among the less-favored and contributed to our misbehavior.

CHAPTER 15

War Years

The Sunday evening meal we sat down to in early December of 1941 was unusual in only one respect. What looked like Mrs. Sampson's radio had been placed on top of the china closet in the dining room. When the meal was ending, and without preamble, Gibsie rose solemnly from her seat, walked with measured pace across the room, and turned the radio on, an event so unusual everyone stopped eating and fell silent. She said nothing but stood by the closet, arms folded, jaw muscles clenching repeatedly, as she surveyed our reaction to the words coming from the radio. What we heard was a frightening description of wholesale death and destruction from a Japanese attack on a place called Pearl Harbor. World War II had begun to register on our childish consciousnesses.

None of us had any idea where Pearl Harbor was, or for that matter the real significance of the startling news. After a few minutes Gibsie turned off the radio and said in grave tones that our country was at war with Japan and Germany. "Is war coming to Sierra Madre, too?" one of the older girls asked in a small, frightened voice. Perhaps realizing she had really frightened us, Gibsie hastened to reply she didn't think so, but that lots of things were going to change in our lives.

Those of us who could remember were dismayed when, a few days later, Gibsie told us the U.S.S. *Argonne*—the ship we had so happily visited on Christmas Day two years before when it was anchored off San Pedro—had been severely damaged in the Japanese attack on Pearl Harbor.

The newspapers I sold and newsreels I'd seen at the movies told of wars raging in other parts of the world, but though frightening, they had seemed remote. Now that our own country had been attacked all that had changed. Living near the coast, we knew Japan was "out there, somewhere" beyond the ocean, and having no real sense of distance, our sketchy knowledge of geography made us feel vulnerable and worried that our town could be struck at any time. This dread seemed even more real when, just before the year ended, for the first time air-raid sirens filled the night air with an ominous wail.

The warning to "blackout!" came suddenly, and we had no idea whether it was practice or the real thing. At school, just before the Christmas holiday break, we'd been instructed to sit on the floor under our desks whenever we heard the air-raid alert. When it sounded, we jumped out of our beds and hid under them, anxious and quaking, awaiting the rumble of exploding bombs. Despite the undercurrent of dread, the urge to mix a little nervous fun in with the exercise was irresistible. So down in the Boys' Building, we pretended to be anti-aircraft gunners and called out the number of enemy bombers shot down. We could make a game out of almost anything.

Not all of us took the air-raid drill so glibly. Up in the Big House when that first siren sounded, the commotion was too much for eight-year-old Ruthie Parra. Laughing, other girls told how Gibsie found her in the upstairs hall "crying softly and twitching all over with fright." Soon after that first air-raid alert, the older girls were assigned windows in the Big House to cover with homemade blackout drapes. But in the Boys' Building when the sirens sounded, we just turned out the lights, stumbled around in the dark, or went to bed.

In the excitement of those early months after President Roosevelt had declared war, the air-raid wardens got a little overzealous about sounding alerts, which came all too often. When the sirens began their mournful warning and there was no following explosion of bombs or even the sound of airplanes droning overhead, they quickly began to lose the thrill they'd generated earlier. It wasn't long before we took them in stride, more often than not sleeping through them.

The excitement and hardship the war ushered in drew our community closer together. Our sense of involvement was made even more immediate in the New Year, when we learned that three former Home boys had already enlisted in the army. Seventeen-year-old Don Lopez, also impatient to enlist, showed up at the Home in March jubilantly waving a letter from his father allowing him to enlist in the U.S. Army Air Corps. The rest of us boys, too young to enlist, could at least take vicarious pride that some of the boys from the Home were "in." Like any other proud mother with sons in the service, Gibsie not only told us of their whereabouts and exploits, but passed on their news to neighbors, merchants in town, and teachers who knew them.

The family restaurant, El Original, *with the author's stepfather, second from the left; the author; his mother; and his older sister, in Los Angeles, circa 1942.*

The war soon began to intrude on our lives in small but important ways. For years, the Women's Society at our church had darned our socks and mended our clothing. But now our needs were subordinated to the sewing the women were doing for the Red Cross and our servicemen. Our clothes and socks that needed attention began to pile up. There was a shortage of men to do ordinary jobs, and, when our cesspool overflowed, there weren't men immediately available to dig a new one. For nearly two weeks the sixteen girls and women living in the Big House chased us out of our building while they used our facilities.

The full impact of rationing wasn't long in coming; it forced everyone to cut back on a great variety of commodities, especially gasoline and meat. For a country accustomed to the freedom of automotive mobility and for which meat was a dietary staple, those shortages soon were the subject of much complaining. My mother and Felipe, who'd been driving out to see us twice a month on weekends, ran out of gas-ration coupons and were forced to come on the streetcar. Then we could only go where we could walk, a serious cramping of our style. Motorcycles became popular, and Mr. Havenhill, the school shop teacher, was only the first of a number of people in the community to use one. Food prices started a slow but relentless climb. Gibsie was always worried about food, and now rationing began to affect the ability of donors to visit the Home. People couldn't replace the tires on their cars when they wore out.

People all over the country were planting Victory Gardens, and even Mother tried her hand at raising a few vegetables in the small plot behind her apartment in Los Angeles. One Sunday after we'd picnicked at the Sierra Madre park, she said she needed to pick up something for her garden, and we walked with her to the nursery located down the street from the park. When the saleslady asked what she wanted, Mother either didn't know or couldn't remember what to call what she needed and tried to describe its function.

"It's that stuff you put on the ground and it makes the plants grow," she explained in slightly accented English.

When the salesperson registered no sign of understanding, Mother tried again. "You know, it comes in bags and you mix it with the dirt."

But at that, the salesperson only shrugged, shook her head slowly to indicate she still didn't understand, and then looked to us for clarification, but we weren't able to help either.

Finally in frustration, Mother blurted, "You know, cow shit!"

"Oh!, oh!," the saleslady said, flustered, "you mean fertilizer." Hiding her embarrassment, she hastily departed to get a small bag of it.

We were also embarrassed and whispered in unison, "Mother!" But she got what she wanted.

◆

As the war effort continued to envelop the country, we were all carried away by the swell of sentimental wartime music. It was unavoidable any time the radio was turned on. Even without the radio, at school we learned and proudly sang patriotic songs, especially the fight songs of the army, navy, and marines. "The White Cliffs of Dover," an import from our ally England, was very popular, as was "Praise the Lord and Pass the Ammunition," and even, "Over There," a song resurrected from the First World War. A growing and steady diet of virulent government-sponsored propaganda in all media did its part to generate a belief in the absolute monstrosity of every Axis soldier we were fighting, all of it designed, of course, to create and maintain a ferocious, uncompromising patriotism. "Sink the Rising Sun!" and "Smash the Axis!" were typical slogans, and posters depicting vermin, like rats and snakes, with the heads of Hitler, Hirohito, and Mussolini were posted everywhere. These were accompanied by an endless stream of other slogans, about every imaginable activity that would contribute to defeating our enemies. One in particular, "A Slip of the Lip Can Sink a Ship," had me wondering what in the world I could possibly know that could have such a devastating impact.

Those enemies were made to seem even more real when the government began the internment of Japanese Americans later in the year. We were made to believe every person of Japanese ancestry was not only a spy for Japan, but an immediate threat to the war effort, as well as to our own well-being. The Santa Anita Racetrack, which was closed for the duration of the war, was one of the sites selected for the internment. After the Japanese Americans had been rounded up and imprisoned at the track, that shameful site became a favorite place to go to gawk. If Mother arrived in a car when she visited on Sundays, Santa Anita Racetrack was usually the first place we asked to be taken. My uncles even drove out from Los Angeles to visit us and have a look, as did a steady stream of other people. Rumors of attempted escapes were rife and recounted with morbid fascination.

Among the Japanese Americans from Sierra Madre interned were the Nomura and the Shimizu families. The head of one of these families, "Charlie" Nomura, was well-known in the town by virtue of the vegetable and fruit vending truck he regularly took door-to-door to his customers. George Shimizu was well-known for the same reason. Both were unimposing and considerate; each man had his route and was careful not to interfere with the other's business. The families had lived in the community for many years.

When Sierra Madre School was built in 1930, the town's small Japanese community donated a beautiful traditional Japanese Garden, which they all helped to construct. It had a fish pond with a bridge over it, stone lanterns, and dwarf trees. The garden was located between the patio, a remnant from the old elementary school, and the back of the new school building, where it could be seen and enjoyed from many of the classrooms. Shortly after the Japanese Americans were interned, some town residents, in a chauvinistic fit, destroyed the garden. Beauty wasn't the only thing the community lost that day.

If there was anyone in our town who thought the incarceration of Japanese Americans was wrong, they failed to speak up. Rather, everyone seemed willing to accept California Governor Earl Warren's rationalization that they should be interned, because "Japanese Americans have not assimilated or embraced American values and traditions."

Gibsie received letters from former Home boys who were in the service, and it was exciting when she shared them with us. When Eliseo Lopez wrote he was with an infantry division somewhere in the Pacific, we made up stories about him fighting heroically against the Japanese. We did same with Angel "Onny" Uribe, who was in Florida getting ready for combat. Edwin Ortiz and Don Lopez couldn't say where they were stationed or what they are doing but still wrote regularly. It was most exciting when the young servicemen came to visit to show off their uniforms. To us they were heroes, even though they had yet to shoot at, much less kill, an enemy soldier. The first such visit was Army Private Edwin Ortiz. Though he had only one eye, the Army still believed there were useful things, such as physical-training instruction he could do, and had allowed him to enlist. He had just completed basic training, and we pressed him for "war stories." Of course he had none, but we happily settled for his less gripping but still fascinating tales of life in the Army.

The well-organized and incessant government propaganda made all of us boys yearn desperately to get into the war ourselves, and we hoped it would last long enough for us to grow into it. Meanwhile, we collected whatever military paraphernalia we could lay our hands on, and while wearing those fragments of gear, played at war. As the fighting progressed and more older brothers, uncles, and even fathers were drafted or joined up, the availability of such war trappings increased. It wasn't long before kids showed up at school with a military unit identification patch, a steel helmet, a cartridge belt, even a whole rifle bullet. The treasures were reverently passed around from one awed boy to the next. Later, souvenirs from the war zones began to show up. The shop teacher, Mr. Havenhill, showed us some sent to him by his son, who was fighting in Europe. One item that his son took from a German prisoner of war was unforgettable: a wallet made from the tanned skin of a woman's breast, including the nipple. It was grotesque, the image haunting me for weeks afterwards.

The community lost no time gearing up to do its part for the war effort. Sierra Madre School soon became the place to bring the scrap metal and paper we were encouraged to collect. We gathered so many bundles of newspapers and magazines that the teachers' parking garage, which by then was mostly empty of cars, was given over entirely to a storage area for them. We also scoured the town picking up discarded metallic wrappings from cigarette packs and candy bars, salvaging and rolling their tinfoil into great, shiny spheres we imagined would be melted down and made into bullets. We did the same with string, zealously collecting and rolling it into huge balls, certain we were advancing the cause.

At school we also made models of German and Japanese war planes, studying their black silhouettes so, if attacked, we could help air-raid wardens identify them. Though we were certain of our expertise, neither I nor any other boy I knew was ever asked to spend the day or night scanning the heavens on the lookout for enemy bombers. War stamps were sold at school, and classes competed to see which could buy the most within a given period. A lot of my earnings from selling newspapers and doing gardening jobs went into those drives. Those of us who earned our money resented the kids who got money from their parents to buy war stamps.

There were things we could do directly for "our boys" overseas, like writing letters and pasting together scrapbooks of cartoons and comic strips from magazines and newspapers. But these we decided were jobs for girls.

◆

Seven years at the Home had not erased my sense of betrayal and abandonment. But those feelings had been pretty well submerged by July, 1942, when I learned Henrietta was leaving the Home for good. Gibsie told me that Henrietta had to leave because she'd reached the age at which the Center required it. There was truth to what she said, as other kids had left at the same age. But it didn't explain why my remarried mother couldn't take both of us. Her explanations all sounded like excuses, simply other ways of saying she didn't want me. In the end, I was left behind to nurse my anger and dejection.

From the day we arrived at the Home, I'd been willing to stay as long as Henrietta was there. But now that she was leaving, remaining became intolerable. Angry and desperate, I decided to run away, thinking if I simply went "home," my determination would convince Mother to let me stay with her.

I decided to go on a Sunday Mother and Felipe weren't scheduled to visit, and when for nearly three hours everyone would be at church; I wouldn't be missed until dinner. Even though I'd never before tried to make the trip to Mother's house alone, I didn't think getting there would be difficult, as I'd been there often enough to know which streetcars to ride. The fare wasn't out of reach either. If I couldn't collect enough in tips, I'd use the money parceled out to us for the church offering.

The next Sunday when everyone began straggling off to church, I hung back before heading for the streetcar station, where I hid until I could catch the ten o'clock run. The rail line ran right past the Congregational Church, and once on board, there were a few anxious moments as I hunkered down in my seat. When we were well past it, and I sat up to watch the passing scene, I experienced a wonderful sense of exhilaration. The thrill lasted the rest of the trip, which was as easy as I'd expected.

In what seemed like a short while later, smug and triumphant, I walked in the door of Mother's house, surprising her and Felipe, who were just sitting down to a late breakfast. Both exclaimed their surprise, but Mother clearly was not pleased to see me. Still, I took heart in the look on Felipe's face, which seemed to say he was delighted at my gumption, and briefly I thought he might take my side. To deflect attention from me, I asked for Henrietta, but instead of an answer Mother offered me something to eat. Always enticed by food, I sat with Felipe while she prepared a plate of *huevos rancheros,* eggs with chile sauce. But any elation I might have felt when I walked in was short-lived; as the minutes ticked by, the tension failed to abate. Mother told me I couldn't stay and called Gibsie to let her know where I was. Sunk in gloom as they drove me back to Sierra Madre later that afternoon, I was thoroughly disheartened.

Back at the Home, while Felipe visited with his son and Billy, Gibsie sat with Mother and me. She appeared unruffled, but I knew she was very angry because of the steely, unsmiling look in her eyes and the way those prominent jaw muscles of hers were flexing. In a quiet voice she told us how worried she was when I didn't show up for dinner. But knowing my state of mind, she'd guessed what I'd done. She explained to me it wouldn't be much longer before Mother would be able to take me home, too. I wasn't mollified, and decided they both just needed more convincing.

Mother left before I remembered to ask again why Henrietta hadn't been at home. A few weeks later I learned she actually hadn't gone to live with Mother, but to the Francis DePauw Home for Girls. It was a shocking revelation, one that convinced me Mother really didn't want us, any of us, to live with her. But that didn't stop me from running away again. I did so never thinking that, like Henrietta, I could end up at the Spanish American Institute, another Methodist home for Latino teenagers and young men.

After my second attempt a few weeks later, Mrs. Sampson kept a close eye on me and on the money I turned in from selling newspapers. I was furious at Mother and Gibsie for not letting me leave. Though I wasn't consciously looking for ways to get myself thrown out, I needed to hit back somehow. It didn't take long to find a way. I was always mischievous, but the things I did ordinarily only warranted a scolding or privileges denied. What I thoughtlessly undertook next was destructive and dangerous.

The Home was outfitted with a number of fire extinguishers. When a town fireman came to recharge them, I learned they were filled with a solution of bicarbonate of soda and a small container of acid just under the screw-on cap. The two mixed when inverted, producing a froth that spewed out under tremendous pressure. As the fireman discharged the extinguishers in the backyard, he warned us never to tamper with them, as the acid could burn, even eat through metal. That was all I needed to hear. Later, I removed the acid bottle from one of the basement fire extinguishers to see for myself what the acid would do.

Before she finally caught me, Mrs. Sampson began to notice a variety of metal objects turning up mysteriously corroded and discolored. Fortunately, I hadn't yet injured myself or anyone else, but sooner or later a serious injury to someone—most likely me—would have been inevitable.

This reckless prank was too much for Mrs. Sampson to handle, and I found myself standing before a furious Gibsie, fully expecting a severe beating. Her usually pallid face flushed, those telltale jaw muscles of hers flexing, I knew she was fighting for control, and I was probably just seconds away from the thrashing of my life. But to my amazement Gibsie instead only gave me a "talking to," though it was heated and seemingly endless. There was no doubt she was alarmed by the potential catastrophe, but knowing how upset I was about not being able to live with my mother, she apparently decided one of her "terrible whippings" wouldn't help the situation.

Of course my mother was told of what I'd done even before she visited us the next time. Mother seemed more exasperated than really worried about me, and any hopes I had she'd decide to take me home with her evaporated. Instead, she warned about how easily I could have hurt myself or someone else. Her parting words were, *"No seas malcriado, Roberto,"* Don't be a badly raised boy. Once again, I got the distinct feeling she had more pressing concerns than me.

While raking the East Yard a short while later, I spied the remnant of a doorbell at the entrance to the basement of the Big House, its twin wires protruding from the door casing wrapped with black electrician's tape. If I'd noticed it before, it never attracted my interest, but this time it drew me like a magnet. In a flash I'd peeled off the sticky black covering and gingerly touched the exposed wires. I was rewarded with a charge that danced and prickled alarmingly through my fingers and up my arm. Fascinated, I touched it repeatedly before finally getting up the nerve to grasp the wires firmly between thumb and forefinger. The shock was stronger, but I could easily stand it. When I realized I'd not electrocuted myself, both fear and excitement abated and I foolishly held the wires with one hand while grabbing a nearby water spigot with the other. The shock this time traveled through my entire body and made my arm feel like it would explode. It was all I could do to disengage myself. Though frightened, I decided this was too much fun to enjoy alone and soon got others involved.

This escapade came to a climax when I got a number of other kids to hold hands so the current could pass through us. But when I grabbed the water pipe for the final thrill, one of the girls in the circle fell to the ground writhing and gasping for breath, mostly from fright. The rest of us fled. When Gibsie heard what had happened, she was alarmed and enraged. This time when I was called before her, she was actually pale and trembling in her fury. I was certain I'd be expelled.

"Bobby, what are you using for brains?" she said, her voice deadly calm. "Did it ever occur to you someone might have been injured, even killed?"

I only shook my bowed head in answer. I realized that I wasn't going to be flayed within in an inch of my life and was puzzled as to why not, since I certainly deserved it. Maybe Gibsie felt responsible for not having had the wires removed.

An electrician removed them the next day.

◆

I was acutely aware of Gibsie's and Mrs. Sampson's concern about the marked change in my behavior, often imagining I could feel their eyes on me even when they weren't physically present. A short while later, I knew they'd decided on a new tack when Mrs. Sampson called me to her room to say she was planning a week's camping at a state park and had decided to take me with her. It wasn't unusual for a matron to take one or more of us along on their vacations, but usually those taken were girls. I wasn't pleased. Spending a week alone with Mrs. Sampson was definitely not my idea of a good time. I let her know I didn't want to go, but it wasn't as though the choice was mine.

Grudgingly, I spent the next week helping her prepare our bedrolls and packing the camping equipment she'd collected from friends in Huntington Park. Saturday morning she gathered together our food, we loaded her car, and together we departed for the campground. I was angry and for the entire drive in a deep gloom. But camping was Mrs. Sampson's element, and when we arrived a few hours later, she had me hustling with unpacking and setting up the tent and cots.

The campsite was situated in a grove of tall pines that scented the air with a wonderful fragrance and completely carpeted the ground with their needles. The slightest breeze set the trees soughing, the comforting sound and the natural beauty raising my spirits in spite of myself. The campsite had a picnic table nearby, a water spigot, and even a makeshift campfire pit with seating logs arranged around it. We spent the rest of the day getting settled. After supper, though we hadn't needed it for cooking, she showed me how to build a small fire in the campfire pit, and we sat in the twilight gazing into the flames and embers. She talked, I listened. In the deepening dusk, Mrs. Sampson told me we'd go to bed and rise with the birds each day. As dark enveloped us, she lit a candle and went into the tent to change for bed. A few minutes later she called me to follow.

After breakfast the next morning, we spent the day hiking and exploring. A seasoned camper, Mrs. Sampson seemed to know a great deal about the rocks and plants we encountered along the trails, and kept up a steady commentary. At the same time she tried to draw me into conversation, which wasn't easy, determined as I was to wallow in unhappiness. That night after we'd cleaned up from supper, we repeated the campfire chat of the first night. It became a nightly ritual, during which she gradually got me to vent some of my anger and frustration. By Tuesday we'd explored all of the nearby area, and I hoped we could cut the trip short. But Mrs. Sampson, despite my melancholy, seemed to be enjoying herself immensely and was determined to stay the whole week.

The next afternoon after hiking an hour or two alone, I returned to the campsite to find it apparently deserted. I entered the tent and in the dim light found Mrs. Sampson seated on her cot, stripped to the waist, in the midst of a sponge bath. Unperturbed, she paused and looked at me. I was speechless, transfixed by her nakedness, which she made no effort to cover. Her pale, blue-veined breasts with brownish-pink, distended aureoles, hung flat and pendulous almost to her lap, and I couldn't take my eyes from them.

I had enough presence of mind to stammer an apology for barging in on her, and started to back out. But to my amazement she stopped me and, yet without the slightest embarrassment or attempt to cover herself, asked if there was a problem. Still too stunned to speak, I could only shake my head in reply, after which she directed I also take a sponge bath when she was finished. I seemed to have trouble getting my legs to back me out of the tent. She resumed her bath.

Outside, my embarrassment was suffused with a mixture of distaste and wonder. I fully expected her to fly into a rage, as she had one night a few weeks earlier when she'd caught Adelberto Lopez, one of the older boys, peeping into her bedroom window. Yet, she hadn't shown the slightest anger. Though titillated, I felt like I'd violated her. The encounter at first left me confused, unable to clear it from my mind; I replayed it again and again. Still, I was aware that as brief as it was, the episode in the tent had scored a neat division in my life. While I didn't understand how or why, I had the feeling that before I entered it I was one way and when I came out I was another. And I was keenly aware something between us had changed, but too rattled right then to realize what it might be. Part of what I felt was the falling away of an invisible barrier, the event bringing with it a sort of familiarity. The sense of intimacy was strengthened that night when, instead of the care she'd taken previously, she called me in to change before she'd entirely finished herself, the two of us changing in the gathering darkness, as if it were a perfectly natural thing to do. Her relaxed manner continued for the rest of our stay and, despite the unattractiveness of her aging body, I found it impossible to keep from conjuring erotic fantasies.

During our week together things between us were transformed. In one sense I felt slightly mesmerized by Mrs. Sampson, the result of seeing her partially nude and the air of intimacy afterwards. But there was something else. In the remaining days of our stay, the fact that she never mentioned the "incident" implied a trust that I wouldn't mention it to other boys—or anyone else—when we returned to the Home. Given my propensity for mischief, telling about such an event was something she might well have expected of me. But we now shared a secret; for me one of momentous proportions. I clutched it like a found thing of value, one I needed to hold onto for the simple reason no one had ever trusted me this way before. The interlude had affected me profoundly in other ways, too. I no longer felt like Mrs. Sampson was my warden, and if the excursion was intended to dissuade me from running away again, it succeeded.

CHAPTER 16

Reality

It was the shock of learning my father's identity that stirred up the sediment of memory and started me on this journey of remembrance and discovery. Since embarking on the project, I'd been astonished that my siblings and other former Home mates recalled so much more detail of life at the Home than I did. Even more amazing was the picture of the Home's daily life that emerged from Gibsie's diary and her monthly reports. Indeed, it was so different from what I could recall I could have been reading about another place entirely. This I knew was partly the result of denial, of suppressing memory, and of being so withdrawn that much of what went on at the Home simply failed to register.

I had by now re-read and studied everything I'd been able to gather about the Home. But more than simply clarifying what went on, I wanted to pin down what it was about life there that had left me with such awful feelings about myself. Certainly there were the facts of being a charity case, of wearing hand-me-downs, of performing for our supper. But there had to be more. Probing deeper I began to understand there were a number of deliberate, troubling policies and practices—some apparent by inference, others by omission—-that had harmful effects. At first what I got from my "reading between the lines" didn't seem all that significant. But taken as a whole, I saw a not-so-subtle pattern of teaching us to devalue our group and ourselves.

It began with small things like anglicizing our names. That was always the first step for each of us: Enriqueta became Henrietta, Racquél got changed to Rachel, Roberto to Bobby, Francisco to Frank, and even Jesús to Billy. This also happened at school, where some teachers, to make it easy for themselves, went so far as to make us pronounce our family names as they preferred, a practice not only jarring to our ears, but demeaning.

Then there was the matter of being reprimanded for speaking Spanish and being looked down upon for being Spanish-speaking or for not speaking English well. That, too, was harmful to our self-image. I'm not saying we shouldn't have learned English—we all did and rightly so—but implying that one language was qualitatively "better" than the other degraded Spanish and the cultures that speak it. When I think about how much time I've spent trying to regain fluency in Spanish, it saddens me to realize how easily I could have learned both languages and grown up bilingual.

No doubt all this was done with the best of intentions. But when your rightful name is taken from you, then your language and your religion, you lose your heritage—one piece at a time.

There were other instances of cultural bias, too. It was obvious from the Diary and monthly reports that important dates in Mexican history were deliberately ignored, while at school and in the country at large, important dates for other groups—St. Patrick's Day and Bastille Day come to mind—were and are celebrated. *El Cinco de Mayo,* the date inaugurating the insurrection that resulted in Mexico's defeat of the French, was celebrated only once at the Home in 1932, but never again. Interestingly, for years Gibsie noted in her diary each May 5 that it was a day of celebration for Mexicans. Yet she never mentioned it to us. That she bothered to remember the date at all suggested someone at the Center instructed her not to celebrate it. Similarly, during the early days after the Home was established, there was some discussion at the Center of celebrating the anniversary of the Home's founding on September 16, the date associated with Mexico's independence from Spain. But the idea was dropped. Clearly our guardians were aware of the potential significance of these dates to us, and then deliberately suppressed them. Of course, such commemorations didn't jibe with the goal of making "real Americans" of us.

Since they were made at the expense of what we were, the Methodist Church's efforts to develop in us a sense of self-worth had exactly the opposite effect. How could we be expected to take pride in our heritage, much less ourselves, when every scrap was deliberately removed or blocked from consciousness?

Both Gibsie's diary and her monthly reports to the Center described the difficulty she had finding and keeping help. But not until near the end of the Home's thirty-year existence, when it was virtually impossible for the Center to hire someone else at the low salaries it was willing to pay, did it turn to a Latina. Clearly the Center didn't want to have anyone in a position of authority who looked or sounded like us. There was no one in authority like us at the Home, and certainly no one at school, at church,

A group portrait of the Home kids taken just prior to the author's leaving the Home, circa spring 1945. The author is the left-most boy.

or in the town for us to look up to. In such an environment, it was a short, subliminal step to infer that Latinos were incapable of being leaders, or that only Anglos could be. What a difference it would've made in the perception we developed of ourselves to have had a model in those roles.

I could see how those prejudices, implied and inferred, insidiously made their way into my young mind, there to do their destructive work engendering self-hatred.

Overt and blatant discrimination—including often hearing Mexicans stereotypically depicted as lazy and dirty—were not missing from my experience, either.

Early June, 1943, began like the months preceding it, news of the war continuing to rivet our attention each day. There was no reason to expect succeeding days would not follow suit. The year's interval since Henrietta's departure had done little to ease my resentment about being left behind. As I'd grown older, the sense of being second-class, if anything, had been magnified, as had my awareness of the low esteem in which others held Mexican Americans. The resulting poor image I'd developed of myself was reflected in my personality. Even so, as a kid going on age twelve, I was treated at school in most things like any other child. My reputation and popularity, both of which I believed were pretty good, were helped by my accomplishments in the classroom and on the playing field. The kids I believed were my friends were among the most popular.

But at school on a Monday in early June, my brittle self-confidence was shattered. At the first recess, I gathered with my usual coterie of buddies in a favored spot, which had been the patio of the old school. Our conversation as usual rambled from subject to subject. Suddenly, and with the same vehemence reserved for the hated Germans and Japanese, Gary, one of my best friends, blurted, "Boy, we really showed those dirty Mexicans!"

Everyone froze and looked at me. Gary was referring to the confrontation the previous day between some servicemen and Mexican Americans in Los Angeles.

He quickly tried to salvage the situation and stammered, "I, I don't mean you, I mean the *Pachucos.* You, you're different."

But the damage had been done. I'd heard disparaging references to Mexicans before, but they'd never come from a friend in my presence. And hadn't he said, "We?" In my already overly sensitive state, the hurt was penetrating, the effect devastating.

My response was an automatic, defensive attempt to save face—to his suggestion that I was different, I defiantly replied, "No, I'm not!" Wounded, angry, and feeling rejected, I stalked off.

I knew *Pachucos* were Mexican zoot-suiters, but not much about what they'd supposedly done. Even though I sold newspapers in the evenings after school, I did little more than look at headlines so, if asked, I'd have an answer to, "What's new?" There was nothing in the paper on Friday about the fight between a few *Pachucos* and a small group of sailors on shore leave, who had driven into East L.A. to pick up girls. Their zoot-suiter boyfriends had taken offense and fought them off.

The full story about the fight between servicemen and *Pachucos* was in the paper on Saturday, and I found it all extremely upsetting. I felt worse, even alarmed, when I read on Monday afternoon about the much larger battles that had taken place on Saturday and Sunday nights involving many hundreds of soldiers, sailors, and civilians. Those servicemen and their supporters had hired a fleet of taxicabs and driven to East L.A., where, unimpeded by the police, they'd stopped and beaten up anybody they saw wearing a zoot suit.

When Mother and Felipe visited us on Sunday afternoon, they seemed fearful and were reluctant to talk about what was happening in the city.

When I asked about *Pachucos,* all they said was they were a bunch of no-goods giving all Mexicans a bad name. Nothing at all was said at the Home.

In the recesses of my mind I knew Gary hadn't meant to include me in his epithet, but my pride was another matter, and as far as I was concerned, I was no longer part of the group. Paranoia had set in, and besides hurt, I felt alienated and somewhat sullied. The looks I thought I got from my classmates only contributed to my sense of isolation and rejection. A simple syllogism played repeatedly in my mind: *Pachucos* were Mexican and hated; I was Mexican, so I was hated. I suffered a helpless rage at the injustice, and I desperately needed somehow to salvage my esteem. My mother branded the *Pachucos* as bad, but it wouldn't be until much later, when I knew more about what had happened, that I'd learn they were the ones being preyed upon—and being punished for it.

At the Home no one had ever instilled us with pride in ourselves as Mexican Americans. Nor had my mother. I supposed because we lived apart from them, she and my stepfather did little to educate us about the value and virtue of being who we were. As immigrants, they kept a low profile, not wanting to stir up the hatred toward Mexicans of which they were keenly aware. So I was growing up ignorant of the stories, traditions, and achievements that might give me pride in our heritage. I felt certain there were thousands of Mexican American soldiers and sailors fighting in the war; my uncle was one and so were some of the Home boys. But if any of them were performing well or were heroes, there was never any mention. And no one bothered to tell us that, measured by the number of Medal-of-Honor winners who were Mexican American and the rate at which they were suffering casualties, no other ethnic group was serving with greater courage.

That was precisely what I needed to know at that awful moment. But there was no way for anyone at the Home, much less my mother, to know it. I was as excited as anyone by Hollywood's movies about the wartime heroics, real or imagined, of other Americans. But they never included a word about the real contributions of Mexican Americans. When I saw the propaganda-like film about the Bataan Death March there wasn't a mention that fully a quarter of the U.S. soldiers on that hellish journey were Mexican Americans.

During that awful weekend in June, not many miles from us, hundreds of young Mexicans and Mexican Americans were beaten up by our soldiers and sailors. The Los Angeles police looked the other way. So much for heroism, fidelity, and sacrifice.

Mexicans were friendless everywhere in Los Angeles, and I cringed when I saw the prejudice reflected in the *Sierra Madre News,* as well as in the newspaper I sold. To my relief, I noticed no immediate change in the way we were treated by the merchants or the townspeople. Interest in those events was soon overtaken by news from the battlefronts, but I sensed a change that was manifested in a variety of subtle ways.

Though teachers continued to treat me as usual, I imagined I was being avoided by my classmates. But it wasn't just my imagination that school friends were having parties to which I wasn't invited. "Hey, Bobby, I had a great party Saturday night. You should've been there," one of them said, as he walked away laughing. Some friends. Anxiety, resentment, and mistrust became my companions in their stead.

◆

It was one thing to be ostracized by kids at school, but really devastating when a community leader, like the young, highly respected minister at our church, did it. Dr. Frederic Groetsema had replaced Dr. Pritchard three years before at the Sierra Madre Congregational Church. I didn't know for sure whether events involving Mexicans in Los Angeles had influenced him or not. But an episode at church one Sunday evening a short while later made it seem so.

Dr. Groetsema had organized a young people's Bible study group, which for some was also preparation for confirmation. A few of us from the Home, who were twelve or older, were required to attend. At the first meeting Dr. Groetsema read Bible passages and explained their meaning. At the end, he assigned readings for the next meeting and said we'd then take turns reading aloud and explaining the assignments. So that we'd make a good showing, each night during the week Gibsie worked with the two girls, and Mrs. Sampson spent time preparing Adelberto Lopez, Margarito Flores, and me.

The following Sunday evening, more than a dozen children were seated around the periphery of the study room, the five of us from the Home clustered together at one end. As the session began, Dr. Groetsema again explained the procedure and had the first of the town children begin. The Bible passages were of varying difficulty, and when a child had difficulty interpreting them, Dr. Groetsema would ask for volunteers to help out. One or two of us raised a hand to volunteer, but he ignored us. When the turn arrived at our little group, but before the first of us could begin reading, he raised a restraining hand and said, "No, that's all right, you don't need to read, we understand about you."

We looked at each other in confused silence as if to ask, what was it he understood about us? that we didn't speak English? that we couldn't read? that we were too stupid to understand that stuff? Humiliation and embarrassment quickly set in, immediately followed by anger. I was furious and wanted to tell him what I understood about him! He tried to make his patronizing attitude appear as though he was doing us a favor by letting us off the hook. But it was clear to everyone in the room it was nothing less than belittling prejudice. And since he'd said "We understand," I could only guess what he might earlier have said about us to the other children, whose embarrassment was also clearly evident. In the stony silence of the moments that followed, I had no way of knowing what my mates were thinking. But then, as if on cue, we all stood and stalked from the room.

Afterwards, Gibsie defended Dr. Groetsema, minimized what had happened and tried to talk us into going again the next week. I refused. I was convinced Dr. Groetsema intended to have the Home kids quit the class anyway.

The contempt I read on Dr. Groetsema's face and heard in his voice that evening was crushing, particularly since he expressed it in the presence of the town children. I couldn't speak for my mates, but in the instant he gave in to his prejudices, he undid years of work by his predecessor and others to bring me into the Protestant fold. That devastating experience did more to turn me away from religion than anything else could have. For me, that event was just one more drip in the constant flow of humiliation forming and hardening into stalagmites of anger and bitterness. Dr. Federic Groetsema couldn't have chosen a more certain way to be immortalized in my memory.

◆

Release from the demoralizing events of the past few weeks finally came with the end of school in late June. I couldn't wait to go "home." Mrs. Sampson, perhaps realizing my depressed state, suggested this time I be allowed to spend a whole month with my mother and stepfather and they agreed.

They lived in a small, rented house in the Echo Park area of Los Angeles. It only had one bedroom, so Henrietta, also home for vacation, slept on a sofa bed in the living room; I used a mattress on the floor.

Although they probably could have afforded a larger house, Mother and Felipe were saving every dollar for the business they'd started. The war effort was by now under a full head of steam, and anybody who had anything to sell stood to make money. For Felipe, who was already past forty when the war started and too old to enlist, this was another opportunity to exercise his entrepreneurial bent by opening a restaurant a few miles away, on the Western Avenue side of the city.

The restaurant was still in the early stages of being decorated and outfitted with kitchen and other equipment when I arrived at the end of June, and since I couldn't work there, Mother suggested I find a job and earn a little money. At the start of the next week, I went to a busy commercial street nearby and immediately found a job in a market. My first task each day was to rinse the returned soft-drink bottles and sort them into the appropriate cases by size and brand. The rest of the day I stacked goods on shelves. Things went very well for most of the week, and at the end of it, I looked forward to taking home an actual paycheck for the first time in my life.

On Saturday morning a truckload of watermelons arrived. The floor manager gathered all of us male employees in the back, where we began unloading the melons, passing each one hand to hand bucket-brigade fashion. Once the unloading was under way, the manager left. Being a bunch of boys, it wasn't long before we began horsing around. Predictably, we dropped a couple of the melons, and when we finished the job, we sat around feasting on the fragments. I assumed this was normal procedure and was enjoying what I believed was our just reward for a job well done. But suddenly and without a word to me, everybody else scattered, leaving me in the midst of the evidence, a reddish juice on my face and hands and a pile of watermelon rinds. I found myself looking up at a very angry floor manager.

"Come with me and pick up your paycheck, you little sonuvabitch, then get out!" he shouted at me. At first I was speechless, and on the way to the office I tried to explain what had happened. The furious manager would hear none of it and sent me ignominiously on my way, my small paycheck clutched in a sweaty hand. Being called a foul name was bad enough, but the injustice was outrageous and I was sorely in need of sympathy. When Mother returned that evening, I did my best to tell her my sad tale without crying, but when I got to the part about being called a sonuvabitch, she and Felipe roared with laughter; my dammed-up tears burst out in a torrent. Clearly, I wasn't ready for life in the big city, and spent the remaining weeks trying to make myself useful in the restaurant-to-be.

◆

The holidays yielded substantial money donations at the Home that year. When she had added it all up, Gibsie discovered that, at least for a while, there was enough money for us all to buy our lunch at the school cafeteria.

At about the same time, in exchange for our lunches, Margarito Flores and I, along with two girls from the Home, got our turn to work in the cafeteria. This opportunity was one of long-standing for older girls and boys from the Home, as well as other seventh and eighth-graders from the community. Working there was highly prized, as there was always plenty to eat, certainly far more than we normally got.

It didn't take us long to realize that the first student-helper to arrive in the cafeteria got some special extra, like the residue from cake pans or the juices left from fruit salads. Each day the race was on to see who would collect that day's treat. The prize was always left in the same spot, so we could be sure whatever was at that place was meant for us. But there was a cost associated with being first to claim the reward. The staff liked to have a little fun at the children's expense, and they often set some sort of trap for the unsuspecting.

One day, shortly after I'd started working there, I raced to the kitchen just a step or two ahead of my classmates and spied in that special place a full glass of yellow-colored juice. I assumed it was pineapple and claimed it as mine. Scooping it up triumphantly, I quickly drained its contents in a few large gulps, discovering too late it was pure lemon juice! It was all I could do to keep from vomiting, much less keep my composure. For a few minutes, head shaking, stomach recoiling, my face distorted in an ugly grimace, I ran to a nearby sink and tried to rinse the awful taste from my mouth. My performance exceeded the staff's expectations and was roundly applauded. Worse, I had to bear their laughter and jibes until the next unsuspecting newcomer was tricked. But in the end, I more than made up for the insult by eating well.

◆

The only thing on my mind when the summer of '44 arrived was going home again, and in July, after enduring four weeks of Vacation Bible School, I got my wish. The restaurant Felipe and Mother had opened the previous year was going full blast and I was put to work as a busboy.

Felipe named the place "El Original," after a famous restaurant in Mexico City. Though it seemed so to us, it probably wasn't all that special, the space actually just one long room with a counter and a dozen stools on the right, a row of booths along the opposite wall. It might be true Felipe was still a cook and Mother a waitress, but now they played those roles in a place of their own. Felipe and Mother were proud to have their own business, and I was proud right along with them. It changed them; they were full of hope and exuberant optimism. Their new attitude was reflected in the way they decorated the restaurant, adorning the walls with colorful Mexican serapes, ornate sombreros, and travel posters of historic and vacation spots in Mexico. Felipe and a hired chef did the cooking, while Mother and Henrietta served.

There was good reason for optimism. We opened the restaurant each day at eleven, in time for the lunch trade, and a rush of diners packed the place until about three in the afternoon. At about five, the supper rush began and continued until we closed at ten. The exhausting workdays were offset by the gratifying knowledge that we were making a profit substantial enough for Felipe to start thinking about finding a larger place. Mother's and Felipe's discussions also included hopes of making enough money to bring all of us kids home for good.

As busboy I set up the tables and cleared them. Once a customer's order had been taken, I also brought water and served the soup and salad courses. For this I received a share of the gratuities left for Mother and Henrietta. When Billy arrived for a week's stay in August, he wanted to share in the earnings and began vying with me for the privilege of clearing tables and serving customers. To eliminate the competition and avoid the problems that might develop, Mother decided I would set the tables and serve the soup course, and Billy would serve the water and salad. Both of us would clear.

This arrangement worked just fine for a while. But Billy and I got a little overzealous about our duties. Inevitably, the time came when Billy, serving salad at the same time I was serving soup, jostled my arm; I spilled a full bowl of steaming vegetable soup into a customer's lap. This brought an end to our careers as waiters. Even so, we managed to earn what was for us a stupendous amount of money. And we ate our fill of Mexican food, which we loved. Judging by the crowds that flocked to the restaurant, it was excellent.

Before Billy and I returned to the Home in August, I argued energetically to be allowed to stay on. Though again I was unsuccessful, returning to the Home was tolerable, because I knew this time would be the last.

◆

It was already late August when I returned to the Home. I was nearing the end of a ten-year stay, years that had left me with a sticky residue of anger, resentment, and longing. In the Boys' Building it was customary for the two oldest to share a small room apart from the main dormitory. At age thirteen, having achieved that lofty status earlier in the summer, I shared the room with Adelberto Lopez, the other boy my age.

My bed was on the south side of the room next to a window whose sill was at almost the same height as that of my bed. It was there I awoke uneasily one late-summer night. I didn't know what had broken my sleep, though I was dimly aware of remnants of a dream that might have disturbed it. I emerged from slumber to find moonlight streaming in the window, its silvery glow imparting a bluish-white cast to my skin.

Because of the heat, I was dressed only in pajama-bottoms, my chest and arms bared to the moonlight. It took only the smallest stretch to imagine I could feel it bathing my naked skin. I'd no idea what time it was, but the stillness, broken only by the chirp of insects and the soft snores of my roommate, told me it must be very late. Fully awake, I lay for a while fascinated by the play of light on my hands as I moved them like flying things in the lunar brilliance. Rising on one elbow, I looked out at the expanse of the South Lot, made magical by the moon's glow. Some night creature, a bird or a bat perhaps, caught my eye for fleeting seconds as it soundlessly flapped by, and I sat up to see where it had gone. The moonlight-transformed landscape into which it disappeared was breathtaking and hypnotic. For a few moments I was transfixed; then I decided to go outside to be part of the strange, surreal world the summer moon created.

Unsure exactly what I would do, the daring novelty of my impulse thrilled me, so much so it set my heart pounding. Fear and audacity fought for dominance, but only briefly did I question the urge to go. Soundlessly I slipped out of bed to the floor and stood for a few seconds before taking the first tentative steps across the room. The floor's linoleum was cool under my bare feet. There was nothing actually wrong in what I was doing, yet how to explain if caught? With great care I tiptoed down the short hallway toward the door fronting on the expanse of the yard in back of the Big House, where the girls slumbered. As I neared the matron's room, which lay just beyond the washroom, I was almost panting, my pulse pounding madly in my head. I paused to listen for the sound of anyone who might have heard me.

The knob and hinges of the door leading to the outside were well-oiled, and I was able to pull it open without making any noise. At last I stepped out onto the landing, my excitement at such a level I could hardly breathe. I stood there for a short while calming myself, again making sure I hadn't been discovered. Satisfied the dormitory continued its slumber, I descended the two steps into the gentle warmth of the summer night. The gravel of the yard seemed to feel different to my naked soles. Only the night creatures noticed my presence, stopping their chirping for a few seconds before welcoming me into their midst, resuming their night-song.

I gazed awestruck at the emptiness of the yard space, devoid of any other being, remade by a monochromatic coating of silvery-blue. I realized I'd never really looked at the yard before, surely never seen it like this. And I was unlikely ever to have it all to myself again. I was filled with a need to do something, anything, to celebrate the revelation. Despite a sense I was engaging in the forbidden, I looked full-face into the silent moon and untied my pajamas, letting them fall to the ground. This simple act brought a wild, erotic joy unlike anything I'd ever known. I surveyed my slim, moonlit nakedness. Pulse racing, I stretched my arms upward as if to embrace the seductive object that had brought me there.

Moon-shade created dark and secret places in the yard. Some of these seemed benign and even inviting. I took the first few watchful steps. Fairly certain now I remained unseen, I began moving around the yard, mindful to avoid the yawning black entrance to the cellar of the Big House. Still cautious, I stepped in and out of the inky shadows cast by the large pepper tree at the yard's center, my footfall light and soundless on the still-warm sandy gravel. I was fearful Rico, the Home's pet dog, who bedded with the girls in the Big House, might begin barking and put an end to my adventure. But there was no sound from him. My fears diminished, in a burst of exuberance I began to run, at intervals jumping, my arms extended, as if by leaping and moving fast enough I could fly. With wildly beating heart I continued my jump-skipping dance to the summer moon, electric, erotic feelings surging through me. A straining erection testified to my excitement. I wanted to fly in the moonglow, to be part of it and have it envelop me. Back and forth I ran, a skip-running bounding that carried me from one end of the yard to other, until I was out of breath.

Without realizing it, I'd stopped at the set of swings at the edge of the yard, found myself sitting in one, scarcely aware of the seat's coolness against my backside. I pushed off with my feet to begin a cautious slow back and forth, testing for any noise the swing's chains or hinges might make. There was none. I began pumping with my legs, slowly at first then progressively more rapidly, each pump increasing the arc until I could go no higher, aflame with the thought of prolonging the magic by using the swing to fly, to actually launch me into my own unassisted flight. The warm flow of night air rushing around my nakedness increased the sensation of moonlight washing me, splashing on my face and chest and against my back. The higher I went the more aroused I became, with a need to vent the elation of my rapture, to find release for my almost-unbearable carnal longing. I could only pump harder, mouthing silent screams, on into the night until I was exhausted.

I sat motionless in the seat, hands gripping the chains, head hanging, allowing the swing to slow on its own, slower and slower, until it came to rest. Spent, I sat for a time slumped in the seat, then slid out to rest on hands and knees before lowering myself to the ground, mindless of the gravel's roughness. The moon had moved westward. Rolling over, lying spread-eagled on my back, I stared still enraptured into its full face until a chill from the cooling ground sent a shiver through me, ending my reverie.

Rising and brushing myself off, I groped my reluctant way back to where I'd stepped out of my pajamas and put them on. With a last wistful look back at the scene of my revel, I tiptoed to my room.

For a while, back in bed, I relived the bliss of my escapade. For the first time I could recall, I was at peace, for the moment drained of the rage and bitterness so long with me, surely a gift from the summer moon.

CHAPTER 17

Mainstreaming

Nearly ten years of life at the Home came to an end in mid-June 1945, when I left Sierra Madre to live with my mother in Los Angeles. I was quite aware how lucky I was to have a home to go to, as many kids went to foster homes or a place like the Spanish American Institute. I knew I should have been grateful for all that had been done for me, but so intense was my dislike of the Home, I left it without a backward glance, resolving never to return. Nor was there a person at the Home or in the town I wanted to seek out to say good-bye to, or ever see again.

Much later, in a more reflective frame of mind, I regretted not thanking Gibsie and Mrs. Sampson before leaving. But gratitude was not in me that day. The stigma of dependence on charity generated an engulfing sense of shame. And, as if feelings of second-class status weren't enough, there was the stinging awareness of the low esteem in which I believed I was regarded for being Mexican American. The result was a crushing self-loathing. Whatever else the Home may have done that was good, it was mainly those damning feelings I associated with being there. I found it impossible to forgive, much less thank, those who'd taught me to feel that way.

I vowed then that no one would ever know I'd grown up in an orphanage. I could at least leave that humiliation behind, make a fresh start.

As the time for departure drew closer, I fantasized about how wonderful life would be with Mother and Felipe. I'd already been many times to the modest rented house on Plata Street in north-central Los Angeles where they lived, and I'd explored it with a proprietary eye. That it was small mattered not at all, for I'd at least have a room of my own!

I wasted no time decorating my new room with hand-built model airplanes, heroic pictures cut from magazines, and my own drawings of horses and airplanes. The pictures of nude women I was copying from the art-school sketch book left behind by the former owner stayed hidden in one of the built-in closets to be pored over in private. An old battered radio provided a finishing touch. The house had a lawn and small backyard whose care I happily assumed, a sense of pride coming to the fore.

When Henrietta had come home from the Francis DePauw Home for Girls the previous summer, I had no reason to know she was unhappy. But she later told me coming home had been a great disappointment, mainly because she couldn't have Mother all to herself. Felipe, it turned out, was the love of Mother's life, the soul-mate for whom she'd so long been searching, and her relationship with him left no possibility for the kind of intimate connection Henrietta had once shared with her and expected to have again. Instead, my sister learned the unhappy lesson that the fulfillment of a dream could be quite different from a dream of fulfillment. If I was to have a similar disappointment, it would come later; my immediate reaction to being "home" was euphoria.

◆

At the end of the previous summer, my parents sold El Original and leased a larger space closer to the city center. They named the new restaurant, El Café Orizaba, after another famous counterpart in Mexico, and that's where I went to work. As the new place seated more people, Felipe hired two cooks to work with him, along with two waitresses to help Mother, who doubled as cashier and general watchdog. Henrietta, who seemed barely able to get along with Felipe, worked when she felt like it.

Besides being busboys, Billy and I were sent out each morning to drum up business by passing out handbills advertising the place in the surrounding neighborhood. Billy was much better at this than I and allowed no one to pass without getting a handbill. If someone declined the offer, he simply stuck the advertisement in a pocket, a purse, or the crook of an arm. Anyway, it soon became apparent the handbills weren't necessary, because the restaurant quickly filled to capacity when it opened at eleven each morning and stayed that way until it closed. For the ten to twelve hours we worked each day, we were each paid the enormous sum of $30 a week. We spent it all on Tuesday, our day off, on rides and games at one or another of the amusement parks at nearby beaches. Though Billy hated to see his vacation and access to all that money come to an end, he happily returned to Sierra Madre at the end of July.

In mid-August, Japan's surrender ended the war and with it the rationing and other hardships associated with wartime. We closed the restaurant early on V-J Day and went to Long Beach to join the throngs already joyously and largely drunkenly celebrating victory. But when a group of exuberant sailors good-naturedly made a pass at my mother, whose beauty usually drew attention, our revelry came to an abrupt end. Felipe, a little high himself, was determined to defend Mother's honor. He stood scant inches over five feet and weighed all of 120 pounds, but despite his size, he tried to take on all of the sailors single-handedly. Fortunately, my soldier-uncle, who had accompanied us in uniform, decided such gallantry was better saved for another day. He maneuvered us out of the crowds and home.

◆

News of life at the Home was now limited to what Mother and Felipe reported after visiting Richard, Billy, and Connie, who were still there. Although we were invited to go with them, Queta, as Mother now insisted Henrietta be called, and I left no doubt about our feelings and always declined. After one of those visits, Mother told me Mrs. Sampson had left, that at nearly sixty, a combination of age and declining health had forced her to retire. Privately I suspected it was all those beatings she'd given Danny Meza that had finally worn her out. In any case, she had gone to live in Upland with her recently widowed brother. They said Gibsie, looking older and more tired than ever, was very upset about losing her sister's companionship and moral support.

I was more interested in the news about Rico, the Home's aging pet dog. Rico's age was anybody's guess, but he was certainly very old. It was evident he was living out his final days, and Gibsie had agreed to find a puppy as a replacement. She had been reluctant to get another dog and for a while it seemed fate might decide in her favor. Rico's first successor-to-be, another mongrel pup, died shortly after it arrived at the Home.

It wasn't until the following June that another replacement for Rico arrived, a seven-week-old puppy. While it may not have been a purebred, the pup nevertheless had been well cared-for by its owners, and as Gibsie said, "arrived in excellent health, along with a schedule like a baby's." It had already been named Rover, and so it remained. A few days after Rover's arrival, Rico went for a one-way trip to the dog pound. I heard it took just a matter of seconds.

The other bit of news I found interesting was that for the first time in many years, fewer children were arriving at the Home to take the places of those who'd left it.

The rest of the summer of '45 I spent working in the Café Orizaba, but when school started again in the fall, I was amazed to learn I would only be expected to go to school and do my chores at home. Except on weekends, when I was to help out at the restaurant, the rest of the time would be mine for homework, sports, and participation in the one or two organizations I might join at school. Incredibly, I'd be living pretty much as I'd dreamed I would. But my new life was not without its jolting realities.

My parents, having no idea where I was supposed to go to school, left me to fend for myself. Another kid on our street, whom I judged to be my age, told me the nearest one was Virgil Junior High School. Fortunately, it was close enough to walk to. When I fully realized I'd be going to a new school in the fall, I experienced an alarming sense of insecurity. As much as I'd disliked the Home, it had been a place of shelter, and its protective aura extended to wherever I happened to be. Now I was fearful and vulnerable, especially when I started at Virgil. The school was large and had a fair representation of Mexican American children, whom I viewed with curiosity and some apprehension. Besides those at the Home, this was my first exposure to large numbers of others who supposedly were like me, but I soon discovered I felt anything but kinship toward them. Not only did most of them seem to be among the poorest students, both academically and economically, but some of them were pretty tough and spent the lunch hour intimidating other kids. Their favorite tactic was to go along the line of those waiting to buy milk and ice cream asking menacingly for the "loan" of a dime or quarter. They traveled in groups of three or more, and the kids in line had little choice but to give up their change.

The first time I was accosted, I naively refused; the boy "asking" was so startled he just looked at me quizzically and went on to the next kid. When they were well past me, the girl behind me whispered, "You must want to get yourself beaten up. That's what they usually do if you don't give them something." And sure enough, moments later I saw the three Mexican kids pull a boy out of the line and rough him up until he gave them money. A few days later, another group was shaking down the line again. When they came to me and one asked for a "loan," I quickly handed him a coin. But as he took it, he looked more closely and said, "Hey, are you Mexican?" When I say I was, he said, "I'm sorry, man, I didn't know. Here's your money back." A part of me felt relieved, but the encounter also made me burn with shame for being what I was, and now for yet another reason.

In the classroom things weren't going so well either. At the Home, we were encouraged to do our best in school, the matrons checking to see that we did our homework. And if we were having problems, one of them would go to the school to confer with the teachers. Their interest and praise for good grades made it clear how they valued education. But now that kind of concern and supervision stopped, and the consequences began to show when classes got under way at Virgil. The very large school with indifferent teachers left me foundering. I found algebra incomprehensible, and as the end of the semester approached, there was no doubt I was failing it. I wasn't doing so well in other subjects either, and by the Christmas break I not only believed I was pretty stupid, but my sense of inferiority had been reinforced.

Meanwhile, business was booming at the Orizaba, which had turned out to be even more successful than El Original. With two winning ventures to his credit, Felipe began to see the possibility of a business and a home where all of us could live—and work. Deciding the time was right, he sold the restaurant in early January 1946 and bought a property in Baldwin Park, a small community located some forty miles east of Los Angeles. We moved there shortly afterwards.

◆

Life in Baldwin Park centered around growing oranges—the community was surrounded by hundreds of acres of orange groves. Our property was located a couple miles east of town on Ramona Boulevard, the main east-west road that ran along the foothills of the San Gabriel Mountains. It was a beautiful and generally peaceful site, even with the rumble of heavy trucks incessantly whizzing past along the roadway. Mother and Felipe had picked the spot specifically for that traffic, which would be good for business, and also because it was a better place than Los Angeles to raise children.

The main attraction on the four-acre property was a tavern catering largely to truck drivers and laborers, some of them migrant workers hired to pick oranges in season. The property also came with a gas station and garage on its west side, which Felipe leased to a married couple who lived in a mobile home in the back; a vacant lot was on the property's east side. The plan was to convert the tavern to a full-fledged Mexican restaurant and build a home for us on the vacant lot; part of the lot could also be used to grow vegetables for the restaurant, a job Felipe informed me would be mine. Buying the property had taken most of my parents' cash, and they planned to delay the conversion so they could replenish their coffers from the gas station lease and by continuing to operate the tavern for a time as it was.

The plan was a prudent one, but it turned out to be unworkable. The tavern's clientele were a rough crew, whose drunken brawls erupted with discouraging regularity. I spent many a night crouched behind the bar with my terrified mother watching, until the police arrived, my diminutive stepfather bravely try to restore order while ducking flying beer bottles, some of which smashed against the walls and on people's heads.

One night after an especially bad brawl, Mother, visibly shaken, surveyed the damage and said, "*Aye* Felipe, *no más,* we can't go on like this." He agreed he'd had enough, too. Within a month, Felipe shut down the tavern, borrowed more money, and proceeded with its conversion.

By March, the building had been gutted and given a fresh coat of paint inside and out, the bar replaced with booths and tables, and new equipment installed for the kitchen. When the new sign was finally erected out front, proudly proclaiming "Cerrillo's Tavern," the name they'd decided upon, we all went out to admire our handiwork, believing the metamorphosis to a restaurant was complete. But almost immediately it became apparent that keeping the word "tavern" as part of the new name was a big mistake; it misled former patrons into thinking they could still stop in for a quick drink or while away the night carousing. When told they could only have beer or wine with a full meal, some of our erstwhile customers took offense, a few becoming disruptive.

It took months to rid the place of those former patrons, who were always surprised to find the bar gone and the place filled with a different clientele, mostly families. In time, most of those former customers accepted the new order and found a watering hole more to their liking. But on one occasion, an unsuspecting truck driver came in and demanded a drink. "I'm sorry," Mother told him, "This is no longer a bar. You can have a drink, but only with a full meal." At that the man became abusive. Hearing the noisy disruption, Felipe burst through the kitchen's swinging doors brandishing a heavy knife sharpener like a sword. He charged at the startled truck driver, energetically parrying and thrusting until the hapless man had been fenced back outside. Meanwhile, the restaurant full of diners watched, mouths agape. For his heroics Felipe got smiles and applause. I was pretty proud of him, too.

◆

When the school year ended in June, Billy and Richard come to Baldwin Park for the summer. Money being in short supply after the renovation, work on our new house had not yet started, and we were all making do trying to live in the restaurant's storage room. Though it at least had a full bath, the quarters were extremely cramped and reeked of beer and other supplies. Fortunately, the room was large, and even though a good part of it was taken up with those supplies, we were still able to section off the remaining space into sleeping areas, a measure of privacy managed by hanging sheets from clotheslines strung across the room. But with the addition of the two boys, living conditions became intolerable. Arguments over use of the bathroom were endless. The two boys shared a bed while I grudgingly moved to a mattress on the floor. Nonetheless, Mother was so taken with the idea of having her family nearly intact again, she pestered Felipe into agreeing to keep Richard and Billy permanently rather than returning them to the orphanage at summer's end. Felipe had misgivings, but he could rarely deny Mother anything and reluctantly agreed, though the new house wouldn't be available until later in the year.

During one of our days off at the end of August, Mother and Felipe drove to Sierra Madre with the boys to pick up their belongings. Connie had been spending the summer at the Home, where she preferred to be. While the boys were packing their things, Mother—seemingly on the spur of the moment—decided to bring her back, too. Billy, who considered the orphanage his real home, was still in tears when he got back to Baldwin Park, hoping his weeping would convince Mother to let him return. He was out of luck—her mind was made up. Because the move was so sudden, Connie made surprisingly little fuss; the full realization that she was never returning to the Home came to her later.

At the time, Mother's decision to take Connie out of the orphanage seemed pure impulse, a whim of the moment. Later it was clear she hadn't been impulsive after all. While she admitted she had a lot to thank Gibsie for, she had for years resented the way Gibsie had alienated Connie's affections—how she'd all but "stolen" the child from her. "Enough is too much," as she liked to say.

With all of us now at home, life was even more crowded and hectic. To relieve our cramped quarters, Felipe decided it was time to build the new house. It turned out to be a triumph of practicality over comfort and esthetics. He had only the part with the bedrooms and bath built, the rest to come later. The "house," a long, narrow structure, went up surprisingly fast and looked for all the world like a barracks. Still the improvement in our living arrangements was marked, with us boys now in bunk beds in one room at the back end of the house, the girls in their room at the front end, and our parents in a room in the middle. But there was no improvement in the bathing facilities; we still had only one bathroom, albeit with a shower, and in desperate moments the one in the restaurant's back room was available.

Meanwhile, there was the restaurant. Felipe expected all of us to work there any time we weren't in school. He and Mother imbued us with the notion that our very survival depended upon making a success of the business. Except for Tuesday, when the restaurant was closed, we worked every day and evening after school and all weekend. Felipe taught me to cook all the food we served, and I often stepped in to help him when things got rushed. To my surprise, I liked working with him and learned quickly. He in turn praised me when I did things the way he wanted, patiently explaining when I didn't. I knew he appreciated my efforts and I worked the harder for it. More than anything else, it was the respect he showed me that made me willing to do even other somewhat less desirable tasks.

We seemed to use vast quantities of sauce made from long red chili peppers, and making it was one job I really despised. The peppers arrived in great dried bundles, which Felipe first boiled for a few hours in a large steel pot to reconstitute them. When they cooled and their stems were pulled off, they were put through a hand-cranked food mill. That was my job and difficult enough, since the mill was always getting clogged. But the hardest part was separating the soft pulp from the bits of tough outer skin by forcing the soggy ground mass through a conical stainless steel sieve by hand. The chili burned and left my hands stained red for days after one of those sessions. Billy and Richard refused to share the task, and though I complained at the unfairness of being the only one to do it, Felipe was unmoved. After months of this work, when I was on the verge of revolt, Felipe finally decided he could afford to buy a machine that did the entire job quicker and better.

I took the success of the business so seriously that after school each day I'd rush to the cash register to see how much money we'd taken in. If the total was just a few dollars, my anxiety could only be relieved if we had a good crowd show up for supper. But often the register showed no sales at all, and my distress grew. I developed a stammer, especially noticeable when I tried to ask a question. Months went by, and the stammer grew worse.

One afternoon as I was checking the register, I overheard Mother in the kitchen laughing. "*Míre,* Felipe, Roberto is out there checking the register again," she said. "I zeroed it out before he got home from school." She laughed again and added, "He gets so worried when he thinks we've made no money."

It dawned on me she'd been deliberately keeping the sales total low to manipulate me. Furious, I stormed into the kitchen to confront her. "Is this your idea of a joke?" I said. She just laughed off my anger. It was months before I got over the hurt and disappointment, but at least the stammer stopped.

◆

School kept getting in the way of work that had to be done, so Felipe decided to hire a cook and a waitress to take our places. But Mother and Felipe were both jealous types, and soon each was accusing the other of flirting with the hired help of the opposite sex. They voiced these imagined betrayals as soon as the last customer and the employees were out of the door. Their fights were loud and unpleasant, and we worried and wondered among ourselves, fearful our newly reconstituted family might once again be shattered and our future put in doubt. The jealous outbursts, lasting into the early morning hours, left us all exhausted from emotional distress and lack of sleep. The only solution was to fire the help.

But running the place alone was difficult without having us kids do a lot of the work. And Felipe's concern with making a success of the business was in conflict with my hopes of doing better at school. He and Mother were from a culture in which children were expected to work for the benefit of the family, and they expected me—all of us—to work as long as the restaurant was open. Neither came from educated families, though education might have been prized, and I had to fight for time to do my homework. After many arguments, Felipe finally agreed I could quit work at eight o'clock each night, after the peak of the evening mealtime, to do it. But when I managed to make the football team, which meant staying a few hours after school for practice each day and traveling with the team for our games, the battling started all over again. Mother knew how much I wanted to play football—-it was one of the few ways I seemed able to gain acceptance at school—and for once she went to bat for me. Though grudgingly, Felipe finally agreed to let me play and even came up with $20 for the pair of cleated football shoes I needed.

After a period of adjustment for all of us, things finally seemed to settle down. Somehow we managed to work out our differences. The addition of an enclosed patio behind the restaurant doubled its capacity, and with all of us working very hard, the restaurant was more successful than any of us imagined it would be.

Despite the business success, Mother and Felipe were still squabbling. Then the drinking started. I didn't know whether it was to celebrate our good fortune, due to problems in their relationship, or because of the stress of having all of us with them. On days the restaurant was open, they usually limited themselves to a drink or two to unwind after closing. But on Tuesday, the day the restaurant was closed, their drinking increased significantly. Felipe bought supplies for the restaurant at the big central wholesale market in downtown L.A. He left early and was usually back by mid-afternoon. When we got home from school, we all piled into the car and drove back to Los Angeles to have supper at one or another of their favorite restaurants. Though it meant I'd be up late getting my homework done for the next day, I still appreciated having someone else do the cooking, serving, and cleaning up for a change.

The place we liked best was a family-style French restaurant called Les Freres Taix, where we sat in a roomy enclosed booth. The soup arrived in a large tureen, which Mother, actually playing the role of mother for a change, ladled into our bowls. Felipe served the other courses, all of which arrived on large platters. It was very cozy, and I liked the feeling of family the ritual evoked.

It was what accompanied those evenings out that made me dread them. Felipe included a fifth of rum in the purchases he'd made earlier in the day, and by the time we headed for L.A., I could tell he and Mother had already begun nipping from the bottle concealed in a brown paper bag. Their imbibing, now at least done from drinking glasses instead of directly from the bottle, continued all through supper. By the time we started home, they were both pretty drunk and arguing loudly—about who knows what, and always in Spanish so we wouldn't understand. Felipe's driving was frightfully erratic, and we were stopped more than once by the police, who never seemed inclined to ticket him, only to chuckle at his condition.

On one of those trips back from a night out, Queta and I decided we had to do something to stop their drinking. "Maybe you can get the bottle away, and throw it out of the window," Queta whispered. The bottle was lying on the front seat and I managed to snatch it while Mother and Felipe were busy hollering at each other. I rolled down the window next to me and threw out the bottle. But when they missed the rum, Felipe stopped the car and turned to look at us in the backseat.

"Did you take the bottle?" he demanded angrily looking at me. I shrank under his glare and confessed. "What have you done with it?" When I told him, he turned the car around, ordered me out, and retraced a mile or two of our route, while I walked along beside it searching for the bottle, the whole time wondering what they'd do if it were broken. Luckily, the bottle had landed on someone's lawn intact.

Those Tuesday nights could be terrifying, and all of us kids were anxious until we got home. I was always fearful around people who were drinking, and for me those trips were especially troubling. My anxiety usually faded within a day or two, but began to mount again as the next Tuesday approached. To our great relief, the weekly drinking bouts, which continued for a few months, stopped as abruptly as they'd started.

At first the move to Baldwin Park only seemed to disrupt my school life further. In Los Angeles, Mother and Felipe were preoccupied with making a go of their business and neither knew nor seemed to care much about how their children were doing at school. This time, the couple who sold them the Baldwin Park property provided the information about the schools we were to attend. Queta and I immediately started classes at Covina Union High School, which served the surrounding rural area. But Queta, still smarting over her resentment at Mother's and Felipe's relationship, took advantage of their preoccupation with work and dropped out. Though she left with me for school each morning, she never went to class. Instead, she detoured to the bus station and went to L.A., spending the day at the movies and other diversions. Even after her truancy was exposed, she refused to return to school and instead went to work for the phone company.

Queta missed out on the genuine interest the teachers had in their students at this much-smaller school. On my first day, the math teacher, Mr. Corbin, reviewed my dismal transcript and asked me to return after school to discuss it. When he asked what I didn't understand about algebra, I said, glumly, "Everything." Unruffled, he replied, "We'll fix that, together." For the next few weeks I stayed an hour after school each day to review, which meant missing the last bus, Since we lived five miles away, I hitchhiked or often had to walk home. Felipe wasn't pleased that I was missing work, but Mr. Corbin's interest was inspiring and I was determined to take advantage of it.

In the few weeks it took to catch on and catch up, I discovered I actually had an aptitude for math; I did so well that I started tutoring other kids who were having trouble. That Mr. Corbin could teach me something I really believed I'd never master was nothing short of miraculous. I was in awe of him as a teacher. I had similar if less dramatic experiences in my other subjects. Taken all together, that academic year was the most affirming I'd ever had, and it began to undo the poor appraisal I'd developed of myself.

But offsetting the joy of discovering that my mind actually worked was the decidedly negative attitude toward Mexicans I encountered. Migrant and temporary workers brought in from Mexico picked the oranges grown in the orchards of Baldwin Park, Covina, and surrounding area. Though the growers depended upon the pickers for the success of their orchards, they despised them, treated them poorly, and otherwise had nothing to do with them. It was no surprise that the growers' attitude was reflected in that of their children, as well as in the community.

Rather than return to Mexico, over time some of these workers had remained and settled their families in the small nearby town of Irwindale. The few Mexicans attending Covina Union High School were the children of these former migrant workers. Dark-skinned and mostly speaking heavily accented English, they were shunned and made the object of ugly, cruel remarks by many of the other kids. Understandably they clustered together for moral support.

I was terribly torn about whether to befriend them. But fearful I'd be ostracized as they were, I stayed away and did my best not to be regarded as one of them. I felt awful about myself for avoiding them. The hostile climate also increased my own feelings of self-loathing; when asked about my heritage, for a while I claimed to be Italian or Portuguese, which made me feel even worse. But it wasn't long until I was unmasked; my schoolmates soon discovered my parents owned a Mexican restaurant, the only one for miles around. But strangely, that fact seemed to give me a certain amount of status, since many of my classmates' families dined at our place.

The Christmas of '46 was our first together as a family under our own roof, but Mother and Felipe hadn't reckoned with trying to provide the kind of celebrating we'd become used to at the Home. I was glad no longer to be involved in all that revolved around the holidays at the orphanage—especially performing—but Billy and Connie were particularly unhappy about all the parties they thought they were missing. We kept Cerrillo's Tavern open right up until Christmas Eve, and there were no plans for a tree, besides the tiny one in the restaurant, or even a trip to church, not that we missed it. But because of all their crying and complaining, Mother finally agreed to a quick visit to the Home on Christmas Eve, the first Billy and Connie had not spent there. They cried most of the time, and when it came time to leave, they begged Gibsie to get Mother to let them stay, knowing gifts would be opened after the caroling and storytelling. But we left before the first gift was passed out, further adding to their disappointment. Queta and I couldn't leave soon enough.

◆

The new year seemed like a fresh start for all of us, our new surroundings taking on the sheen of the familiar and the acceptable. Even my younger brothers and sister quit fighting the inevitable and took to their new situation. In the days and weeks that followed, we all settled into a workable routine, one in which I began to take a little joy.

Doing well in school also helped to ease my anxiety about the prejudice I saw all around me. I even achieved a degree of popularity as quarterback of the junior-varsity football team. But if I was beginning to think my schoolmates accepted me, it was evident some of their parents didn't. This was made vividly clear when a girl in one of my classes asked me—I was too afraid of rejection to ask anyone myself—to take her to the junior prom.

Nancy was blond, blue-eyed, pretty enough, and one of the most popular girls at school. I was surprised and flattered she wanted me to be her escort. Borrowing Felipe's good blue suit—his only suit—and the family car, I arrived on prom night to meet her parents, deliver a corsage, and pick her up. If I'd known Nancy was the daughter of a wealthy grower I might have turned her down when she asked. She lived in a grand house in a conspicuously wealthy Covina neighborhood, and when I saw it I almost turned around and drove back to Baldwin Park.

Already nervous, I was ushered into the living room, where Nancy's mother wanted to have our picture taken before we went on to the prom.

Nancy's father, who was eyeing me with distaste, positioned us by the grand piano, while her mother pinned on Nancy's corsage. The room seemed filled with grinning family friends who'd been invited to observe the rite of passage. My tentative smile belied my extreme discomfort. The moment before he snapped the picture, Nancy's father pointed and said to me, "Look, your shoe is untied." Just as I looked down, the camera flashed. I knew exactly what he'd done and why he'd done it, as no doubt did everyone else. When Nancy's mother protested and asked him to take another picture, he refused, smiling contemptuously at me.

Unable to deny his daughter her choice of date, nor pass up recording the milestone the junior prom represented, Nancy's father had resorted to a cheap trick to avoid having to explain later what she was doing with a Mexican boy. It was a cowardly act, and I could only hope someday he'd feel as badly about himself as he'd made me feel. On our way to the prom, Nancy cried and told me how delighted her parents were at first that her prom date was a member of the football team. But when she told them more about me, mentioning that mine were the people who owned the Mexican restaurant, the conversation had turned into a violent, screaming argument, which ended with her mother finally, if grudgingly, taking Nancy's side. I was amazed Nancy thought enough of me to stick to her guns. Later, when I showed Mother the picture of Nancy and me—a great shot of the wavy hair on the top of my head—she muttered something in Spanish I was sure was a bad word and told me I should tear it up. I needed no further prodding.

It's difficult to know exactly when I had the dream the first time. But it had to have been after I'd been at the Home for a few years, because the incinerator in the backyard seemed to be a major feature in it. When I awoke, all I remembered of the dream was that it had to do with something buried. And, as so often happens with dreams, it seemed to pass completely from my consciousness. But sometime later, maybe a week or two, when I was playing in the yard, I suddenly stopped, gazing transfixed at the incinerator's soot-coated, brick mouth gaping open like a frozen scream. Then the dream came flooding back, and I shuddered with the lurking fear that something or someone was buried in the ground beneath it, and worse, that somehow I was responsible.

The incinerator, a simple brick-and-mortar structure made in the shape of a large, rectangular box, stood as tall as a man. At its front end there were in fact two openings, one above the other. Trash was fed into the top opening, where it rested on a steel grating while it burned. The lower opening provided a flow of air and was also the means by which ashes could be removed. There was really nothing very mysterious or ominous about it, as every boy had at some time or other climbed inside to use it as a hiding place during a game of hide-and-seek. This burning receptacle held no inherent fear for me, but as I gazed at it now, it assumed a portentous quality it hadn't had before.

Perhaps because of my recollection during the day, I had a variation of the dream again that night. But this time, though no one else was present, I still had the sense that everyone was looking for a man who was missing, a man whom somehow I knew. What was especially disturbing was that I knew where he was and had reason to be frightened about saying so. His grave was no longer the incinerator, but in this dream had been moved to a spot under the porch of an old frame house. The porch was high enough off the ground to permit a person to walk upright under it, so that burying a body there would be an easy enough thing to do. The dream was so upsetting it woke me in the dark of early morning, and for a while I lay awake wondering if I really had killed someone, but couldn't remember who it was, how and why I had done it, or when it had happened. I also tried to visualize the old house, but couldn't bring it back into sharp enough focus to picture anything more than that its flaking paint was gray with white trim. In subsequent days and weeks I was periodically shaken by the feeling that maybe I was a killer. I strained to remember, but could not.

With increasing intervals between, the dream has recurred through the years, and in it someone is always missing. Each time the burial site is also different. Sometimes it's in the crawl space under the Big House, and other at times it's in a garden. For a time, in each dream he—for it was always a man—was buried in the ground under the plant-filled benches of a greenhouse, stifling from its artificially created humidity and vivid with the colors of the blooming flowers growing in it. While no one else was ever physically present in these dreams, I was still aware I had to hide my guilt from those absent people, whose presence was nonetheless palpable.

As I grew older and went on with life, the intervals between the dream sequences also lengthened. But their impact never diminished; the sense that I had killed someone remained. Usually, after I had dreamt it again, I simply brushed away the remembrance, which was easy to do as my life became more crowded with the demands of work and family. In spite of those efforts, I would still wake from a deep sleep and stare into the darkness, knowing I'd had the dream again and had been unable to push it away. It was conceivable the dream might have to do with an infantile desire symbolically to kill. If so, whom could I have wanted out of the way so badly I would wish him dead?

◆

During the two years we lived in Baldwin Park and despite my differences with him, Felipe had come to fill a large hole in my life. For as long as I could remember I'd yearned for a father. But it wasn't until the Flores boys came to the Home in the summer of '38 that I'd become aware of how deeply I wanted one. Every time Mr. Flores came to see his sons, I'd find it next to impossible to resist hanging around to be near him. He was an older man, already past sixty, and he seemed to embody everything I could want in a father. I liked the way he treated his boys and the way they beamed when they were with him. He seemed so understanding, giving them his full attention, and when he roughhoused with them a bit it was always done lovingly. The warmth he radiated was wonderful to be around, and all the children sensed his attraction. I didn't really want him to be my father; I just wanted one of my own, one like him. I was jealous of his boys and would have resented their father's presence if he had not also been so nice to me. He always brought his sons what seemed to be great things to eat, and he was mindful others of us would be around, so he usually made sure he had enough for us as well. What I liked best were the small red bananas he brought, the sweetest I'd ever eaten. As long as they lasted, he passed them out to any nearby child, saying reassuringly, "Here, have a banana. They're good for you. They'll put oil in your blood." Presumably the oil made the blood flow more smoothly. He seemed so earnest and sincere I actually believed him.

When Mother married Giuseppi Pertusatti in 1940, I briefly entertained the notion that he might become the surrogate father I yearned for. My longing for a father substitute continued even after Felipe began showing up at the orphanage on Sundays with her. He was a man who had many of the same attributes that had endeared Mr. Flores to me, and these became evident over the course of the next few years.

But in my brief life I had learned not to trust, to be suspicious of everyone, particularly any man who might be associated with my mother. I was not only fearful Mother would leave me again, but jealous of any such relationship, and despite his many endearing qualities, that put Felipe at a large disadvantage. I suspect he realized it. Wisely he neither ignored me nor went out of his way to be charming or winning—which might have deepened my suspicions—instead allowing time for our association to develop slowly and naturally. Queta, on the other hand, was not only distrustful but resentful, and she held Felipe at arms' length even after he and Mother had married and the rest of us had pretty much accepted him.

By 1946, after I had lived with him and Mother for nearly a year, I realized that I had grown to love Felipe. I had no difficulty thinking of him as my father and readily called him, "Papa," as did the others; I resented Queta's refusing to call him anything but "Felipe," sarcastically at that. And even though he was something of a taskmaster, he set an example as a hard worker and was usually reasonable, ultimately willing to resolve our differences. He had shown himself to be courageous as well as understanding and compassionate. Nor did he lack a sense of humor, which he used to ease all of us past difficult periods. More importantly, he was the first adult male who ever took any real lasting interest in me; the only man who took the trouble to explain how to do things and why it was necessary to do them in a particular way, how to be a man. I could tell he respected me and I returned the favor.

Of course, any man who was willing to teach me to drive even before I turned sixteen was due my gratitude. When he went so far as to trust me with the car when I announced I was ready to solo, he was bound to win my admiration. And when, after one of those early solo drives ended in a ditch, Felipe responded with sympathy, not the chewing-out I deserved, he definitely had my lasting affection and esteem.

Because of him, I also gradually came to occupy a special place in the family. One reason was traditional among Latinos—I was the oldest male child. The other was that I was becoming the best-educated family member, the one presumed to be learning things the others didn't know. Felipe acknowledged me in both regards, often deferring to me and at least giving the impression he valued my opinion regarding most family matters that came up. This treatment pleased me, but often set me at odds with Richard, who felt that as Felipe's natural son he deserved the deferential regard I was being shown. Though Richard and I continued to be friends, his relationship with his father deteriorated to the point that ultimately he felt he had to leave us and return to live with his own mother. For all those reasons, I felt very lucky to have ended up with a man like Felipe. When he died years later, I doubt my grief and sense of loss could have been deeper if he'd been my natural father. I mourn him still.

Felipe was Mother's fourth and last husband, and while I'd known little about how she got along with the others, I did know she and Papa had loved each other deeply. Increasingly less able to breathe because of the encroaching emphysema paralyzing his lungs, he took his own life in May, 1974, with his last breath asking Mother's and Bill's forgiveness. His death was a great shock to all of us. Although Mother understood the great pain and agony he'd been enduring, she still couldn't forgive his leaving her. She was devastated and remained profoundly depressed for years afterward. I saw his suicide as an act of courage and selflessness.

It's at times of crisis when we are most prone to give up our secrets, and with Papa's death, that time had come for Mother—to a degree. A few days after we buried Papa, Bill and I took Mother to the local Social Security Administration office to apply for her benefits. I was helping her fill out the necessary forms, which among other information called for the dates of her marriages and divorces. She had little trouble remembering the dates she had married, but seemed totally unable to recall when she had divorced any of her former spouses.

"Mother," I began, "we have to fill in the names of your former husbands and the dates you married and divorced them on the form. O.K.?"

"Yes, *Mijo,*" she said. "Do you want to start with Papa?"

"No," I said. "We already have that information, so let's start with your first husband, Rodolfo Batres."

She told me approximately when they were married, but when I asked for the date of her divorce, she thought for a moment and replied, "I can't remember exactly, *Mijo.*"

"Can you just guess at an approximate date?"

She shook her head.

"O.K.," I went on, "when did you marry Jesús Sanábria?"

"*Mijo,*" she said, her expression plaintive, "I'm upset and it's hard to remember all these things. Just put 1931."

"O.K., that'll do. Now when were you and he divorced?"

Again she shook her head, and then answered that she couldn't remember. So I said, "Well, you must remember the dates you married and divorced Joe Pertusatti." But again she mumbled she could not.

So far I'd written nothing on the form, and by now it was dawning on me there must be more to this than she was revealing.

"Mother, did you divorce any of them?" I asked in a cautious whisper.

Guiltily, she looked at the floor and slowly shook her head again. "My God!" I thought, "what do we do now?" Then she looked up at me sheepishly and, in hushed embarrassed tones, explained what to her mind had been good reasons why she'd repeatedly ignored that bothersome legal technicality. Amazed, I listened as she recounted again how her first husband had abandoned her in El Paso and returned to Mexico never to be heard from again; how her common-law husband, Jesús Sanábria, had abused her and she'd had to flee to escape him. And as far as her marriage to Joe Pertusatti was concerned, she said she was not really married to him, anyway.

"Mother, wait a minute," I interrupted. "What do you mean you were never married to him?"

"No, that's not right. I did marry him," she corrected. "But he couldn't, well, you know, do it," she said, embarrassed.

"Do you mean you and he never made love?"

"Yes, that's it."

"Why, what happened?"

She said it was too embarrassing for her to talk about. But when I insisted Mother finally told me that poor Joe, who'd fought in World War I, had most of his genitals shot off and neglected to tell her of this sad fact until it became evident on their wedding night. At first she did her best to be sympathetic, but being of a somewhat fiery nature herself, she soon found it impossible to overlook this requirement for conjugal living. "I was still a young woman, after all." Eventually, her fury at having been misled overwhelmed any feelings of sympathy she might have had for his plight. She simply went her own way, leaving Joe to his misery.

All of this, of course, was far too complicated to explain to the clerk who was handling her case, so I did as Mother asked, left well enough alone, and simply ignored the information about the other husbands. She was in fact entitled to the meager benefits she was applying for, and we let it go at that.

CHAPTER 18

Final Years

"The Pasadena Symphony Orchestra is giving a concert in Sierra Madre tomorrow evening," Sherry announced hopefully, reading from an item in the *Los Angeles Times.*

"Is that right? And I suppose that means you want to attend," I said, uninterested.

It was a Friday morning in early June, 1996, and we were ensconced in the Residence Inn in Ontario, California. Sherry had accompanied me to this inland city where I was to make a presentation later in the day on my proposed sculpture for Ontario's new convention center. The cheap airfare carried with it the requirement we stay through Saturday; Sherry was looking for things to do.

"On our way back from the beach, we could drive to Sierra Madre in the late afternoon, find a nice place to eat, and then stay for the concert," she outlined.

"What is it you find so intriguing about Sierra Madre, anyway?" I said. "You know how I feel about going there."

Ignoring my reaction she said, "I really like the place, and a concert would be fun, something we haven't done in ages. Besides, what else have we got to do?"

Good question.

A stage had been set up at the city park, the same one where as a child I went during the Depression to see the silent films the city sometimes screened. There was a good turn-out for the concert, an annual event. The available lawn space was rapidly filling up. In the largely white upper-middle-class crowd, there were a few Asian-looking faces, and even fewer black ones; I scanned for Latinos, but saw only one possible. Where we live in Virginia, on Sunday evenings during the summer there are concerts like this on the courthouse lawn. There are only a few more dark faces at those concerts than here. There are also more children because the Virginia crowds are younger, but otherwise the two crowds could be interchangeable.

There was something else missing here, too, I realized. When the city turned out for those silent movies, there was a real feeling of community, one that even I could feel and participate in. But we've become a nation of transients, and today people keep more to themselves, so that feeling of community seemed entirely absent here. I felt as out of place as ever. After the first selection, a rousing rendition of "The Charge of the Light Brigade," Sherry saw the distraught look on my face and said, "You're really not enjoying this, are you?"

"In a word, no," I grumbled. "But I guess I can stand it if you really want to hear the rest of the concert."

"Oh, such a martyr. No, I don't particularly want to, either."

On the way back to Ontario, she asked, "Was it anything in particular that was getting to you back there?"

"Well, besides the fact that it's where I grew up and the unhappy feelings the place recalls, yes, there were a couple of things. I'm sure you noticed what the crowd consisted of."

"You mean 'white bread'?"

"Exactly. But the other thing that came to my mind, as I watched the people filter in, was the book, *Sierra Madre Vistas*, that history of Sierra Madre in pictures I arranged to get through an interlibrary loan a couple years ago."

"Was there something wrong with it?"

"Yes, at best it should have been entitled a 'selective' history. You know, that book was put together for the country's bicentennial observance by the Sierra Madre Historical Society and published only twenty-two years after the Home closed. There's not a picture or a word in it about the Children's Home, even though it existed in the city for thirty years."

"Why's that important?"

"After wading through all the documentation I have about it, I know the Home was an important part of life in Sierra Madre. And we're not talking about something that existed in the nineteenth century, either."

"You're suggesting that mention of the Home was deliberately left out?"

"Yes, exactly. The Home was covered regularly by the town's newspaper, and all anyone had to do was look at their archives. By contrast, there was another home in Sierra Madre, called the British Home, that was included in *Sierra Madre Vistas*. It was established in the fall of 1931 for elderly residents of British Commonwealth birth or parentage. So doesn't it strike you as odd that one was included and not the other?"

"I can see how one might reach the conclusion you have. But maybe those archives were destroyed before work began on that book. You don't know it was deliberate."

"No, I don't, but based upon what I now know about Sierra Madre, I wouldn't doubt it. In any case, from both historical and sociological perspectives, I think it's a serious omission and certainly sloppy research."

"Really? What's so serious about not including the Home?"

"Well, by choosing to ignore its existence, the historical society obscured an important aspect of the city's image and lessened the character of those who lived in and developed Sierra Madre during that time period." From the look on Sherry's face I couldn't tell whether I'd convinced her or not.

◆

Despite my personal feelings about the place, I still experienced a sense of sadness as I pieced together the circumstances surrounding the closing of the Home only nine years after I left. Despite the exigencies of the Great Depression and World War II, in many respects the ten years I was there were its best. After Mrs. Sampson left it in the fall of 1945, the boys never again had a permanent matron, and the tenure of cooks was never very long either. Indeed, during the ensuing five years, the jobs of cook and boys' matron were more like revolving doors. Of the six women the Center sent to fill the positions, only one managed to stay more than three months. I found references in her reports about how disheartening all of this was for Gibsie, who knew the Board's inability to find more permanent help was a sign all was not well at the Center. It was this difficulty in finding and keeping adequate help that finally moved the Center in 1947 to hire Mrs. Eloisa Garcia, the first of three Latinas to be part of the staff during the Home's remaining years.

By 1948, more and better jobs created by the postwar boom meant fewer families needed the kind of help the Home offered. At the same time, state and county welfare agencies had switched their preference to placing destitute children in foster, rather than institutional, homes. The result was a gradual but persistent decline in the number of children coming to the Home. Postwar inflation also had an immediate effect on the cost of feeding, clothing, and providing the health care for the children who were there. The aging Big House needed ever-increasing amounts of money to operate and keep in repair; sometimes so many things needed fixing at the same time, Gibsie felt like she was under siege, she wrote.

By mid-December 1950, when Gibsie celebrated her fifty-seventh birthday, it was evident she was disgruntled with the lack of support from the Center, and not only when it came to supplying adequate help. Also grating to her was the knowledge that the Center was trying to keep expenses down, as it had for years, by underpaying her and Re. And she suspected the spate of unacceptable help she'd been receiving was because the Center couldn't pay the going rate for prospective cooks and matrons.

The Home was inexorably on the way out. But before it closed its doors for the last time, I saw it again, despite my earlier vow never to do so.

When North Korea invaded the South in June 1950, a number of us former Home boys were caught in the military draft. Gilbert and Rudy Martinez were inducted into the U.S. Army. Adelberto Lopez and Margarito Flores shipped out to Korea with California's 40th Infantry Division. Other Home boys had their turns in the military: Richard Cerrillo in the Army, Frank and Arthur Flores in the U.S. Air Force.

I'd dropped out of college earlier in the year and, knowing I would soon be drafted anyway, joined the U.S. Air Force, with some of my friends along for moral support. In January 1951, we left for basic training in San Antonio, Texas. It had been six years since I'd left the Home, and when I returned from having completed "basic" and a few months of duty, I decided I was ready to show Gibsie my proud new status. Without realizing it, I still needed and wanted her approval, her recognition of the potential sacrifice I might be making. Well remembering the inordinate pride she'd had in "her boys" who'd served in World War II, I fully expected similar treatment.

I showed up in uniform, a starched and pressed airman first class. In the years since I'd last been there, everything about the Home seemed to have shrunk; the result, I supposed, of the change in my eye level. The Big House certainly appeared less grand than it had seemed, the signs of deterioration evident in many places. Except for obvious signs of aging, Gibsie didn't seem to have changed, at least in manner or in her attitude toward me. While she was civil enough and even invited me to stay for supper, she could barely muster a minimum of tolerance, let alone cordiality, and otherwise made it clear she was totally disinterested in me. I really wasn't surprised, as I'd never been one of her favorites—far from it. I'd vented my anger at having been left at the orphanage in so many ways and so consistently, I knew she must have often wanted to get rid of me. She seemed

The author when lieutenant colonel, U.S. Army, at the Defense Intelligence Agency, the Pentagon, circa 1970.

certain I'd never amount to much. Disappointed in her reception, I got one more to my liking from Re, who seemed more impressed.

At the Home I'd lusted after Re, and in the year or so before I left, she had sometimes even been accepting when I'd tried to kiss her. So I thought the visit might still be salvaged by spending some time with her, and was encouraged when she agreed to go with me for a drive in the nearby hills after supper. But my "date" with her also ended disastrously. While we were parked in a star-lit mountain trysting spot, I misinterpreted her intent and got a complete rebuff when I tried to do more than kiss her. I left Sierra Madre no better disposed to the Home than I'd been before, and I was sure I'd seen it for the last time.

A year later I was stationed at Walker Air Force Base in New Mexico, disillusioned with my assignment as a weapons handler, an awful job that involved cleaning black grease from an endless supply of stored pistols and carbines. A buddy, equally unhappy with the assignment, suggested we transfer to the Army, which was then looking for infantry platoon leaders—cannon fodder, some said—and attend Officer's Candidate School. With the somewhat tarnished view I had of myself, I'd never entertained the possibility I could become an officer and was hesitant. I went anyway, and discovered in the process I was in fact well-prepared for the strict regimen of keeping myself, my clothing, and my equipment neat and orderly; I'd already had years of such training at the Home. With the pressure of military classes and the hard physical demands, other "candidates," as we were called, nearly went crazy trying to keep up; indeed, many dropped out. I was virtually serene. I graduated in March, 1953, and felt pretty damn good about the fact that, out of the 249 men in my company who'd started, only ninety-seven graduated, and I ranked seventh in the class. For one of the few times in my short life, I'd been given a chance to compete on the basis of merit alone and had succeeded very well. The experience marked the beginning of a profound change in my life, not least in the way I viewed myself.

In early fall I visited the Home for the second time since I'd left it nine years before. I was on pre-embarkation leave prior to shipping out to Korea, having been commissioned a second lieutenant of infantry six months before. I knew no other boy from the Home had ever been a military officer, and I wanted to show Gibsie that her suppositions were wrong about my ultimate failure in life. I showed up once again in full regalia, shiny gold bars and all, sure now she would certainly be impressed. But my reception this time was as frigid as the previous one had been. I got the distinct impression that, unpersuaded by my accomplishment, she still wasn't convinced I would amount to anything. For Gibsie, my uniform with all its brass and symbolism did nothing to hide the boy she'd known for so long, and apparently viewed with such distaste. It was obvious there was nothing I could say or do that would ever change her mind, a sad revelation. I'd done many mischievous things, but none I knew of that could have had such a profound and lasting effect on her. This time, she was at least somewhat attentive, a change I thought might have been motivated by the fact I might well be going off to my death. As I left for what would be the last time, I finally realized I no longer needed her approval, and what she thought about me didn't really matter either.

◆

Judging from the last of Gibsie's reports to the Center, it was evident she didn't know Christmas, 1953, would be the last for the Home. There were only fourteen children left, less than half of its possible thirty, and these included only four boys. When it came to gifts, Gibsie found herself in the strange position of having more donors for children's Christmas boxes than there were children, and the schedule of performances and parties was as full as ever. The Elks Club again provided a tree, and the Kiwanis Club held its annual luncheon at the Home, paying for their food and leaving a substantial check as it usually did. But the Nash's traditional

Christmas party was not held, nor would it ever be again; the couple were too old and infirm to host it anymore. Miss Higgins, then seventy-three, was present for the Home's own Christmas Eve supper and party, and if she knew what the New Year held in store for the Home, she said nothing about it.

In fact, in the closing months and weeks of 1953, the Center's Board had all but decided to close it down. So it was that, with considerable trepidation about her future, Gibsie arrived at the Center in late February, 1954, when the Board of Trustees met to decide the Home's fate—and hers.

Lack of money was the main reason the Board wanted to close the Home. The number of children also had steadily declined, so that as the Board was meeting, only ten children were still in the Home. And now there were other Methodist-sponsored institutions, like the David and Margaret Home, that would take Latino children and were eager to take those at the Home in the event it shut down.

By the end of the review, it was clear to Gibsie and everyone else that closing the Home was inevitable. The time for closure was ultimately set for August first, a date that would allow the children still there to finish the school year. The Center's executive secretary would send appropriate letters to the Center's constituents, especially to the larger donors, "thanking them for their prayers, their interest and their support." Gibsie would do the same for her "contacts" and the Home's supporters in Sierra Madre. Gibsie was acknowledged for her long and faithful service, and both she and Re were given the month of August as a vacation with pay. There was, however, no mention of severance pay, nor mention of any retirement fund for Gibsie.

In Sierra Madre, there were rumors the Home was to be closed, and while she declined to confirm them, Gibsie acknowledged there were growing difficulties in trying to meet the ever-changing requirements of the county and state welfare departments. When the closing was formally announced, reaction in the town was indifferent, although as might be expected it made the front page of the *Sierra Madre News.* In his column, Lee Shippey, the *News*'s long-time feature writer, recounted the Home's history and Gibsie's role in it. It was a very sympathetic article, among other aspects noting, "In most homes for children, the first thing a visitor sees is the office. In this home the first thing one sees is children, romping with their dog or riding their pony or playing in the front yard. They are clean, respectful boys and girls, but they show no evidence of being institutionalized." He expressed the skepticism of some in the town about the Center's plans for continued services to the children in their own homes, especially since many of those remaining had no home to go to. He also voiced the townspeople's doubts "that as much good for the children and the community can be done anywhere else for as little money. They think Miss Gibson has not only been inspirational to the children, but to the entire community." But despite these fine sentiments, no one came forward to protest the closing, and no one wrote to the Center, as Mr. Roberts had done on behalf of Sierra Madre's citizenry in the 1930s, to suggest the city be allowed time to see what it could do to keep it open.

In the months that followed, Katherine Higgins, who had long since retired as the Center's executive secretary, volunteered her services to provide whatever help might be needed at the Home to ease its closure. It must have been with a heavy heart she oversaw the shuttering of the institution she had been so instrumental in bringing to life. With Gibsie and Re, she planned a final homecoming celebration for all the former children and former staff members they could contact. This event, held on Sunday, July 18, 1954, was also a front-page feature in the *Sierra Madre News.* Some eighty people showed up, including many former children, and their spouses and offspring, for one last look around and a meal. They came from near and far.

I knew nothing about the closing. I had just returned from Korea and was still in an Army hospital in Denver where I was being treated for TB. Of the Home's former matrons, only Kathleen Sampson, Gibsie's sister, and Mae "Fuller" Zlatnik were there, as were Miss Higgins and other staff people from the Center. The reporter covering the event quoted Gibsie's estimate that the former children in attendance "represented 237 years residence at 72 West Alegria Street."

The following Friday at the home of Martha Pritchard, daughter of the late Dr. Arthur Pritchard, the Women's Society of the Congregational Church held a reception honoring Gibsie, which was open to all Sierra Madre residents who had known her. In addition to thanking longtime supporters directly, Gibsie thanked the community as a whole in a letter published in the *News.* She wrote in part:

> There are no words adequate to express to you our deep feeling of gratitude for the wonderful way in which you accepted us and always gave us a sense of belonging.
>
> The personal interest taken by all the organizations, churches, school staff and PTA—even the business houses—has been indicative of the spirit of Sierra Madre which we will always cherish.
>
> Now that we have come to the parting of the ways, we want you to know we appreciate your many expressions of affection and concern. Thank you, everyone.

With some exceptions, the Home's furnishings, most of which were secondhand, were divided up. Gibsie and Re got first pick. Some of the remaining furnishings, books, and articles of clothing were given to former Home children when they came to attend the final homecoming. Three of the nine children who were still at the Home were transferred to the Methodist Margaret and David Home. On their last day, each of the remaining six children was allowed to take with them the sheets and blankets from the bed they'd slept in. Theirs were the last cries of laughter, the last sounds of one child calling to another, the fading noise of feet padding through the halls and running in the yard. No more would a ringing bell wake the children to greet a new day or to call them to meals. When they were gone, there was only the echo of a door slamming shut for the last time.

CHAPTER 19

Insight

I once heard the writer, Gore Vidal, suggest that the memory of an event is the one you had the last time you thought about it. In other words, I took that to mean that our memories are constantly changing, shifting in the way of sand dunes; each time we revisit them the dunes are still there, but blown by the wind, their shapes and positions have changed relative to the landscape and to each other. Like those dunes, the images I now have of Sierra Madre and my life there are no longer entirely the ones of my childhood. I've returned to the place and my memories of it often enough during the past few years to have the recent mingle with the past, and the inevitable result is potpourri.

My recollections have also been modified if not supplanted by what I've read in the pages of Gibsie's diary, her monthly reports, other records, and in obituaries and newspaper articles, as well as by talks with and letters from my former Home mates and other people who lived in the town. Now I wonder which are my memories and which are those of others. Someone else might be saddened to have their memories distorted or even destroyed. But I am not, for much of what I experienced I deliberately blocked from memory and the rest, what I can recall consciously, isn't all that pleasant.

This now years-long journey of discovery, this rooting out of what happened to me, to know better who I am, has been both revelation and catharsis. At the outset, I hoped that learning about what happened at the Home would allow me to put the whole experience in better perspective, if not put it to rest. Though I've gained a better view of the personalities involved and the context, having so much of that experience made explicit has not been pleasant, nor has much been put to rest. Memory is selective; we remember a person or an event for a reason, the understanding of which reveals its real significance. In many instances it's that kind of "memory understanding" that this search of mine provided. As one consequence, the view I now have of my mother, a woman I'd idolized all my life, is one of a person made more human by her imperfections; but some of her actions I can't help but regard as self-serving and thoughtless, and that's not easy to accept. Realizing and understanding the effects of the Home experience also has been disquieting at best.

◆

For every child who lived at the Home for any extended time, the experience was a major turning point. And given the circumstances from which we came, I doubt there is one of us who would not agree the alternative could easily have been markedly different, if not disastrous. As it did for my mates, the Home gave me a roof over my head, food to eat, clothes to wear, and started me on the road to a religious and secular education. For that I'm more than grateful. But none of what I uncovered showed any awareness, much less concern about what happens to children when they are raised by people not their parents. A child who grows up believing he was unloved or neglected by parents often becomes an adult who is never convinced of anyone's real affection. I am one of them. The legacy of the Home experience reinforced my distrust, with repercussions in all my intimate relationships. To lay blame is pointless, but to understand is both important and necessary.

By imposing a culture different from my own, the Home distorted my image of who and what I was. There was no appreciation of what it meant—and means—to be Latino, particularly Mexican American, in a part of the country where Mexicans have been despised from the outset. As for religion, the Methodist Church succeeded in turning me away from Catholicism, but it also succeeded in starting to turn me away from any religion at all.

In many respects, living in a small town was ideal for accomplishing the Methodist Church's goal of turning us into "real Americans." There were myriad examples of white, middle-class Americans on whom to model ourselves, but few if any examples of exemplary Latinos. Of course our parents could be considered exemplars, but for that critical time their lives, too, were supported by the generosity of others. As for the townspeople, most of us recall that Sierra Madre turned a friendly and accepting face to us, usually without the prejudices that were—and still are—rampant in the

The author, now a sculptor, with his work, "Moment of Flowering," in 1982

Southwest, not to mention nationally. As we got older there were social pressures against associating with us, and occasionally we might hear ugly names connected with our group, but these were rarely directed specifically at us. For the most part we seem to have been well regarded.

It's not surprising we left Sierra Madre thinking there wasn't much racial or ethnic hatred in the town. If we were treated as "different," we thought it was mainly because we were kids from an orphanage, that it was a matter of class. But in 1992 when I visited a woman who had lived for many years across the street from the Home, my suppositions were shaken. I was curious about how she and others had perceived the Home and its children. When I mentioned how seemingly little prejudice there was, she fixed me with a skeptical look.

"Believe me, it was there," she said. "The reason you thought otherwise is because you were all pretty well-behaved. But more importantly, everybody knew you were children and would leave the community before you became adults. If you had continued to live here after you were grown, you would have seen how people really felt about you."

Then she told me about a Mexican American veteran who moved into the town after World War II and started a construction company. For a long time he was shunned by the townspeople, and it was years before his business really thrived. Eventually he became a successful businessman and a pillar of the community, but his experience was an object lesson in bigotry.

The Home and the Center showed little understanding of how it feels to be a charity case or to be regarded by oneself and others as second-class. The Home's money-raising operation relied heavily on our participation. "Singing for our supper" itself wasn't necessarily bad, since we at least gave something in exchange for what we got, but performing was a constant reminder of our charity status. We were continually singled out in the community as people who needed help and for whom "allowances" had to be made, a condescension of which we were well aware. Wearing the castoffs of others was particularly ego-shattering, especially when the donors, full of pity and self-righteousness, showed up to make the offering in person. Being always on the receiving end of charity is ultimately debasing. I learned to hate the donor and myself, which was why for a long time I was scrupulous about hiding the fact I grew up in an orphanage. But it also contributed to my drive to make something of myself, a result for which the Methodist Church can take little credit.

A variety of orphanages existed in the country from the 1920s through the 1950s. But this one was different, a home for Latinos run by Anglos, one designed to purge and revamp us completely. There were far-reaching effects on language, culture, religion, and the image we developed of ourselves. A Jewish child growing up in the Jewish orphanage in Los Angeles at that time didn't have to unlearn anything about being Jewish, nor learn to be anything other than what he or she already was. That child might emerge feeling second-class for having been dependent on charity, but this was a condition later independence and economic self-sufficiency could erase. Otherwise he or she was culturally intact. Not we Home kids. I emerged from the experience bereft in all ways. I fit in nowhere, not welcome in the mainstream society, nor comfortable among Latinos, whom I largely rejected. I've never quite shaken this sense of living in a cultural purgatory.

The Methodist Church firmly believed in the idea of America as a melting pot and did its best to make us measure up as Americans. Because most of us entered the Home at such young ages, the mechanics of assimilation came easily. We learned to speak English—forgetting Spanish in the process—embraced American values and traditions, and otherwise adopted and adapted ourselves to the larger society's habits and mores. According to the myth, we should have readily melted into the pot. Yet despite its pride in being a nation of immigrants, America has traditionally scorned and rejected those in its midst who are "different." Being different, we remain lumps in the stew, unable to dissolve into the blend. When Gerard Stanley Lee said "America is a tune. It must be sung together," not everyone was listening. Too many still aren't.

◆

My former mates have all reacted to their early experiences in their own ways. Some, like me, did their best to assimilate and even intermarried. Others withdrew to the friendlier environments of Latino enclaves in Los Angeles or other areas. A few even returned to Mexico—for better or worse—to resume life in the culture from which they were separated as children. I chose to "escape": to live in other areas of the country; to be myself; to be regarded and treated as an individual, rather than as a member of a group, reviled or not. The U.S. military initially provided me the way out, and though I often returned to Southern California, my visits convinced me I should stay far away, not only from the environment, but from my family, which, sadly, I could see would always hold me back.

For the most part that move has worked for me. Even so, I've found that it hasn't been enough to be native-born, to speak English without an accent, to believe and do all those things that should make me as much American as anyone else. Even without dark skin, being regarded as different starts with having a family name that ends in a vowel. I've often been asked "what" I am before being asked "who" I am. For the same reason and in spite of my accentless English, it's not unusual to be asked patronizingly by non-Spanish speakers, *"¿Habla español?"*—an unsubtle effort to pigeonhole me. For a long time I believed I'd be more acceptable if I rejected my ethnicity. It took years to see this was not only self-destructive, but that I was less respected and liked for doing so. Since then, sad to say, I've often recognized the same syndrome in people of other ethnicities.

My mother and stepfather, both naturalized Americans, worked hard to realize what they could of the American dream. They were proud to be Americans, but they always knew they were outsiders, retaining a sense of disaffiliation for all their lives. Whether this was due to an unwillingness to "let go" of Mexico or to a sense that America made them feel unaccepted were questions I never asked them. It was likely a combination. Probably because of their appearance and accents, even when they became American citizens, they were still treated like outsiders, if not immigrants;

no one ever let them forget it. Could they be blamed for sometimes acting that way? I'm sure I absorbed some of their sense of apartness. In my case, it was mainly, if not entirely, because of the way I'd been made to feel I was different, one of the "other." And I didn't have the advantage, if it can be called that, of affiliation with another country. This is my country, and I reject those who try to make me feel it's not.

◆

For me, as for other first-generation Americans, my parents' homeland had existed as a sort of mysterous beacon distantly beckoning. Though I knew I was American, I hadn't always completely felt like one. For that reason I'd often thought of Mexico as a place that would welcome me as one of its sons, should I ever go there. But what I discovered the first time I heeded its supposed call was totally unexpected. I traveled there with my mother and stepfather, who wanted me to see their birthplaces before I went off to Korea. The late Mexican painter Rufino Tamayo often spoke about straining to hear the voices of Mexico's ghosts, who he believed roam the country. With my first step across El Rio Bravo, as Mexicans call the Rio Grande, I expected a welcoming, enveloping embrace from those ghosts, to feel something *puro mejicano* rise up out of the earth and connect with my core being. Instead, and for the first time in my life, I truly felt American! Why? Because here I was not, could not be, was not allowed to be Mexican; because here I was American. I felt even more so when I tried to find something in common with the people. They were amused at my halting Spanish and treated me as a foreigner. They likewise were foreigners to me, for the country was strange and alien; if my so-called "roots" were there, I didn't find them.

Years later, when I was stationed in Germany, and for that matter anywhere I traveled abroad, I had the same experience: I was American, no doubt about it. Not only that, but I was warmly greeted as such by other Americans I encountered. As I reflect on it now, it really strikes me as absurd that I had to go anywhere to feel American, that it's been so difficult to feel that way at home.

◆

It was the revelation about my father that began this inquiry, this journey into the past in search of myself. At this late date, it has been especially unsettling to be unable to discover the part of my heritage that is Italian. Regretfully but not surprisingly, I feel no connection with it at all. For devoid of contact with my father or with others of Italian ancestry as I was growing up there is no way for me to feel Italian in any respect, except for an intellectual awareness. Yet when I look at a reflection of my face, I can't help but wonder how much of my father's image I'm also seeing, and considering the many times during my life I've been mistaken for Italian, how much that heritage is manifest there. Now and then I allow myself to dwell on that Italian father I never knew. I can blame him for robbing me of his presence, of his love, if indeed he even knew of my existence and might have loved me. But to what end?

Finally, I'm left wondering who the "real" Americans are. Maybe people like my children, whose mother is scarcely aware of her English/German/French extraction. Like her, our children, now adults, are barely conscious of their ethnic heritage, and given my upbringing, I'm as much the cause of that as she is. Like America, they are the sum of many parts, even as I am. But when I think of myself as an American it is almost never without the consciousness of my heritage. It has taken most of my life to feel I belong. I'm still not completely there. That's not only because of how I perceive my countrymen regard me, but because the American in my head is, and always will be, at odds with the Mexican in my soul.

Afterword

After the Plaza Community Center Children's Home was closed, the Center itself continued as an activity of the Methodist Church, but functioned on a much-reduced scale. The church's need for funds later forced it to sell the property on which the Center stood and its activities, providing health care primarily for impoverished women and children, were moved to its present site on Indiana Avenue in East Los Angeles. Virtually all of its financial support now comes from Los Angeles County and State of California welfare agencies, rather than the church. The United Methodist Ministries does provide a small portion of its funding, however, along with the Community Chest, foundations, and other private philanthropies. Despite the critically essential services the Center provides, it struggles to stay afloat.

The property at 72 West Alegria Street was sold soon after the Home was closed; the Big House demolished by the developer who bought it. He built houses on each of the two lots on which the main building had stood, remodeled the Boys' Building, and then sold all three structures. All that remains of the orphanage is a portion of the brick staircase that once led from the East Yard to the portico of the Big House. What had been the South Lot, which actually had never been part of the Home's property, was also eventually developed, as was the vacant lot across the street from the

Big House. Otherwise, though it seems much shorter to me, West Alegria Street remains little changed.

Elsie Nora Gibson was in her sixty-first year when the Home closed its doors for the last time. She went directly to the town of Upland, California, where her sister, Kathleen Sampson, had built a home for herself the year before, and where her brothers, Ernest and Donald Gibson, had homes and families. For the next few years she lived with her sister and became active in the Upland Methodist Church, teaching Sunday School and otherwise living a quiet life of retirement. In the spring of 1962, Kathleen underwent major surgery from which she never fully recovered, and it fell largely to Elsie to care for her. But on November 10, days short of her sixty-ninth birthday, Elsie died suddenly. Her death was a severe shock to Kathleen, and that trauma was magnified when, only nine days later, their elder brother, Ernest, died just as abruptly. Kathleen survived for only two more months before joining her siblings in death in late January, 1963.

When the Home shut its doors, Regina Rivera, who had not only spent her childhood at the Home but a good deal of her adult life there as well, had no family to whom she wished to go. She had refused to accompany her father to Mexico when he, like other Mexicans, had been forcibly deported during the Great Depression, and had since lost contact with him. Still a young woman of thirty-six when the Home closed, she moved for a time to Santa Ana, California. But after a few weeks she returned to Sierra Madre, where she had friends, and found lodging and employment locally. She lives there still. Like her mentor, Gibsie, she never married.

Following her retirement from the Plaza Community Center, Katherine B. Higgins continued to do volunteer work among Latin Americans in Los Angeles. Even in her declining years, she devoted time to collecting food and clothing for the church-sponsored La Casa de Todos, "The Home for Everyone," in Tijuana, Mexico. After a long life filled with service and accomplishment, she died in Pasadena, California, in December, 1967, at the age of eighty-seven.

Dr. William T. Gilliland continued his interest in the activities of the Plaza Community Center long after he left it to become minister of a Methodist Church in the Echo Park district of Los Angeles, an area heavily populated with Latinos, predominantly Mexican and Mexican American. After forty-three years of service to his church, which included subsequent assignment in Douglas, Arizona, and another, his last, as minister of Bethel Church in Los Angeles, he retired in 1946. He continued to live in L. A. until his death in 1970.

After stepping down as superintendent of the Plaza Community Center in 1925, The Reverend Dr. Vernon M. McCombs continued to work and write in Southern California. In that year he summarized his years of working with Mexicans in a book, *From Over The Border—A Study of the Mexicans in the United States*, which was published by the Council of Women for Home Missions and Missionary Education Movement, New York, N.Y. He continued as superintendent of the Latin American Mission until its conversion to the Southern California–Arizona Conference in 1939. From then until his retirement, he was superintendent of the Latin American Provisional Annual Conference. Already in less-than-robust health from his years in Peru, Reverend McCombs retired in 1946 in Los Angeles, where he died in March, 1951.

Except, of course, my siblings, I had little contact with my former Home mates until I began research for this book. Consequently, I know about the outcome of the lives of only about one-fifth of them. Even so, I feel safe in making these generalizations about how far the Methodist Church succeeded in making "real Americans" of us.

Despite the handicaps of our origins, the majority of the 180 Home children successfully took their places in American society. They became self-sufficient, productive citizens, their lives generally paralleling in variety and accomplishment that of the mainstream population. Many of the boys served proudly and honorably in World War II or in the Korean War. Two of our young men died while in military service, and during the twenty-two years of my U.S. Army career, I served both in Korea and Vietnam. A number of others took their turns in the country's defense as well.

Among our group are at least three attorneys, including a judge; two dentists; a gifted musician and composer; a sculptor; a former Golden Gloves champion; a California state policeman; a number of successful businessmen; a municipal-level politician; and two commercial printers. Former Home girls mainly followed traditional roles as housewives and mothers. Many if not most worked outside the home as clerks, secretaries, telephone operators, or in the food-service industry. Two were nurses, and some had successful careers in real estate, while others married businessmen and joined them as partners. There are undoubtedly others who ended up on the other end of the spectrum, but I know of only one.

Acknowledgments

To round out the historical background of the Mexican Revolution and that surrounding my mother's childhood in Chihuahua, Mexico, and El Paso, Texas, which she related to me, I relied upon the works of various authors, including:

Aguirre, Manuel J. *Ensayo Histórico de Teocaltiche.* Edited by B. Costa-Amic. Mexico City, Mexico: Casa JAL Culturas Indigene, 1971.

Altamirano, Graciella and Guadalupe Villa. *Chihuahua—Una Historia Compartida, 1824–1921.* Mexico: Gobierno del Estado de Chihuahua, Instituto de Investigaciones Dr. José María Luís Mora, Universidad Autónoma de Cuidad Juárez, Mexico, D.F., 1988.

Kandell, Jonathan. *La Capital.* New York: Random House, Inc. 1988.

Sonnichsen, C.L. *Pass of the North—Volume II, 1918 to 1980.* El Paso, Texas: Texas Western Press, 1980.

◆

To gain a basic understanding of the Methodist faith and in particular its motivations in serving the Mexican and Mexican American community, as it did in establishing the Plaza Community Center Children's Home; to learn about the history of orphanages in the United States; and to learn about the Methodist personalities who were principally involved in the Southern California effort, I relied upon:

El Rodeo, Los Angeles: University of Southern California, 1924.

McCombs, Dr. Vernon M. *From Over The Border—A Study of the Mexicans in the United States.* New York: Council of Women for Home Missions and Missionary Education Movement, 1925.

Servín, Manuel P. and Iris Higbie Wilson. *Southern California and its University—A History of USC, 1880–1964,* Los Angeles: The Ward Ritchie Press, 1969.

Hudson, Winthrop S., *Religion in America,* 4th ed. New York: MacMillan Publishing Co., 1987.

Weisman, Mary-Lou. "When Parents Are Not in the Best Interests of the Child," *The Atlantic Monthly,* July, 1994, 42–63.

I was also fortunate to have available most of the Plaza Community Center's annual reports to its members, *The Plazagram,* which included information on the status and activities of life at the Home from that perspective. Additionally, I am indebted to Geraldine Zapata, the then–executive director of the Plaza Community Center, for allowing me to research the Center's archives, in particular the minutes of the monthly meetings of the Board of Directors; as well as the "Community Survey of the Plaza District" written by Katherine B. Higgins for the Plaza Community Center, dated circa 1918.

My experience and those of the other former residents of the Home was one of relative isolation from the rest of the Latino community, at least during the first 14 to 17 years of our lives. For that reason, it was important for me to understand how our experience differed from that of the general Mexican American population during the same time frame and subsequently. More generally, it was also important for me to know and understand how and why American society had come to regard Mexican Americans with the contempt it did and does. These insights were provided in large measure by the works of these authors:

Hoffman, Abraham. *Unwanted Mexican Americans in the Great Depression; Repatriation Measures, 1929–1939.* Tucson, Arizona: University of Arizona Press, 1974.

Lind, Michael. *The Next American Nation: The New Nationalism and the Fourth American Revolution.* New York: The Free Press, 1995.

Riding, Alan. *Distant Neighbors—A Portrait of the Mexicans.* New York: Alfred A. Knopf, 1985.

Samora, Julian, and Patricia Vandel Simon. *A History of the Mexican American People.* Notre Dame, Indiana: University of Notre Dame Press, 1993.

Shorris, Earl. *Latinos—A Biography of the People.* New York: W.W. Norton & Company, 1992.

Sowell, Thomas. *Ethnic America—A History.* New York: Basic Books, Inc., 1981.

Valdéz, Luis, and Stan Steiner, eds. *Atzlán—An Anthology of Mexican American Literature.* New York: Alfred A. Knopf, 1972.

This book, then, is the work and experience of many others. The list includes some of my former mates at the Home, who took the time to answer my questions and provided documentation I could not otherwise have had. I was also fortunate to have available a majority of the monthly reports of the Home's manager to the Plaza Community Center for the years 1936 until it closed its doors in 1954. These, though somewhat sanitized, were nonetheless rich in the details involved in child-rearing on a fairly large scale, as well as providing information on the operation of an institution and all that entails. Having access to the personal diary of the Home's manager, which she maintained during the years 1932 through 1938, provided a treasure trove of insights, which otherwise could only have been available through interviews with her; she had died more than thirty years before I began the research for this book.

From the Children's Home, those who were especially helpful and to whom I am grateful: The Hon. Edwin (Ortiz) Beach, Dr. George A. Cabrera, Richard J. Cerrillo, Frank Flores, Donald S. Lopez, Eliseo Lopez, Angelita Parra Palascios, Rachel Parra Quick, Regina Rivera, Anita Avila Rodriguez, William J. Sanabria, Ruth Lopez Seedborg, Margaret Gonzalez Trejo, and Angel Uribe. I am especially indebted to my sister, Henrietta Sanabria Martinez, who provided details about our family's history I could otherwise have not known.

To round out my recollections of the City of Sierra Madre, I relied upon:

Keith, Elizabeth P. *Sierra Madre Vistas—A Pictorial History of Sierra Madre.* Sierra Madre, California: The View, 1976.

I also received valuable information from former and current residents of the City of Sierra Madre, including Margaret Buckner, Phyllis Chapman, Cynthia Rondeau Cook, Helen Obazawa, and Elwood and George Williams.

Many others helped once I began writing. They included: Dr. Joseph Mancini, Genelle Paschall Nicholson of the Sierra Madre Congregational Church, and Betty Clements of the Claremont Theological Seminary.

I'm indebted to Mary Callahan who edited the manuscript; and last, but by no means least, my wife Sherry Zvares Sanabria, who encouraged me, made constructive suggestions, provided a counter to my sometimes disjointed viewpoint, and otherwise kept me on an even keel throughout.

Appendix: List of Children

During the thirty-one years of its existence, 180 children lived at the Plaza Community Center Children's Home for periods varying from a few weeks to a number of years. After consulting the manager's record, her diary, and her monthly reports to the Plaza Community Center, I could only account for the following 163 children; they are listed by date of entry.

NAME	**ENTERED**	**AGE (upon entry)**	**DEPARTED**	**DOB**
Quiroz, Frances	8/5/23	7	8/?/27	8/5/16
Gomez, Ezekiel	9/25/23	6, 1 mo	9/?/30	8/?/17
Madero, Pedro	?/?/23	?	?	?
Madero, Luis	?/?/23	?	?	?
Najera, Rosa	10/6/23	4, 10 mo	11/?/33	12/?/18
Najera, Ruby	10/24/23	10, 3 mo	10/?/27	7/4/13
Becera, Theresa	9/29/23	8, 7 mo	10/?/30	?
Becera, Amalia	10/1/23	5, 8 mo	7/?/32	?
Becera, Alberto	3/12/24	4, 7 mo	7/?/33	?
Portillo, Alfredo	4/4/24	2, 9 mo	12/?/32	?
Hauffen, Carlos	5/28/24	7, 10 mo	9/10/33	6/?/16
Hauffen, Ester	5/28/24	9, 2 mo	10/?/32	3/24/15
Hauffen, Sara	6/2/24	11, 6 mo	8/?/26	?
Cortez, Alfonzo	9/15/25	6, 10 mo	6/?/27	?
Ibarra, Carmen	9/15/25	8, 9 mo	5/20/33	12/15/16
Salazar, Salvador	9/?/25	6, 9 mo	6/?/33	?
Uribe, Angel	1/20/26	7	6/27/34	?
Ballesteros, Victoria	5/27/27	8, 1 mo	6/?/36	4/27/19
Rivera, Regina	11/11/27	9, 2 mo	To close	9/7/18
Uriarte, Berta	1/17/28	4, 5 mo	6/?/43	8/?/24
Uriarte, Mario	1/17/28	2, 5 mo	6/?/40	9/?/26
Avila, Anita	1/7/28	8, 5 mo	9/?/34	?
Lopez, Ruth	9/29/28	2, 7 mo	10/?/35	?
Lopez, Donaciano	9/29/28	5	5/?/35	9/15/23
Lobo, David	10/30/28	5, 4 mo	6/?/35	?
Lopez, Eliseo	10/13/30	8, 8 mo	10/18/35	?

NAME	ENTERED	AGE (upon entry)	DEPARTED	DOB
Ortiz, Betty	9/10/31	8, 6 mo	7/?/36	3/19/23
Ortiz, (Beach)Edwin	9/10/31	7, 4 mo	7/?/36	5/19/24
Gonzalez, Carmen	2/23/33	12	7/?/34	1/16/21
Gonzalez, Nellie	2/23/33	9, 2 mo	9/?/39	?
Gonzalez, Margaret	2/23/33	5	9/?/40	7/5/27
Gonzalez, Ruben	2/23/33	6, 11 mo	9/?/40	3/26/26
Reyes, Rosita	2/23/33	2, 8 mo	6/10/33	?
Sandoval, Margarita	8/20/33	9, 6 mo	7/?/37	?
Castillo, Sylvia	10/26/33	4, 3 mo	7/?/35	?
Cano, Jane	12/30/33	5, 9 mo	6/19/34	?
Palacio, Anita	8/24/34	?	?	?
Gurena, Esther	9/15/34	6, 8 mo	4/27/35	?
Gurena, Joel	9/15/34	4	4/27/35	?
Macias, Elena	9/17/34	?	12/?/34	?
Valdez, Cruz	9/12/34	7, 2 mo	6/?/36	?
Valdez, Elena	9/17/34	7	?	?
Sanabria, Enriqueta	10/10/35	7, 3 mo	7/?/42	7/4/28
Sanabria, Roberto	10/10/35	4, 2 mo	7/?/45	8/20/31
Sanabria, Jesús (William)	10/10/35	2, 2 mo	7/?/46	8/1/33
Sanabria, Concepción	10/10/35	0, 10 mo	7/?/46	12/1/34
Valéncia, Frances	10/?/35	7	6/?/36	?
Reyes, Manuel	1/5/36	?	8/?/37	?
Lozano, Ofelia	5/9/36	9	12/?/37	?
Yanez, Sara	7/5/36	10, 6 mo	10/?/36	?
Franko, Teddy	7/?/36	6	10/?/36	?
Meza, Victoria	7/21/36	?	8/?/43	?
Meza, Daniel	7/21/36	3, 9 mo	8/?/43	?
Castorena, Jose	9/?/36	?	12/?/37	?
Castorena, Richard	9/?/36	?	12/?/37	?
Sellers, Byron	3/?/37	?	7/?/37	?
Sellers, Dolores	3/?/37	?	7/?/37	?
Sellers (?), Armando	4/?/37	?	7/?/38	?
Sellers, Tiny (?)	6/?/37	?	7/?/37	?
Lopez, Consuelo	9/23/37	?	11/?/38	?
Villareal, Alvino	10/?/37	?	11/?/38	?
Flores, Margarito	7/19/38	7, 8 mo	7/?/46	12/?/30
Flores, Frank	7/19/38	6	7/?/47	?
Flores, Arthur	7/19/38	5	7/?/47	?
?, Rose Marie	8/5/38	4, 6 mo	4/?/39	?
Gonzalez, Margaret	3/20/38	3, 1 mo	12/?/38	?
Frutas, Beatrice	9/28/38	?	6/?/42	?
Martinez, Gilbert	9/11/38	?	8/?/42	?
Martinez, Rudy	9/11/38	?	7/?/43	?
Meza-Garcia, Leroy	11/?/38	?	7/?/40	?
Mendoza, Josephine	12/17/38	?	5/?/42	?
Mendoza, Adela	12/17/38	?	5/?/42	?
Mendoza, Angela	12/17/38	?	5/?/42	?
Mendoza, Gloria	12/17/38	6	5/?/42	?
Parra, Rachel	3/20/39	7, 4 mo	7/1/50	12/?/32

NAME	ENTERED	AGE (upon entry)	DEPARTED	DOB
Parra, Jose	3/20/39	6	7/?/47	?
Parra, Marie	3/20/39	?	12/?/48	?
Parra, Rebecca	4/6/39	11	6/?/42	?
Parra, Angelita	4/6/39	8. 4 mo	1/?/48	?
Parra, Ruth	3/11/40	7, 5 mo	6/?/52	5/28/?
?, Julia	4/?/40	5	?	?
Cerrillo, Richard	5/23/40	7, 6 mo	7/?/46	11/20/32
Lopez, Marianna	7/31/40	11, 6 mo	6/?/43	?
Lopez, Adelberto	7/31/40	9, 1 mo	7/?/46	6/?/31
Lopez, Alicia	7/31/40	6, 4 mo	6/?/48	?
Chavez, Alfred	9/23/41	8, 7 mo	6/?/42	?
Soto, Shirley	1/17/42	4, 6 mo	5/?/52	?
Estrada, Alfonso	8/21/42	?	8/1/45	?
Estrada, Henry	8/21/42	4, 5 mo	8/1/45	?
?, David	9/?/43	4, 6 mo	?	?
Melendez, Lucy	9/19/42	12	9/?/45	?
Silva, Emerita	11/?/42	?	?	4/28/?
Imperial, Diana	11/15/42	5	8/?/45	?
Matamoros, Alfa	11/20/42	5	6/?/46	?
Matamoros, Reynaldo	11/20/42	3, 9 mo	6/?/46	?
?, Lupe	?/?/42	?	?	?
?, Sally	?/?/42	?	?	?
Salazar, Olivia	?	?	?	?
?, Yvonne	?/?/43	?	4/?/44	?
?, Herlinda	9/?/43	6, 10 mo	2/?/44	?
Martinez, Elsa	3/1/44	3, 6 mo	5/?/44	?
?, Bobby	2/?/44	?	?	?
?, Celia	4/?/44	5	?	?
Reyes, Ester	6/?/44	6	?	?
Reyes, Elvinia	6/?/44	8	?	?
Clayton, Yolanda	6/?/44	4	1/?/48	?
?, Shirley	?/?/44	?	5/?/45	?
Silva, Raymond	12/15/44	5, ?	?	?
Silva, Rosalia	12/15/44	4	?	?
Silva, Robert	12/15/44	3	?	?
Walker, George	9/?/45	?	1/?/47	?
Walker, Bobby	9/?/45	?	1/?/47	?
Silva, Johnnie	11/?/45	4, ?	8/?/50	?
Silva, ? (girl)	11/?/45	?	?	?
Silva, ? (girl)	11/?/45	?	?	?
Silva, ? (girl)	11/?/45	?	?	?
Torres, Luis	1/15/46	5,	?	?
Torres, Manuel (Tony)	1/15/46	4,	?	?
Valdez, Raymond	4/?/46	?	6/?/46	?
?, Luz	?/?/46	?	?	?
Masqueda, Arthur	9/?/46	4,	?	?
Morales, Rachel	9/?/46	6	?	?
Diaz, Diana	?/?/47	?	6/?/49	?
Diaz, Martha	?/?/47	?	6/?/49	?

NAME	ENTERED	AGE (upon entry)	DEPARTED	DOB
Castillo, Jacob	12/?/47	8, 2 mo	4/?/53	?
Lopez, Bertha	4/25/48	8, ?	?	?
Lopez, Mary	4/25/48	4, 10 mo	?	?
Blackburn, Kenneth	?/?/48	?	7/?/49	?
Lopez, Manuel	?/?/48	?	8/?/50	?
Fraijo, Enid	9/?/49	?	?	?
Fraijo, Steven	9/?/49	?	?	?
Arocha, Arthur	9/?/49	?	6/?/50	?
Martinez, Georgina	10/?/49	10, ?	6/?/52	5/3/39
Kayo, George	5/?/50	?	?	?
Kayo, Lillian	5/?/50	?	?	?
Perez, Joe	?/?/50	?	2/?/51	?
?, Mona	?/?/50	?	3/?/51	?
Cabrera, Martha	9/?/50	7	6/?/54	?
Cabrera, Beatrice	9/?/50	5	6/?/54	?
Ochoa, Ofelia	9/12/50	6	?	?
Corrales, Hector	3/?/51	4	?	?
?, William	?/?/51	?	?	5/20/?
?, Lily	?/?/51	?	?	?
Amenta, Linda	?/?/51	?	?	?
Gonzalez, ? (boy)	?/?/51	?	?	?
Veas, Loretta	?/?/51	?	6/?/52	?
Veas, Leonard	?/?/51	?	6/?/52	?
Cabrera, George A.	9/?/51	5, 1 mo	6/?/54	8/2/46
Moran, Mario	?/?/52	?	?	?
Monterrey, Martha	?/?/52	8	?	?
Madrigal, Crispin	4/?/52	5	?	?
Madrigal, Edward	4/?/52	6	?	?
Duran, Irene	5/?/52	5	10/?/5	?
Gonzalez, Albert	6/?/52	5	?/54	?
Hooper, Rita	8/?/52	10	?	?
?, Fred	?/?/52	?	?/54	?
?, Tony	?/?/52	?	?/54	?
Ramirez, Diana	8/?/52	11 ?	4/?/53*	?
Ramirez, Carolyn	8/?/52	?	4/?/53	?
Moreno, Adria	10/?/52	5	?	?
Figueroa, Luis	10/?/52	5	?	?
Martinez, Leandro	4/?/53	5	?	?
?, Lydia	?/?/53	?	?	?

*—Died while at the Home.